ON TO C

Patrick Henry Winston

Professor of Computer Science

Massachusetts Institute of Technology

Addison-Wesley Publishing Company

Reading, Massachusetts ■ Menlo Park, California ■ New York
Don Mills, Ontario ■ Wokingham, England ■ Amsterdam ■ Bonn
Sydney ■ Singapore ■ Tokyo ■ Madrid ■ San Juan ■ Milan ■ Paris

Library of Congress Cataloging-in-Publication Data
Winston, Patrick Henry.
    On to C / Patrick Henry Winston.
        p.   cm. -- (Programming languages library)
    Includes index.
    ISBN 0-201-58042-X
    1. C (Computer programming language).   I. Title.   II. Series.
QA76.73.C153W57   1994
005.13'3--dc20

                                                    93-49603
                                                    CIP

Reprinted with corrections January, 1995

Reproduced by Addison-Wesley from camera-ready copy supplied by the author.

2 3 4 5 6 7 8 9 10-MA-9695

CONTENTS

ACKNOWLEDGEMENTS

The cover photograph, the cover design, and the interior design are by Chiai Takahashi, with counsel from Karen A. Prendergast. The bull in the cover photograph resides near Wall Street, New York.

Lyn Dupre was the developmental editor, and Boris Katz was the chief technical editor. Both have a special gift for rooting out problems and suggesting improvements.

In addition, Sundar Narasimhan provided invaluable advice on C's subtleties, Thomas Stahovich helped to test the programs, and Lisa Freedman found grammatical and typographical errors that were introduced in final editing.

1 HOW THIS BOOK TEACHES YOU THE LANGUAGE

1   The purpose of this book is to help you learn the essentials of C programming. In this section, you learn why you should know C and how this book is organized.

2   Early versions of the UNIX operating system were written in a language named B, which was based, in part, on a language named BCPL. The implementers of UNIX then developed another, better language, based on their experience with B. They decided to name that new language C inasmuch as it superseded B.

3   Today, just about all computers are organized around bits, bytes, and collections of bytes. Instruction sets vary greatly, however. Accordingly, C allows you to refer to bits, bytes, and collections of bytes explicitly, but C does not allow you to specify computer-specific instructions. Instead, your computer-independent, higher-level function descriptions are translated for you into sequences of computer-specific instructions.

4   **Assembler languages** allow you to specify functions at the level of computer-specific instructions, which operate on memory chunks of various sizes. Thus, programs written in assembler languages are not portable.

C, by contrast, allows you to specify sequences of computer-independent, conceptual instructions, which operate on memory chunks of various sizes. Thus, programs written in C are portable.

By encouraging you to think in terms of memory chunks, yet discouraging you from thinking in terms of computer-specific instructions, C provides a sensible tradeoff, enabling you to write programs that are both fast and portable. Accordingly, C is sometimes called a **portable assembler language**.

5   C has became popular by virtue of attractive characteristics, such as the following:

- C is easy to learn.
- C programs are fast.
- C programs are concise.
- C compilers—programs that translate C programs into machine instructions—are usually fast and concise.
- C compilers and C programs run on all sorts of computers, from small personal computers to huge supercomputers.
- UNIX, a popular operating system, happens to be written in C.

6   There are two principal reasons to learn C:

- C is often the right language to use in situations requiring maximum program speed and minimum program size.
- The supply of powerful off-the-shelf C software modules, both free and for sale, is huge.

Also, because C is so widely used, you often hear programmers debate the merits of other languages in terms of their advantages and disadvantages relative to C.

7 Four principles determined this introductory book's organization and style:

- The book should get you up and running in the language quickly.

- The book should answer your basic questions explicitly.

- The book should encourage you to develop a personal library of solutions to standard programming problems.

- The book should deepen your understanding of the art of good programming practice.

8 To get you up and running in C quickly, the sections in this book generally supply you with the most useful approach to each programming need, be it to display characters on your screen, to define a new function, or to read data from a file.

9 To answer your basic questions explicitly, this book is divided into parts that generally focus on one issue, which is plainly announced in the title of the section. Accordingly, you see titles such as the following:

- How to Do Arithmetic

- How to Define Simple Functions

- How to Process Data from Files

- How to Create Structures and Objects

- How to Organize a Multiple-File Program

10 To encourage you to develop a personal library of solutions to standard programming problems, this book introduces many useful, productivity-increasing, general-purpose, templatelike patterns—sometimes called **cliches** by experienced programmers—that you can fill in to achieve particular-purpose goals.

Cliches are introduced, because learning to program involves more than learning to use programming-language primitives, just as learning to speak a human language involves more than learning to use vocabulary words.

11 To deepen your understanding of the art of good programming practice, this book emphasizes the value of such ideas as *data abstraction* and *procedure abstraction*.

12 In this book, single-idea segments, analogous to slides, are arranged in sections that are analogous to slide shows. The segments come in several varieties: **basic segments** explain essential ideas; **sidetrip segments** introduce interesting, but skippable, ideas; **practice segments** provide opportunities to experiment with new ideas; and **highlights segments** summarize important points.

13 Finally, the book develops a simple, yet realistic C program, which you see in many versions as your understanding of the language increases. In its ultimate version, the program reads

data from a file containing recent stock-market information, computes the average price per share and number of shares traded, and predicts the next-day's price using a straight line fitted to previous prices. The statistical flavor of the example is meant to suggest the popularity of C as a language for implementing statistical-analysis programs.

- C is a programming language that encourages you to think in terms of memory chunks of various sizes, but not in terms of computer-specific instructions.

- C enjoys considerable popularity, because C is easy to learn, C programs are fast, C programs are concise, C programs allow you to think intimately in terms of bits and bytes but not in terms of computer-specific instruction sets, C compilers are usually fast and concise, C compilers and C programs run on all sorts of computers, off-the-shelf C programs are widely available, and UNIX, a popular operating system, happens to be written in C.

- This book gets you up and running in C quickly; it answers your basic questions explicitly; it equips you with program patterns that you can adapt to your own purposes; and it deepens your understanding of the art of good programming practice.

2 HOW TO COMPILE
AND RUN A SIMPLE PROGRAM

15   In this section, you learn how to compile and run a simple program that computes the average of three prices. You also review much of the standard terminology used throughout the rest of this book.

16   Working with C is like working with most programming languages. First, you **write** a program using an editor. Next, you **compile** your program, translating it into machine instructions.

In its original form, your program is called **text** or **source code**. Once translated, the source code becomes **object code**.

Your program's source code may be distributed among several files, which you can compile into separate object-code files. Subsequently, you **link** the separately compiled object-code files to produce **executable code**.

Finally, you **run** your executable code, or, said another way, you **execute** your program.

17   As usual, you generally go around two key loops many times as you search for bugs:

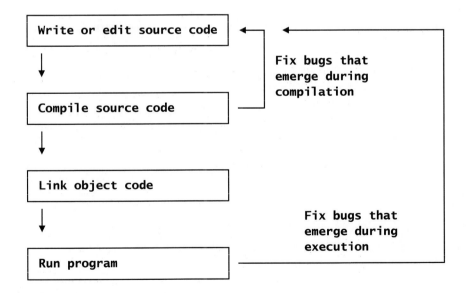

18   Typical C programs contain many **function definitions**, each of which contains a sequence of **variable declarations**, which tell the C compiler about the variables you intend to use, followed by **statements**, which tell the C compiler about the computations to be performed.

Every C program must contain a definition for a function named main. When you start a C program, that program starts to perform the computations specified in the main function.

19 In mathematics, a *function* is a set relating input variables uniquely to output variables.

SIDE TRIP In C programming, the word *function* is used differently, inasmuch as the functions in C programs may have side effects, or may not produce consistent outputs for all inputs, or may not even produce outputs at all. Accordingly, many authors of books on programming prefer to use the word *procedure* instead of the word *function*. Recognizing, however, that the word *function* is solidly entrenched in the vernacular of C programming, this book uses *function* throughout.

20 The following program, which computes the average of three prices, consists of just one function, the `main` function:

```
main ( ) {
   (10.2 + 12.0 + 13.2) / 3;
}
```

This `main` function consists of the **function name**, `main`, followed by matched parentheses—which you should ignore for now—followed by a single statement sandwiched between matched braces that delimit the function's **body**.

The one and only statement in the body of the `main` function contains two instances of the **addition operator**, +, and one instance of the **division operator**, /. Note that this statement, like most C statements, is terminated by a semicolon.

The semicolon, the parentheses, and the braces act as punctuation. Occasionally, such symbols, in such contexts, are called **punctuators**.

Note also that the sample program is quite catatonic: It accepts no input data and produces no output result.

21 To relieve the sample program of a portion of its catatonia, you can provide statements that tell the C compiler that you want the results of the computation to be displayed, as in the following revised program:

```
#include <stdio.h>
main ( ) {
  printf ("The average of the prices is ");
  printf ("%f", (10.2 + 12.0 + 13.2) / 3);
  printf ("\n");
}
```

The revised program introduces several concepts and syntactical markers, and forces the introduction of the line `#include <stdio.h>`. Accordingly, you need to zoom in, and to look at the revised program piece by piece.

22 The **display function** is `printf`, where `printf` is an acronym for *print f*ormatted. In the sample program, the matched parentheses following the `printf` symbols surround the information that `printf` uses to determine what to display.

In the first instance, the `printf` function displays a **character string**; in C, character strings are delimited on both ends by double-quotation marks:

```
printf ("The average of the prices is ");
```

23 In the second instance, the display function displays the result of an arithmetic computation:

```
printf ("%f", (10.2 + 12.0 + 13.2) / 3);
```

Here you hand the printf function a character string and an arithmetic expression. The character string, in this example, consists entirely of a **print specification**, %f, marked as such by a percent sign, %. The %f print specification tells C that a floating-point number is to be displayed. In the example, the particular floating-point number to be displayed is provided by the expression (10.2 + 12.0 + 13.2) / 3. Thus, the print specification is paired with an arithmetic expression:

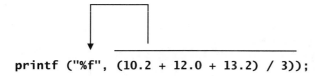

```
printf ("%f", (10.2 + 12.0 + 13.2) / 3));
```

24 The %f print specification, along with those for integers, strings, and other data types, is explained more fully in Appendix A.

25 In the third instance, the printf function appears with \n. You should think of \n as a name for the **newline character**, the one that causes display devices to terminate the current line and to start a new one.

26 To use the printf function, you must inform the C compiler that you plan to use C's standard input–output library by including the following line in your program:

```
#include <stdio.h>
```

There is more to be said about such lines; for now, however, just include the prescribed line before the first instance of the printf function appears.

27 Note that C is **blank insensitive**; C treats all sequences of spaces, tabs, and carriage returns—other than those in character strings—as though there were just a single space. Thus, the following are equivalent:

```
#include <stdio.h>
main ( ) {
  printf ("The average price is ");
  printf ("%f", (10.2 + 12.0 + 13.2) / 3);
  printf ("\n");
}
```

```
#include <stdio.h>

main ( )
{
  printf ("The average price is ");
  printf ("%f", (10.2 + 12.0 + 13.2) / 3);
  printf ("\n");
}

#include <stdio.h>
main ( ) {
    printf ("The average price is ");
    printf ("%f", (10.2 + 12.0 + 13.2) / 3);
    printf ("\n");}

#include <stdio.h>
main ( ) {printf ("The average price is ");
        printf ("%f", (10.2 + 12.0 + 13.2) / 3);
        printf ("\n");}
```

None of these layout options can be said to be "best" or "official." In fact, some experienced C programmers argue heatedly about how to arrange functions so as to maximize transparency and to please the eye. In this book, the functions are written in a style that both uses paper efficiently and lies within the envelope of common practice.

28 Note, however, that C is **case sensitive**; for example, if you write Main or MAIN when you mean main, C cannot understand your intent.

29 At this point, you have seen sample uses of two C **operators**: the multiplication operator and the division operator. These particular operators are built-in functions that work on inputs supplied to them according to the conventions of arithmetic: Such functions are interspersed among their inputs, and those inputs are called **operands**.

30 Generally, you choose a *source-code file name*, such as average, to describe the file's contents, and you choose a **source-code extension name**, such as c, to indicate that the file contains source code, producing a complete file name, such as average.c. By convention, the file extension for C source code is c.

31 Unfortunately, the correct way to compile and link your source-code files depends on your C supplier and on your operating system. Usually, the name of the program that compiles and links is cc, but some vendors elect to use other names. Accordingly, you many need to refer to your compiler manual, or to ask a local wizard, if the instructions given in the following segments do not work for you.

32 On UNIX systems, one representative way to initiate compilation and linking is as follows, assuming that your program is in a file named average.c:

cc -o average average.c

Such an instruction to the operating system has several parts:

- cc means use a program that includes the C compiler and linker.

- average.c means work on the source-code file named average.c.

- -o average means put the executable code in a file named average.

33　On Dos systems, you compile and link programs a little differently. Assuming that your program is in a file named average.c, you produce executable code as follows:

cc -o average.exe average.c

The file name average.exe appears, instead of average, because Dos, by convention, requires files containing executable code to have an **exe** extension.

34　Once the C compiler and linker have placed executable code in the file named average (UNIX) or average.exe (DOS), you can run that executable code by just typing that file's name, followed by a carriage return:

average

35　Although the sample program communicates with you by way of output data displayed on your screen, it does not receive any input data after it is compiled. Instead, it works with data that were supplied as the program was written. Such data are said to be **wired in** or **hard coded**.

36　In this book, you see many templatelike, general-purpose program patterns that you can fill in to suit your own specific purpose. In these patterns, each place to be filled in is identified by a box that contains a description of the item to be inserted, such as this .

When you fill in a pattern, replacing descriptions with specific instances of the general categories described, you are said to **instantiate** the pattern.

37　PRACTICE　Estimate the number of shares traded on the New York Stock Exchange on a typical day; also estimate the average value of each share. Then, write a program that computes the total value of the shares traded on a typical day.

38　HIGHLIGHTS

- When you work with C, as with most programming languages, you write source code, the C compiler translates source code into object code, the C linker then links object code into executable code, and your computer runs that executable code.

- C functions contain sequences of computation-specifying statements.

- All C programs contain a function named main. When you run a C program, you initiate the computations specified in that main function.

- Many statements involve built-in functions and operators such as the display function, printf, and the addition operator, +. Operators do their work on operands.

- To test simple programs, you often use data that you supply when you write the program. Such data are said to be wired in.

- If you plan to use the display function, **then** you must inform C of your intention by including the following line near the beginning of your program:

  ```
  #include <stdio.h>
  ```

- If you want to display characters, **then** instantiate the following pattern:

  ```
  printf (" characters to be displayed ");
  ```

- If you want to display an integer, **then** instantiate the following pattern:

  ```
  printf ("%f", integer-producing expression );
  ```

- If you want to terminate the current line and to start a new one, **then** instantiate the following pattern:

  ```
  printf ("\n");
  ```

3 HOW TO DECLARE VARIABLES

39 In this section, you learn how to declare variables in C. You also continue to review standard terminology used throughout the rest of this book.

40 A C **identifier** is a name consisting of letters and digits, the first of which must be a letter; underscore, _, counts as a letter.

A **variable** is an identifier that serves as the name of a chunk of computer memory. Thus, each variable **refers to** a chunk of memory.

The variable's **data type** determines the size of the chunk and the way the bits in the chunk are interpreted. If the variable belongs to the int data type, a kind of *int*eger, the chunk of memory involved is likely to contain 32 bits, one of which determines the integer's sign and 31 of which determine the integer's absolute value.

The chunk of memory named by a variable is said to hold that variable's **value**. As a program runs, a variable's value may change, but a variable's data type never changes. Thus, the value of an integer variable named size could be the integer 600 at one time and the integer 200 at another, but size's value could never be a floating-point number—a number that includes a decimal point—such as 10.2.

41 Because every variable is associated with a data type, the C compiler can allocate a memory chunk of the right size for each variable, once and for all, taking advantage of the fact that the value of the variable always will fit within the allocated memory chunk.

42 When you tell the C compiler the type of a variable inside main, you are said to **declare** the variable. Thus, the following program exhibits three variable declarations—all three variables are declared to be integer variables, because each is preceded by the data-type–declaring int:

```
main ( ) {
   int size_one;
   int size_two;
   int size_three;
   ...
}
```

43 You can combine several separate variable declarations into one, more concise variable declaration as long as each variable belongs to the same data type. In the following program fragment, for example, all three variables are declared to be integer variables in a single declaration:

```
main ( ) {
   int size_one, size_two, size_three;
   ...
}
```

Note the obligatory, variable-separating commas.

44 Storing a value in the memory chunk allocated for a variable is called **variable assignment.** Accordingly, whenever C places a value in such a memory chunk, the variable is said to be **assigned a value** and the value is said to be **assigned to the variable.**

45 You can **initialize** variables, as in the following program:

```
#include <stdio.h>
main ( ) {
  int size_one = 600;
  int size_two = 100;
  int size_three = 200;
  printf ("The average number of shares traded is ");
  printf ("%i", (size_one + size_two + size_three) / 3);
  printf ("\n");
}
——————————————— Result ———————————————
The average number of shares traded is 300
```

Note that the print specification for integers is %i, rather than %f, which is appropriate only for floating-point numbers.

46 You can combine several initializations into one, more concise variable declaration, as in the following example:

```
#include <stdio.h>
main ( ) {
  int size_one = 600, size_two = 100, size_three = 200;
  printf ("The average number of shares traded is ");
  printf ("%i", (size_one + size_two + size_three) / 3);
  printf ("\n");
}
——————————————— Result ———————————————
The average number of shares traded is 300
```

47 For the moment, the sample programs use test data that are wired in by way of initialized variables. Later on, in Section 5, you learn how to use test data that you provide using your keyboard or a file.

48 To change the value of a variable, you use the **assignment operator,** =. Three assignment statements appear in the following program:

12

```
#include <stdio.h>
main ( ) {
  int size_one = 600, size_two = 100, size_three = 200;
  sum = size_one;          /* Sum assigned a value */
  sum = sum + size_two;    /* Sum assigned a new value */
  sum = sum + size_three;  /* Sum assigned a new value */
  printf ("The average number of shares traded is ");
  printf ("%i", sum / 3);
  printf ("\n");
}
```
————————————————— Result —————————————————
The average number of shares traded is 300
___

Of course, this program is a bit awkward—the only reason to split the computation of price into three separate statements is to demonstrate that a variable can be assigned and then reassigned.

49 For storing integers, C provides a range of data-type possibilities, including char, short, int, and long. C compiler writers are free to choose the number of bytes associated with each type, provided that the following constraints are obeyed:

> The number of bytes for the char type
> $\leq$ The number of bytes for the short type
> $\leq$ The number of bytes for the int type
> $\leq$ The number of bytes for the long type

The char data type ordinarily is used for storing characters, but because character codes can be viewed as integers, char is viewed as one of the **integral data types**, along with short, int, and long.

50 For storing floating-point numbers, C also provides a range of type possibilities, including float, double, and long double, which obey the following constraints:

> The number of bytes for the float type
> $\leq$ The number of bytes for the double type
> $\leq$ The number of bytes for the long double type

51 The implementation used to test the programs in this book allocates bytes as follows for the various data types:

Type	Bytes (typical)	Stores
char	1	character
short	2	integer
int	4	integer
long	4	integer
float	4	floating-point number
double	8	floating-point number
long double	8	floating-point number

52 For most integers, the `short` integer type is slightly small, and any data type larger than `int` is unnecessarily large. Analogously, for most floating-point numbers, the `float` floating-point type is slightly small, and any data type larger than `double` is unnecessarily large. Consequently, most programmers use `int` and `double` more than they do any other integer and floating-point types, and all the programs in the rest of this book use `int` and `double` for all integers and floating-point numbers. Conveniently, the `%i` print specification works for both `short` and `int` integers, and the `%f` print specification works for both `float` and `double` numbers.

53
SIDE TRIP Because the `long` and `long double` data types usually are unnecessarily large, and are not supported directly by instructions in computer hardware, many C compiler writers arrange for `long` to be synonymous with `int`, and for `long double` to be synonymous with `double`.

54 Experienced programmers occasionally use `short` or `float` when maximum execution speed is of prime importance.

55 Whenever your C compiler encounters a slash followed immediately by an asterisk, /*, the compiler ignores both characters and all other characters up to and including the next asterisk that is followed immediately by a slash, */. Thus, /* and */ delimit comments:

```
/*
This line is a sample comment · · ·
*/
```

If you want to test how a program works without certain lines of source code, you can hide those lines in a comment, instead of deleting them.

56 Note that you cannot place a /* · · · */ comment inside another /* · · · */ comment. If you try, you find that the inner comment's */ terminates the outer comment, and your C compiler cannot compile your program:

```
/*   ◄─────────────────────────────────┐
                                         │
First part of outer comment ···         │
                                         │
/*   ◄── Commented out                   │       */ of inner comment
                                         │       terminates /* of
Inner comment ···                        │       outer comment
                                         │
*/ ──────────────────────────────────────┘
Second part of outer comment ···
*/   ◄── Dangles
```

57   Finally, note that `printf` statements can contain more than one print specification. Generally, print specifications are interspersed among ordinary characters in the character string. The character string acts as a template into which expression values are inserted at places marked by print specifications.

    The following, for example, contains both an instance of %i and an instance of %f:

```
printf ("The average of the %i prices is %f.\n", count, average);
```

58   Some experienced C programmers like to arrange the arguments in `printf` statements so that the arguments line up with the corresponding print specifications, as shown in the following examples:

```
printf ("The average of the %i prices is %f.\n",
                            count,          average);
```

    Such alignment makes `printf` statements easier to read—especially `printf` statements that contain many print specifications or `printf` statements with complex arguments.

59   If you are curious about how much memory your C implementation allocates for the

SIDE TRIP   various data types, you can compile and execute the following program, which uses the `sizeof` operator to determine data-type size:

```
#include <stdio.h>
main ( ) {
  printf ("Data Type    Bytes\n");
  printf ("char         %i\n", sizeof (char));
  printf ("short        %i\n", sizeof (short));
  printf ("int          %i\n", sizeof (int));
  printf ("long         %i\n", sizeof (long));
  printf ("float        %i\n", sizeof (float));
  printf ("double       %i\n", sizeof (double));
  printf ("long double  %i\n", sizeof (long double));
}
```

60   Write a program that computes the total value of the shares traded on the New York Stock

PRACTICE   Exchange on a typical day. Wire in your estimates of the number of shares traded and of the average value of each share using variables `total_volume` and `average_share_price`.

- A variable is an identifier that names a chunk of memory.

- If you want to introduce a variable, **then** you must declare the data type of that variable in a variable declaration:

  `data type` `variable name` ;

- If you want to provide an initial value for a variable, **then** include that initial value in the declaration statement:

  `data type` `variable name` = `initial-value expression` ;

- If you want to reassign a variable, **then** use an assignment statement:

  `variable name` = `new-value expression` ;

- The integral data types are char, short, int, and long.

4 HOW TO WRITE ARITHMETIC EXPRESSIONS

62   In Section 2, you saw sample expressions involving the multiplication operator, *, and the division operator /. In this section, you learn about additional operators and about the way C handles operator precedence and associativity.

63   You arrange for basic arithmetic calculations using the +, -, *, and / operators for addition, subtraction, multiplication, and division:

```
6 + 3      /* Add, evaluating to 9 */
6 - 3      /* Subtract, evaluating to 3 */
6 * 3      /* Multiply, evaluating to 18 */
6 / 3      /* Divide, evaluating to 2 */
6 + y      /* Add, evaluating to 6 plus y's value */
x - 3      /* Subtract, evaluating to x's value minus 3 */
x * y      /* Multiply, evaluating to x's value times y's value */
x / y      /* Divide, evaluating to x's value divided by y's value */
```

64   When an integer denominator does not divide evenly into an integer numerator, the division operator truncates, rather than rounds, the result, producing another integer. The **modulus operator**, %, produces the remainder:

```
5 / 3      /* Divide, evaluating to 1, rather than to 2 or 1.66667 */
5 % 3      /* Divide, evaluating to the remainder, 2 */
```

Of course, when dividing floating-point numbers, C produces a floating-point result:

```
5.0 / 3.0  /* Divide, evaluating to 1.66667 */
```

65   Arithmetic expressions can contain one operator, but they also can contain no operators or more than one operator:

```
6          /* Constant expression */
x          /* Variable expression */
6 + 3 + 2  /* Produces 11 */
6 - 3 - 2  /* Produces 1 */
6 * 3 * 2  /* Produces 36 */
6 / 3 / 2  /* Produces 1 */
```

66   C follows standard practice with respect to the syntax rules that dictate how the C compiler crystallizes operands around operators. In the following, for example, the C compiler takes 6 + 3 * 2 to be equivalent to 6 + (3 * 2), rather than to (6 + 3) * 2, because multiplication has **precedence** higher than addition:

```
6 + 3 * 2  /* Equivalent to 6 + (3 * 2), */
           /* rather than to (6 + 3) * 2 */
```

67 When an expression contains two operators of equal precedence, such as multiplication and division, the C compiler handles the expression as in the following examples:

```
6 / 3 * 2   /* Equivalent to (6 / 3) * 2 = 4, */
            /* rather than to 6 / (3 * 2) = 1    */
6 * 3 / 2   /* Equivalent to (6 * 3) / 2 = 9, */
            /* rather than to 6 * (3 / 2) = 6    */
```

Thus, in C, the multiplication and division operators are said to **associate** from left to right. Most operators associate from left to right, but some operators do not, as you learn in Segment 76.

68 Of course, you can always deploy parentheses around subexpressions whenever the C compiler's interpretation of the entire expression is not the interpretation that you want:

```
6 + 3 * 2       /* Value is 12, rather than 18 */
(6 + 3) * 2     /* Value is 18, rather than 12 */
```

You can also use parentheses to make your intentions clearer. In the following, for example, the parentheses are not required, but many programmers insert them anyway, just to make the meaning of the expression absolutely clear:

```
6 + 3 * 2       /* Value is clearly 12          */
6 + (3 * 2)     /* Value is even more clearly 12 */
```

Inserting such parentheses is especially useful when you are working with large expressions.

69 Most operators are **binary operators**; that is, they have two operands. In C, those two operands are found on the immediate left and immediate right of the operator. Some operators, such as the negation operator, -, and unary plus, +, have just one operand, found on the immediate right of the operator. Such operators are **unary operators**.

You can always determine whether the - and + denote unary or binary operators by looking to see whether there is any constant, variable, or subexpression to the immediate left. If there is, then - denotes subtraction and + denotes addition; otherwise, - denotes negation and + is handled as though it were not there at all.

70 The precedence of the negation operator is higher than that of +, -, *, or /:

```
- 6 * 3 / 2     /* Equivalent to ((- 6) * 3) / 2 = -9 */
```

71 When arithmetic expressions contain a mixture of data types, they are called **mixed expressions**. The general rule about mixed expressions is that C attempts to convert one number into another in a way that does not lose information. Thus, when given a mixed expression that multiplies a floating-point number by an integer, C converts the integer into a floating-point number first, before multiplying.

72 Sometimes, however, C must do a conversion that loses information, as when an integer variable is assigned a value derived from an expression that produces a floating-point number. Many C compilers issue warnings when they are asked to perform such information-losing, **narrowing conversions**.

73   If you want to tell C to convert an expression from one type to another explicitly, rather than relying on automatic conversion, possibly avoiding a quarrelsome compiler warning, you can **cast** the expression. To do casting, you prefix the expression with the name of the desired type in parentheses.

If, for example, i is an integer and d is a double, you can cast i to a double and d to an integer as follows:

```
(double) i        /* A double expression */
(int) d           /* An int expression   */
```

Note that the original types of the i and d variables remain undisturbed: i remains an `int` variable, and d remains a `double` variable.

74   Generally, you should avoid casting, because your C compiler probably will make conversion choices that are as good or better than those you force by casting.

75   The assignment operator, =, like all operators in C, produces a value. By convention, the value produced is the same as the value assigned. Thus, the value of the expression y = 5 is 5.

Accordingly, assignment expressions can appear as subexpressions nested inside larger expressions.

In the following assignment expression, for example, the assignment expression, y = 5, which assigns a value to y, appears inside a larger assignment expression, which assigns a value to x as well:

x = (y = 5)

When the assignment expression is evaluated, 5 is assigned to y first; then, the value of the subexpression, which is also 5, is assigned to x.

76   The assignment operator, =, in contrast to all the other operators that you have seen so
SIDE TRIP   far, associates from right to left. Accordingly, the expression x = y = 5 is equivalent to the expression x = (y = 5).

Fortunately, x = y = 5 *does not* mean (x = y) = 5, because the value of an assignment statement, such as x = y, is *not* a variable name. Thus, (x = y) = 5 makes no sense, and if the assignment operator were to associate left to right, x = y = 5 would make no sense either.

77   So far, you have learned about arithmetic operators, +, -, *, /, and %, and the assignment operator, =. In general, an **operator** is a symbol, or combination of symbols, that is treated by the compiler in a special way.

Most operators are special in that they receive arguments via flanking operands, rather than via the parenthesized argument lists used by ordinary functions. Some operators, such as the `malloc` function, about which you learn in Section 22, and the `free` function, about which you learn in Section 37, are special in that they do not evaluate their arguments. Still others, such as the conditional operator, about which you learn in Section 10, are special in that they evaluate some arguments, but not others.

78 The precedences and associativity of the operators that you have learned about so far are given in the following table, arranged from highest precedence to lowest. Appendix C provides a complete table.

Operators	Associativity
`- (unary) + (unary)`	right to left
`* / %`	left to right
`+ -`	left to right
`=`	right to left

- C offers negation, addition, subtraction, multiplication, division, and assignment operators, and C follows standard precedence and associativity rules.

- If you want to make your arithmetic expressions clearer, **then** use parentheses to create subexpressions.

- If you want to force C to depart from the standard C precedence rules, **then** use parentheses to create subexpressions.

- If you want to force the conversion of a value of one type into the corresponding value of another type, **then** you must cast the value by instantiating the following pattern:

`( type ) expression`

5 HOW TO WRITE STATEMENTS THAT READ INFORMATION FROM YOUR KEYBOARD

80   In this section, you learn how to use the read function, `scanf`, which enables your programs to obtain information from your keyboard, thus eliminating the need to use wired-in data when you experiment with programs.

81   The **read function** is named `scanf`, an acronym for *scan f*ormatted. The read function, `scanf`, is the complement of the display function, `printf`.

The read function picks up a value for a variable by watching what you type on your keyboard. In the following statement, for example, the read function picks up an integer and assigns that integer to an ampersand-prefixed `size_one` variable:

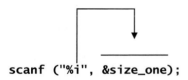

```
scanf ("%i", &size_one);
```

For now, you must think of the ampersand prefix, &, as a language idiom; later, in Section 19, you learn what ampersands do and why ampersands must appear in front of the variables that are assigned values by `scanf`.

82   Note that you use the `%i` read specification in `scanf` calls to read integers, just as you use `%i` in `printf` calls to display integers.

By extension, you would think that you would use the `%f` read specification in `scanf` to read `double` type floating-point numbers, inasmuch as you use the `%f` print specification in `printf` calls to display such numbers.

Alas, no. The `%f` read specification works only with those floating-point numbers of type `float`, and you get weird results if you accidentally use `%f` with a floating-point number of type `double`. For numbers of type `double`, you need the `%lf` read specification:

```
double price;
...
```

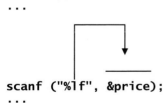

```
scanf ("%lf", &price);
...
```

See Appendix B for a larger discussion of read specifications.

83   The following sample program illustrates how you can accumulate several variable values. When using the program, you would separate each typed integer by a space, tab, or carriage return.

21

```
#include <stdio.h>
main ( ) {
  int average, size_one, size_two, size_three;
  printf ("Please type three trade sizes.\n");
  scanf ("%i", &size_one);
  scanf ("%i", &size_two);
  scanf ("%i", &size_three);
  average = (size_one + size_two + size_three) / 3;
  printf ("The average of the trade sizes is %i.\n", average);
}
```

When you execute the program, presuming you have named it `average_size`, you could witness the following:

```
average_size                       ←—— You type this
Please type three trade sizes.     ←—— The program types this
600 100 200                        ←—— You type this
The average of the trade sizes is 300.   ←—— The program types this
```

When you use the `average_size` program, you can use spaces, tabs, or carriage returns to separate the integers and to mark the end of the final integer.

Note that, if you are using the UNIX operating system, the characters that you type accumulate temporarily in an **input buffer** before delivery to your program. Delivery occurs only when you type a carriage return. Accordingly, the `average_size` program lies inert until you not only type three integers, but also supply a carriage return following the third one.

```
Spaces separate integers
     ↓   ↓

600 100 200 ←—— Carriage return marks the end of a line of input and
                delivers the accumulated characters to your program
```

84 Just as the character-string supplied to `printf` can contain many print specifications, the character-string supplied to `scanf` can contain many read specifications as well. The following `main` function picks up three values:

```
#include <stdio.h>
main ( ) {
  int sum, size_one, size_two, size_three;
  printf ("Please type three trade sizes.\n");
  scanf ("%i%i%i", &size_one, &size_two, &size_three);
  sum = size_one + size_two + size_three;
  printf ("The sum of the trade sizes is %i.\n", sum);
}
```

85 Note that the `scanf` function tolerates whitespace in the first argument. Thus, the following are equivalent:

```
        ┌─── No spaces or tabs
        ▼
        ─────
scanf ("%i%i%i", &size_one, &size_two, &size_three);

            ┌─── Space
            ▼
scanf ("%i %i     %i", &size_one, &size_two, &size_three);
                  ▲
                  └── Tab
```

Later on, in Section 36, you learn about mechanisms that enable you to read data from files. Meanwhile, if you happen to be using UNIX or DOS, you may want to take advantage of the **input-redirection mechanism** that enables you to tell your program to accept input from a file as though that input were coming from your keyboard.

To supply information from a file, you first prepare a file containing the characters that you would have supplied from your keyboard:

600 100 200

The command line that redirects input from your keyboard to the file is as follows, assuming that your program's name is `average_size`, and that your data file's name is `test_data`,

average_size < test_data

Write a program that computes the total value of the shares traded on the New York Stock Exchange on a typical day. Arrange to provide estimates of the number of shares traded and of the average value of each share at run time.

- If you plan to use the read function, **then** you must inform C of your intention by including the following line near the beginning of your program:

  #include <stdio.h>

- If you want to read data, **then** use a read statement:

  ```
  scanf ( a character string ,
         & name of first variable to receive a value ,
         & name of second variable to receive a value ,
         ...
         & name of final variable to receive a value );
  ```

- If you want to redirect input from your keyboard to a file, **then** instantiate the following pattern:

  program name < file name

6 HOW TO DEFINE SIMPLE FUNCTIONS

89 In this section, you learn how to define C functions in addition to the required `main` function. In the process, you learn how to work with arguments, parameters, and returned values.

90 If you want to know how many years it takes to double your money at a given interest rate, and you are willing to live with a good approximation, you can use the **rule of 72**, which gives the time, t, in terms of the interest rate, r:

$$t = 72.0/r$$

The approximation provides an answer that is within 3.5 percent of the correct number of years for interest rates between 1 percent and 15 percent.

Later on, in Section 7, you see how to compute the doubling time exactly. For now, you are to learn how to define your own functions using the approximation formula.

91 Of course, if you propose to use the approximation formula many times, you certainly should define a function, perhaps named `doubling_time`, to do the work:

```
#include <stdio.h>
/* ... Definition of doubling_time belongs here ... */
main ( ) {
   printf ("Your money doubles in about %f years at %f percent.\n",
                                  doubling_time (4.0),
                                             4.0);

}
```

92 In the example shown in the previous segment, the argument is a constant expression, but, of course, arguments can be variable expressions, such as `r`, or expressions containing operators, such as `r + 1.0`:

93 Whenever a call to the `doubling_time` function appears, the C compiler must arrange for the following to be done:

- Reserve a chunk of memory for the value of the argument expression.
- Write the value of that argument expression into the memory chunk.
- Identify the memory chunk with the parameter, `r`.
- Evaluate the expression `72.0 / r`.
- Return the value of `72.0 / r` for use in other computations.

94 You define the `doubling_time` function as follows:

```
double doubling_time (double r) {
   return 72.0 / r;
}
```

Here is what each part of the function definition does:

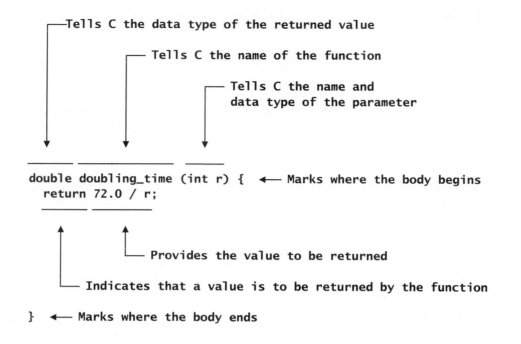

Tells C the data type of the returned value

Tells C the name of the function

Tells C the name and
data type of the parameter

```
double doubling_time (int r) {   ← Marks where the body begins
    return 72.0 / r;
```

Provides the value to be returned

Indicates that a value is to be returned by the function

```
}   ← Marks where the body ends
```

95 Note that a function's **parameters** are just variables that are initialized with argument values each time that the function is called.

96 Note also that you must declare data types for parameters and returned values when you define a C function:

- You declare the data type of each parameter in each function at the place where you introduce the parameter.

- You declare the data type of the value returned by each function at the place where you name the function to be defined.

97 In the following example, the definition of the doubling_time function appears in a complete program:

```
#include <stdio.h>
/* Define doubling_time first */
double doubling_time (double r) {
    return 72.0 / r;
}
```

```
main ( ) {
  double r = 5.0;
  printf ("Your money doubles in about %f years at %f percent.\n",
                                doubling_time (4.0),
                                            4.0);
  printf ("Your money doubles in about %f years at %f percent.\n",
                                doubling_time (r),
                                            r);
  printf ("Your money doubles in about %f years at %f percent.\n",
                                doubling_time (r + 1.0),
                                            r + 1.0);
}
```
———————————————————— Result ————————————————————
```
Your money doubles in about 18.000000 years at 4.000000 percent.
Your money doubles in about 14.400000 years at 5.000000 percent.
Your money doubles in about 12.000000 years at 6.000000 percent.
```

98   The program in Segment 97 produces a result made cumbersome by digits displayed follow-
SIDE TRIP   ing the decimal points. Later on, in Section 35, you learn how to use %f print specifications
in printf statements to limit the number of post–decimal-point digits.

99   The C compiler ordinarily requires C programs to be ordered such that each function's
definition appears before calls to that function appear. Thus, doubling_time must be
defined before main is defined, because main contains a call to doubling_time.

The reason for requiring programs to be so ordered is that such ordering simplifies the
development of efficient compilers.

Later, in Section 15, you learn that function prototypes make it possible to write programs
in which function calls do appear before definitions. Until then, be sure that each function's
definition appears before calls to that function appear.

100   You can leave out the declaration of a function's return value data type if that value is to
SIDE TRIP   be an integer, because if there is no data-type specifier, the C compiler assumes, by default,
that the returned value is to be an integer. Generally, however, most good programmers
declare the return data type for every function, except for the main function, as explained
in Segment 105.

101   So far, you have seen a function definition that exhibits one parameter only. Of course, you
can create functions with many parameters just as easily. When such a multiple-parameter
function is entered, C pairs arguments with parameters.

Suppose, for example, that you want to define a function named trade_price that computes the total price of a stock trade, given the price per share and the number of shares
traded. Now you need two, comma-separated parameters, one of which is a floating-point
price and the other of which is an integer number of shares:

```
double trade_price (double p, int n) {
  return p * n;
}
```

27

Note that you must declare the data type of each parameter individually even if all the parameters have the same type. Data types in parameter declarations, unlike data types in variable declarations, do not propagate across commas.

102 When trade_price is called, a copy of the value of the first argument becomes the value of the first parameter, p, and a copy of the value of the second argument becomes the value of the second parameter, n. Assuming, for example, that the value of the variable p is 10.2 and that the value of n is 600, the copying works like this:

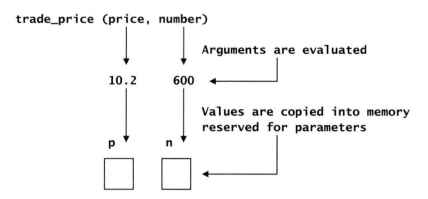

103 Some functions *do not* return values used in other computations. Instead, they are executed for some other purpose, such as displaying a value.

Accordingly, C allows you to use the void symbol as though it were a data type for return values. When C sees void used as a return value data type, C knows that nothing is to be returned.

For example, in the following program, the display of a trade's total price is handled in the display_trade_price function, so there is no value to be returned. Accordingly, void appears instead of a data-type name in the definition of display_trade_price, and display_trade_price contains no return statement:

```c
#include <stdio.h>
/* Define display_trade_price first */
void display_trade_price (double p, int n) {
  printf ("The total value of the trade is %f.\n", p * n);
}
/* Then, define main */
main ( ) {
  double price = 10.2;
  int number = 600;
  display_trade_price (price, number);
}
```
———————————————— Result ————————————————
The total value of the trade is 6120.000000.

104   Because `display_trade_price` has no return statement, it is said to **fall off its end**, returning nothing, which is allowed for only those functions that have a `void` return type.

Some programmers think it inelegant to have functions that fall off their ends. Accordingly, those programmers write empty `return` statements, as in the following amended version of `display_trade_price`:

```
void display_trade_price (double p, int n) {
  printf ("The total value of the trade is %f.\n", p * n);
  return;
}
```

105   Many programmers treat the `main` function specially in that they omit the return type declaration and include no return statement. Such `main` functions are treated by many C compilers as though there were an `int` type declaration in front of `main` and a `return 0;` statement at the end of `main`. The 0 tells the operating system that the program terminated in the expected way, rather than with some sort of error.

Some C compilers issue warnings whenever either the type declaration or the return statement are missing.

106   Note that, because C is case sensitive, the function name `display_trade_price` is different from the function name `Display_trade_price` and different from the function name `DISPLAY_trade_price`. Most C programmers use all–lower-case function names.

107   Write a program that computes the total value of the shares traded on the New York
PRACTICE   Stock Exchange on a typical day. Have the computation performed by a function named `estimate_total_value`. Arrange to provide estimates of the number of shares traded and the average value of each share at run time.

108   The gravitational attraction of the earth on an object is proportional to the inverse square
PRACTICE   of the distance between the center of the earth and the center of the object. Write a program that determines the relative weight of an object at two distances. Write and use a function name `square` in your solution. Use your program to determine how much more an object weighs at sea level than at the top of Mount Everest. Also use your program to determine how much more an object is attracted to the center of the earth at sea level than it would be if it were at the same distance from the center as is the earth's moon.

109
HIGHLIGHTS

- Whenever a function is called, the function's arguments are evaluated and copies of the resulting values are assigned to the function's parameters. Then, the statements in the function's body are evaluated. When a return statement is evaluated, the argument of the return expression is evaluated, and that value becomes the value of the function call.

- When you define a function, C requires you to declare a data type for each parameter and for the value that the function returns.

- If you want to define a function that does not return a value, **then** supply `void` in place of an ordinary data-type declaration.

- If you want to define your own function, **then** instantiate the following pattern:

```
data type  function name ( data type 1  parameter 1 ,
                            ...,
                           data type 1  parameter 1 ) {
   declaration 1
   ...
   declaration m
   statement 1
   ...
   statement n
}
```

7 HOW TO BENEFIT FROM PROCEDURE ABSTRACTION

110 In this section, you review what procedure abstraction is and how procedure abstraction increases your efficiency and makes your programs easier to maintain.

111 When you move computational detail into a function, such as the `trade_price` function defined in Segment 101, you are said to be doing **procedure abstraction**, and you are said to be hiding the details of how a computation is done behind a **procedure-abstraction barrier**.

112 The key virtue of procedure abstraction is that *you make it easy to reuse your programs.* Instead of trying to copy particular lines of program, you—or another programmer—arrange to call a previously defined function.

113 Another virtue of procedure abstraction is that *you push details out of sight and out of mind*, making your programs easier to read and enabling you to concentrate on high-level steps.

114 Another virtue of procedure abstraction is that *you can debug your programs more easily.* By dividing a program into small, independently debuggable pieces, you exploit the powerful divide-and-conquer problem-solving heuristic.

115 Still another virtue of procedure abstraction is that *you easily can augment repetitive computations.* For example, you have seen `doubling_time` defined this way:

```
double doubling_time (double r) {
  return 72.0 / r; }
```

You can easily decide to add a line to `doubling_time` that displays the doubling time:

```
double doubling_time (double r) {
  printf ("The doubling time for rate %f is approximately %f years.\n",
                                    r,                        72.0 / r);
  return 72.0 / r;
}
```

Thus, to arrange for display, you do not need even to bother to find all the places where a doubling time is computed; you need only to change the `doubling_time` function's definition.

116 Another virtue of function abstraction is that *you can improve more easily how a computation is done.* You might decide, for example, that it is wasteful for your `doubling_time` function to divide `72.0` by the rate twice. Accordingly you might decide to do the division just once, using a variable, named `result`, to hold on to the value:

```
double doubling_time (double r) {
  double result = 72.0 / r;
  printf ("The doubling time for rate %f is approximately %f years.\n",
                                    r,                     result);

  return result;
}
```

Again, you do not need to bother to find all the places where the volume is computed using the doubling_time function; you need only to change the doubling_time function's definition.

117 Still another virtue of procedure abstraction is that *you can change easily the way that a computation is done.* If you decide, for example, to replace the 72.0/*r* approximation by an exact computation, you can redefine doubling_time easily to accommodate the change using the following exact formula:

$$t = \frac{log2.0}{log(1.0 + r/100)}$$

Note that the exact formula requires a function, log, drawn from C's mathematics library, as indicated by the inclusion of the #include <math.h> line:

```
#include <math.h>
...
double doubling_time (double r) {
  double result = log (2.0) / log (1.0 + r / 100.0);
  printf ("The doubling time for rate %f is exactly %f years.\n",
                                    r,              result);

  return result;
}
...
```

118 Note that some implementations of C incorporate the mathematics library into the stan-
SIDE TRIP dard library and some implementations do not. For those implementations that do not, you may need to add –lm to the command you use to compile a program that makes use of the mathematics library. Thus you would compile analyze_trades as follows:

```
cc -lm -o analyze_trades analyze_trades.c
```

119 Write a function named c_to_f that transforms an integer argument into twice that integer
PRACTICE plus 30.

Next, amend your c_to_f function such that it displays "Performing an approximate temperature conversion" every time that it is called.

Next, improve your c_to_f function by having it add 40 to the argument, multiply by 9/5, and subtract 40.

Finally, change your c_to_f function such that the argument is in Celsius degrees relative to absolute zero and the result returned is in Fahrenheit degrees relative to absolute zero. Absolute zero is −273 degrees Celsius.

For each change, comment on the corresponding benefit provided by function abstraction.

- *Procedure abstraction* hides the details of computations inside functions, thus moving those details behind an abstraction barrier.

- You should practice procedure abstraction so as to take advantage of the following benefits:

  - Your programs become easier to reuse.

  - Your programs become easier to read.

  - Your programs become easier to debug.

  - Your programs become easier to augment.

  - Your programs become easier to improve.

  - Your programs become easier to change.

8 HOW TO WORK WITH LOCAL AND GLOBAL VARIABLES

121 The **extent** of a variable is the time during which a chunk of memory is allocated for that variable. The **scope** of a variable is that portion of a program where that variable can be evaluated or assigned.

In this section, you learn how C handles extent and scope. In particular, you learn that you can reuse names for parameters and local variables, as long as you do not try to use any name more than once per function.

122 It is important to know that the parameter values established when a function is entered are available only inside the function. It is as though C builds a isolating fence to protect any other uses of the same parameter name outside of the function. Consider `doubling_time`, for example:

```
double doubling_time (double r) {
   return log (2.0) / log (1.0 + r / 100.0);
}
```

When `doubling_time` is used, any existing values for other variables that happen to be named r are protected:

```
doubling_time fence ────────────
   The value of r inside this fence        The values of r
   is isolated from values outside         outside the fence,
                                           if any, are not
   Function computes the doubling          affected by the value
   time using the value of r               inside
   inside this fence
```

123 The reason that C acts as though it builds an isolating fence around each function's parameters is that C reserves a chunk of memory for each parameter every time that the corresponding function is called. In the `doubling_time` example, a new chunk of memory is reserved for the parameters, r, and the argument's value is placed in that chunk, as shown here:

```
Memory reserved for r,              Memory reserved for r,
a variable in main                  a parameter in doubling_time

   ┌────────┐                          ┌────────┐
   │        │ ──────────────────────▶  │        │
   └────────┘                          └────────┘
```

Thus, the reassignment of the parameter, r, inside the function has no effect on the value of the variable, r, outside, even though the names, r and r, happen to be the same.

Because C generally reserves new chunks of memory for parameters and variables, into which values are copied, C is said to be a **call-by-value** language.

The alternative convention, `call-by-reference`, dictates that a variable-only argument, such as r, uses the same memory as the corresponding parameter. Accordingly, reassignment of the corresponding parameter reassigns the argument variable as well.

125 In the following program, for example, r's value is 5.0 before `doubling_time` has been entered, r's value is 10.0 as `doubling_time` is executed, and r's value is 5.0 after the execution of `doubling_time`.

```
#include <stdio.h>
#include <math.h>
/* Define doubling_time first */
double doubling_time (double r) {
   return log (2.0) / log (1.0 + r / 100.0);
}
/* Then, define main */
main ( ) {
   double r = 5.0;
   printf ("The value of r is %f.\n", r);
   printf ("The doubling time at twice that rate is %f.\n",
           doubling_time (r + r));
   printf ("The value of r is still %f.\n", r);
}
```

——————————————— Result ———————————————

```
The value of r is 5.000000.
The doubling time at twice that rate is 7.272541.
The value of r is still 5.000000.
```

126 Because parameters are just variables that happen to be initialized by argument values, you can change the value of any parameter using an assignment statement. For example, you could amend the `doubling_time` function as follows:

```
double doubling_time (double r) {
   /* At this point, r's value is the rate expressed as a percentage */
   r = r / 100.0;
   /* Now r's value is the rate expressed as a fraction */
   r = log (2.0) / log (1.0 + r);
   /* Now r's value is the result of the doubling-time computation */
   return r;
}
```

However, using r to hold three different values is bad programming practice, because such use associates r with multiple meanings.

127 Here are two other important consequences of parameter isolation:

- The values of a function's parameters are not available after that function has returned.

- When one function calls another, the values of the parameters in the calling function are not available during the execution of the called function.

128 In the following program, `doubling_time` is redefined, yet again, albeit awkwardly, to illustrate the limited availability of parameter values:

```
#include <stdio.h>
/* Define doubling_time_aux and doubling_time first */
double doubling_time_aux ( ) {
  /* Following line DEFECTIVE! */
  return log (2.0) / log (1.0 + r);
}
double doubling_time (double r) {
  r = r / 100.0;
  return doubling_time_aux ( );
}
/* Then, define main */
main ( ) {
  printf ("The doubling time is %f.\n", doubling_time (5.0));
  /* Following line DEFECTIVE! */
  printf ("The value r is %f.\n", r);
}
```

In this program, the `doubling_time` function asks a subfunction, `doubling_time_aux`—a function defined with no parameters—to perform the actual computation. The C compiler cannot compile `doubling_time_aux`, however, because no value for r is available to `doubling_time_aux`.

Moreover, C cannot compile the second `printf` statement in the `main` function. The reason is that r exists only during the execution of the function in which it appears as a parameter; r no longer exists once that function has returned.

129 At this point, you are ready to learn about the distinction between a *declaration* and a *definition*. In general, a **declaration** is a program element that provides a compiler with essential information or useful advice. Thus, when you specify the type of a variable or parameter, you are said to *declare* the variable or parameter.

A **definition** causes a compiler to set aside memory at compile time. For example, when you introduce a variable *outside* of any function definition, you both *declare* and *define* the variable, because you inform the compiler about the variable's type and you cause the compiler to set aside memory for the variable at compile time.

On the other hand, when you introduce a variable *inside* of a function definition, you only *declare* that variable, because the compiler does not set aside memory for such variables at compile time.

Generally, when a variable is both declared and defined, you say, as a sort of shorthand, that it is defined; otherwise, it is declared.

Functions are both *declared* and *defined*, because you must specify their return type and because the compiler sets aside memory for functions at compile time.

130 A variable *declared* inside a function definition is said to be a **local variable**; some programmers prefer to call such a variable an **automatic variable**. A variable *defined* outside of any function definition is said to be a **global variable**.

131   What you have learned about parameters also applies to local variables:

- Local variables are available only inside the function in which they are declared. Thus, the assignment of a local variable has no effect on other, identically named variables or parameters that appear in the definitions of other functions.

- The values of a function's local variables are not available after that function has returned.

- When one function calls another, the values of the local variables in the calling function are not available during the execution of the called function.

132   A **compound statement**, also known as a **block**, is a group of statements surrounded by
SIDE TRIP braces. A compound statement can have its own local variables.

The scope of the local variables declared in a compound statement is the compound statement itself. The extent of such local variables is the time during which the compound statement is executed.

Note that function bodies are compound statements. You see other examples in Section 10, because compound statements are used liberally inside C's `if` and `if-else` statements.

133   The rules for global variables—those defined outside of any function—are quite different:

- Global variable values are available to all functions that are defined after the global variable is defined, except in functions in which there is a parameter or local variable that happens to have the same name. Such parameters or local variables are said to **shadow** the corresponding global variables.

- In places where a global variable value is not shadowed, its value can be changed by an assignment statement. The change affects all subsequent evaluation of the global variable.

134   The memory set aside for a global variable is never reallocated, so global variables are said to have **static extent**. The memory allocated for parameters and local variables is reallocated as soon as the corresponding function has finished executing, so parameters and local variables are said to have **dynamic extent**.

Global variables can be evaluated and assigned at any point in a program after they are defined, so global variables are said to have **universal scope**. Parameters and local variables can be evaluated and assigned only in the function in which they are declared. Accordingly, parameters and local variables are said to have **local scope**.

135   Suppose that you want to write many functions that involve, say, the interest rate offered to you by your bank on deposits and your marginal tax rate. You could wire the current rates into such functions, but then you would have to edit and recompile your program whenever rates change. A more efficient alternative is to have your program pick up values for those rates from your keyboard whenever your program runs.

The following program, for example, obtains values for the two rates and assigns those values to global variables, `deposit_rate` and `marginal_rate`, at run time. Those global variables are then used to compute the net rate:

```
#include <stdio.h>
/* Define deposit_rate and marginal_rate to be global variables */
double deposit_rate, marginal_rate;
void display_net_rate ( ) {
  printf ("The net rate for deposits in your bracket is %f percent.\n",
          deposit_rate * (1 - marginal_rate / 100.0));
}
/* Then, define main */
main ( ) {
  scanf ("%lf%lf", &deposit_rate, &marginal_rate);
  display_net_rate ( );
}
```

———————————— Sample Data ————————————

3.5 38.5

———————————— Result ————————————

The net rate for deposits in your bracket is 2.152500 percent.

136
SIDE TRIP **Static global variables** are variables whose scope includes one file of a multiple-file program. Hence, a static global variable can be evaluated and assigned at any point in one file, after it is defined, but that same static global variable cannot be evaluated or assigned at any point in any other file. Static global variables are discussed in Segment 683.

137 Now suppose that you want to write many functions that involve, say, the minimum return on investment you are willing to accept. You decide that you can fix the minimum return before you compile your program, and not only do you never expect to change that minimum return rate, but also you want the C compiler to stop you if you try to change it.

You could, of course, decide that the minimum return rate is a rate such as 2.5, and use 2.5 explicitly wherever you need the minimum return rate. That would make your program hard to modify, however, should your expectations ever change.

Plainly, you need a way to express constants symbolically such that you can change their values but your program cannot. In C, the approved approach is to define what is called a **macro symbol**. Whenever you define a macro symbol, you tell C that you want a symbol, such as MINIMUM_RETURN_RATE, to be replaced by a character string, such as 2.5, wherever the symbol appears in your program. This substitution takes place before the main work of compilation begins.

To declare a macro symbol, you include a line such as the following in your program:

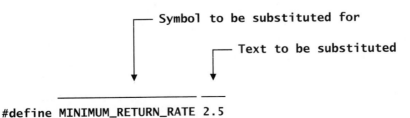

```
#define MINIMUM_RETURN_RATE 2.5
```

39

Note that, by convention, macro symbols contain only upper-case characters. Note also that macro-symbol declarations exhibit no equal sign and no semicolon.

138 Unlike variables, macro symbols cannot be assigned. Suppose you were to write the following:

```
#define MINIMUM_RETURN_RATE 2.5
...
MINIMUM_RETURN_RATE = 5.0;
```

Because the substitution for MINIMUM_RETURN_RATE would be done before the main work of compiling would begin, the compiler would encounter the following altered line, about which it would complain vigorously:

```
2.5 = 5.0;
```

139 The following program uses a macro symbol, MINIMUM_RETURN_RATE, as well as global variables, deposit_rate and marginal_rate:

```
#include <stdio.h>
/* Define MINIMUM_RETURN_RATE to be a macro */
#define MINIMUM_RETURN_RATE 2.5
/* Define deposit_rate and marginal_rate to be global variables */
double deposit_rate, marginal_rate;
void display_analysis ( ) {
  double net_rate;
  net_rate = deposit_rate - deposit_rate * marginal_rate / 100.0;
  printf ("The net rate for your deposit is %f percent.\n", net_rate);
  printf ("The deviation from the acceptable rate is %f percent.\n",
          net_rate - MINIMUM_RETURN_RATE);
}
/* Then, define main */
main ( ) {
  scanf ("%lf%lf", &deposit_rate, &marginal_rate);
  display_analysis ( );
}
```
——————————————— Sample Data ———————————————
```
7.1 42.5
```
——————————————— Result ———————————————
```
The net rate for your deposit is 4.082500 percent.
The deviation from the acceptable rate is 1.582500 percent.
```

140 More sophisticated macros have parameters and take arguments. Consider, for example,
SIDE TRIP the following macro, which you can use when you want to square a number:

```
#define square (x) x * x          /* First version */
```

Once you have defined `square` as a macro, your C compiler will replace any appearance of `square`, and its argument, before actual compilation is done. Suppose, for example, that your program exhibits the following statement:

```
result = square (length);
```

Then, your C compiler substitutes the character string, `length`, for the parameter, `x`, in the macro definition, producing the following statement:

```
result = length * length;
```

141   Note how strongly functions differ from macros:

SIDE TRIP

- Functions are called at run time. Macros are expanded at compile time.

- Function parameters are typed. Macro parameters are not.

- Function arguments are evaluated, and copies of those values are assigned to parameters. Macro arguments are not evaluated; instead, they are viewed as text to be substituted for the macro's parameters before the real work of compilation begins.

Because macro parameters are replaced by text, macros are said to be handled as **call-by-name** parameters.

142   One common error is to write macros with single-symbol arguments (such as `length`) in
SIDE TRIP
mind, only to use those macros with multiple-symbol expressions. Suppose, for example, that you write the following statement, using the macro defined in Segment 140:

```
result = square (x + y);
```

When expanded, your program works as though you had written the following:

```
result = x + y * x + y
```

Because multiplication has precedence higher than that of addition, you might as well have written `x + (y * x) + y`, whereas you probably were thinking you would get the effect of writing `(x + y) * (x + y)`.

The solution is to use parentheses routinely and liberally when defining macros. Consider, for example, the following definition of the `square` macro:

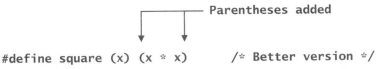

Parentheses added

```
#define square (x) (x * x)        /* Better version */
```

Given the new definition, the problem raised in Segment 142 disappears, because the new macro definition leads to the following, parenthesized expansion:

```
result = (x + y) * (x + y);
```

Note, however, that the definition of `square` as a macro leads to the calculation of `x + y` twice. If you were to implement `square` as a function, `x + y` would be computed only once, as the argument is evaluated, but then your program would be doing a run-time function call. Thus, the use of macros can involve complex performance tradeoffs.

143

SIDE TRIP

You can, of course, define macros with multiple arguments. The following, for example, is a macro that expands to an expression that provides the maximum of two numbers:

```
#define max (x, y) ((x) > (y) ? (x) : (y))
```

One modest advantage of using such a macro, instead of a function, is that the macro works no matter what data types are associated with x and y. One disadvantage is that the macro computes the value of the larger of the two argument expressions twice.

144

PRACTICE

Amend the temperature-conversion function that you were asked to write in Segment 119 such that, each time that it is called, it reports the number of times that it has been called.

145

HIGHLIGHTS

- A local variable is a variable that is declared inside a function definition. A global variable is a variable that is defined outside of any function definition.

- C isolates parameters and local variables, enabling you to reuse their names. Accordingly, the values of a function's parameters and local variables are not available after that function has returned. Also, when one function calls another, the values of the parameters and local variables in the calling function are not available during the execution of the called function.

- You can obtain a value for a global variable everywhere, except in functions in which there is a parameter or local variable that happens to have the same name. You can assign a value to a global variable anywhere that you can obtain a value for that variable.

- You can obtain a value for a global constant everywhere, except in functions in which there is a parameter or local variable that happens to have the same name.

- Macro substitutions take place before the main work of compilation begins.

- If you want to define a macro substitution, **then** instantiate the following pattern:

```
#DEFINE  macro name   text to be substituted
```

9 HOW TO PERFORM TESTS USING NUMERICAL PREDICATES

146　In this and the next two sections, you learn how to do routine testing and branching. You see that C's mechanisms for accomplishing such tasks are not much different from those you would find in just about any programming language. In particular, in this section, you learn how to test numbers.

147　Functions and operators that return values representing true or false are called **predicates**. C offers operator predicates that test the relationship between a pair of numbers:

Predicate	Purpose
==	Are two numbers equal?
!=	Are two numbers not equal?
>	Is the first number greater than the second?
<	Is the first number less than the second?
>=	Is the first number greater than or equal to the second?
<=	Is the first number less than or equal to the second?

148　The value of the expression 6 == 3, in which the equality operator appears, is 0, which means **false** as far as C is concerned.

The value of the expression 6 != 3, in which the inequality operator appears, is 1, which means **true** as far as C is concerned.

Thus, the value returned by the == and != predicates may be either 0 or 1:

Integer Value	Meaning
0	False
1	True

149　A common error is to write =, the assignment operator, when you intend to check for equality. Be sure to remember that the equality predicate is written as a double equal sign, ==.

150　You now know that, whenever the character ! is followed immediately by the character =, the two characters together denote the inequality operator.

Note, however, that the ! character can appear alone, in which case the ! character denotes the **not** operator. The *not* operator is a unary operator that inverts true and false. Thus, the value of !0 is 1 and !1 is 0. Similarly, the value of !(6 == 3) is 1, meaning that it is true that 6 is equal to 3 is false. Also, the value of !(6 != 3) is 0, meaning that it is false that 6 is not equal to 3 is false.

151　Actually, C interprets any integer other than 0 as true. Accordingly, the *not* operator, !, turns any integer other than 0 into 0.

152   Note that you must have a program perform a cast, of the sort you learned about in Segment 73, if you want the program to compare an integer with a floating-point number. The following program illustrates how such comparisons must be performed:

```
#include <stdio.h>
main ( ) {
  int i = 50;
  double d = 50.0;
  printf ("i == (int) d     yields %i\n", (i == (int) d));
  printf ("(double) i != d yields %i\n", ((double) i != d));
  printf ("i > (int) d      yields %i\n", (i > (int) d))    ;
  printf ("(double) i < d  yields %i\n", ((double) i < d)) ;
  printf ("i >= (int) d     yields %i\n", (i >= (int) d))   ;
  printf ("(double) i <= d yields %i\n", ((double) i <= d));
}
```

──────────────── Result ────────────────
```
i == (int) d     yields 1
(double) i != d yields 0
i > (int) d      yields 0
(double) i < d  yields 0
i >= (int) d     yields 1
(double) i <= d yields 1
```

153   The stock value of a company is the product of the price per share and the number of
PRACTICE   shares outstanding. Write a program that accepts the prices per share and numbers of shares outstanding for two companies. Your program is to display 1 if the stock value of the first company is greater than that of the second; otherwise, your program is to display 0.

154
HIGHLIGHTS

- A *predicate* is a function that returns 0 or 1.

- In C, 0 means false, and any other integer means true.

- The ! operator means *not*; the ! operator transforms 0 into 1 and any integer other than 0 into 0.

- If you want to compare two numbers of different types, **then** you must cast one to match the type of the other.

10 HOW TO WRITE ONE-WAY AND TWO-WAY CONDITIONAL STATEMENTS

155 In this section, you learn how to use conditional statements when the computation that you want to perform depends on the value of an expression—possibly an expression involving one or more predicates.

156 Conceptually, a **Boolean expression** is an expression that produces a true or false result. Reduced to practice in C, a Boolean expression is an expression that produces either 0, meaning false, or any other integer, meaning true.

157 An `if` statement contains a Boolean expression, in parentheses, followed by an embedded statement:

```
if ( Boolean expression )
   embedded statement
```

When the Boolean expression of an `if` statement evaluates to *any integer* other than 0, C considers the expression to be true and executes the embedded statement; otherwise, if the Boolean expression evaluates to 0, C considers the expression to be false and skips the embedded statement.

158 Suppose, for example, that you want to write a program that displays a message that depends on a stock's price–earnings ratio. Specifically, if the stock's price divided by the previous year's per-share profit is greater than 30, you want your program to display `It is expensive!`; if the price–earnings ratio is less than 10, you want your program to display `It is cheap!`.

Further suppose that you are able to assign the price–earnings ratio to a variable named `ratio`, using the read function, `scanf`.

One solution is to write a program that uses an `if` statement in which the embedded statements are display statements:

```
#include <stdio.h>
main ( ) {
  int ratio;
  scanf ("%i", &ratio);
  if (ratio < 10) printf ("It is cheap!\n");
  if (ratio > 30) printf ("It is expensive!\n");
}
```
———————————— Sample Data ————————————
```
35
```
———————————— Result ————————————
```
It is expensive!
```

159 The `if-else` statement is like the `if` statement, except that there is a second embedded statement, one that follows `else`:

```
if ( Boolean expression )
   if-true statement
  else
   if-false statement
```

The if-false statement is executed if the Boolean expression evaluates to 0 or, said another way, if the Boolean expression is false.

160   Either the if-true statement or the if-false statement or both may be embedded if statements. Accordingly, another solution to the ratio-testing problem looks like this:

```
#include <stdio.h>
main ( ) {
  int ratio;
  scanf ("%i", &ratio);
  if (ratio < 10)
    printf ("It is cheap!\n");
   else
    if (ratio > 30)
      printf ("It is expensive!\n");
}
```

Note that the first if statement's if-false statement is, itself, an embedded if statement:

```
if (ratio > 30)
   printf ("It is expensive!\n");
```

This second if statement is executed only if the ratio is *not* less than 10. If the ratio is between 10 and 30, nothing is displayed.

161   The layout of nested if statements is a matter of convention. Here is another common arrangement:

```
#include <stdio.h>
main ( ) {
  int ratio;
  scanf ("%i", &ratio);
  if (ratio < 10)
    printf ("It is cheap!\n");
  else if (ratio > 30)
    printf ("It is expensive!\n");
}
```

Whatever convention you use, you should be able to defend it on the ground that you think it contributes to program clarity.

162   Suppose that you want to execute more than one statement when an if or if-else statement's Boolean expression is true or not true. You need only to combine the multiple statements, using braces, into a single **compound statement**.

```
{ statement 1
  . . .
  statement n }
```

In the following if-else statement, for example, you not only want to display a message when the value of ratio is above 30, but also want to assign 1 to a suitable variable so as to record that the ratio has gone above the threshold of 30:

```
if (ratio > 30) {
  high_ratio_switch = 1;
  printf ("It is expensive!  High ratio switch set to %i.\n",
          high_ratio_switch);
}
```

163   Note the ambiguity in the following nested if statement:

```
if (ratio > 10)
  if (ratio < 30)
    printf ("It is in the normal range.\n");
  else printf ("It is ?.\n");
```

With what should you replace the question mark: expensive or cheap? As laid out on the page, it seems that expensive is the right answer. Laid out another way, however, you might have the impression that cheap is the right answer:

```
if (ratio > 10)
  if (ratio < 30)
    printf ("It is in the normal range.\n");
else printf ("It is ?.\n");
```

Because C pays no attention to layout, you need to know that C assumes that each else belongs to the nearest if that is not already matched with an else. Thus, the question mark would be replaced by expensive.

164   Although you can rely on the rule that if-false statements belong to the nearest unmatched if statement, it is better programming practice to use braces to avoid potential misreading.

In the following example, the question mark would be replaced by expensive, because the braces clearly group the if-false statement with the second if statement.

```
if (ratio > 10)
  {
  if (ratio < 30)
    printf ("It is in the normal range.\n");
    else printf ("It is ?.\n");
  }
```

On the other hand, in the following example, it is clear that the question mark would be replaced by cheap, because this time the braces clearly group the if-false statement with the first if statement.

```
if (ratio > 10)
  {
  if (ratio < 30)
    printf ("It is in the normal range.\n");
  }
  else printf ("It is ?.\n");
```

165 Many C programmers use braces in every `if` statement they write, even though the braces often surround just one statement. Such programmers argue that the habitual use of braces reduces errors later on when a program is modified. When braces are not used, it is easy to add a second embedded statement to an `if` statement, yet to forget that the modification requires the addition of braces.

166 Recall that C's `if` statement executes its embedded statement if the value of the Boolean expression is *not* 0. C has no complimentary statement, which might be called *unless*, if it existed, for which the embedded statement is executed when the value of the Boolean expression is 0.

One way to get the effect of the nonexistent *unless* statement is by prefacing the Boolean expression with the *not* operator, !. Thus, the following tests are equivalent:

```
if (ratio < 10) printf ("It is cheap!\n");
if (!(ratio >= 10)) printf ("It is cheap!\n");
```

167 Another way to get the effect of the nonexistent `unless` statement is via an `if-else` statement with an **empty statement**—one that consists of a semicolon only—in the if-true position. Thus, the following tests are equivalent:

```
if (ratio < 10) printf ("It is cheap!\n");
if (ratio >= 10)
    ;
  else printf ("It is cheap!\n");
```

168 So far, you have learned how to use `if-else` statements to execute one of two embedded computation-performing *statements*. You should also know about C's **conditional operator**, which enables you to compute a value from one of two embedded, value-producing *expressions*.

The conditional operator sees frequent service in display statements, where it helps you to produce the proper singular–plural distinctions. Consider, for example, the following program, which displays a price change:

```
#include <stdio.h>
main ( ) {
  int change;
  scanf ("%i", &change);
  if (change == 1)
    printf ("The price has changed by %i point.\n", change);
  else
    printf ("The price has changed by %i points.\n", change);
}
```
———————————————— Sample Data ————————————————
1
———————————————— Result ————————————————
The price has changed by 1 point.

The program works, but most C programmers would be unhappy, because there are two separate output statements that are almost identical. Such duplication makes programs longer, and the longer a program is, the greater the chance that a bug will creep in.

Accordingly, it would be safer to move the variation—the part that produces either the word *degree* or the word *degrees*—into a value-producing expression inside a single display statement.

169 The following is the general pattern for C's value-producing conditional-operator expression:

Boolean expression ? if-true expression : if-false expression

Note that, in contrast to the operators you have seen so far, the conditional operator consists of a combination of distributed symbols, ? and :, separating three operands—the Boolean expression, the if-true expression, and the if-false expression. Thus, the conditional operator combination is said to be a **ternary operator** with **distributed operator symbols**.

Note also the similarity to the if-else statement—it is as though the if became a question mark, and moved between the first two expressions, and the else became a colon.

Finally, note that either the if-true expression or the if-false expression is evaluated, but both are not. Thus, any variable assignments or other side effects in the unevaluated expression do not occur.

170 The value of the following conditional-operator expression is the character string "point" if the price change is one point; otherwise, the value is the character string "points":

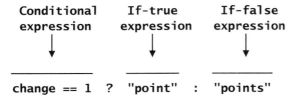

```
Conditional      If-true        If-false
expression     expression      expression
     |              |               |
     ↓              ↓               ↓
_____   _____    _____

change == 1  ?   "point"   :    "points"
```

You can, if you want, employ parentheses to delineate the Boolean expression, but parentheses are not needed in the example, because the equality operator has precedence higher than that of the conditional operator, as shown in Appendix C.

171 Because a conditional-operator expression, unlike an if statement, produces a value, you can place it inside another expression. In particular, a conditional-operator expression can be an argument in a printf expression, because C allows you to insert a character string into the string displayed by printf. You simply place %s in printf's first argument at the place where you want the character string.

In the following, for example, a conditional-operator expression appears inside a printf expression, solving the duplication problem encountered in Segment 168:

```
#include <stdio.h>
main ( ) {
  int change;
  scanf ("%i", &change);
  printf ("The price has changed by %i %s.\n",
          change,
          change == 1 ? "point" : "points");
}
```
———————————————— Sample Data ————————————————
```
1
```
———————————————— Result ————————————————
```
The price has changed by 1 point.
```

If the change is one point, the value returned by the Boolean expression, and subsequently displayed, is "point"; otherwise, the value returned and subsequently displayed is "points".

172 You can, if you want, use conditional-operator expressions in place of if statements, as
SIDE TRIP in the following example, in which one of the two display expressions is evaluated:

```
#include <stdio.h>
main ( ) {
  int change;
  scanf ("%i", &change);
  change == 1
    ?
    printf ("The price has changed by %i point.\n", change)
    :
    printf ("The price has changed by %i points.\n", change)
    ;
}
```

This program not only reintroduces needless duplication, but also introduces a conditional-operator expression that is not inside any other expression that can make use of the value produced. Instead, the conditional-operator expression forms a complete statement. Such use of the conditional operator is considered poor programming practice, and your C compiler should issue a warning.

Write a program that transforms a company's price–earnings ratio into one of three messages: "The company appears to be undervalued," "The company appears to be normally valued," or "The company appears to be overvalued." Your program's input is four numbers: the first is the price of the stock, the second is the number of shares outstanding, the third is the most recent annual earnings of the company, and the fourth is the average price–earnings ratio for companies in the same line of business. The overvalued and undervalued messages should not appear unless the company's price–earnings ratio differs from the average by more than 10 percent.

Write a program that displays a message indicating the deviation of a company's price–earnings ratio from the average price–earnings ratio, truncated to the nearest integer, of the form `The company is` `overvalued or undervalued` `by` `number` `percentage points`. Your program's input is four numbers: price per share, shares outstanding, earnings, and average price–earnings ratio. Be sure that, if the deviation is just 1 percent, the word *point*, rather than *points*, appears.

- If you want to execute a statement only when an expression produces a value other than 0, **then** use an `if` statement:

  ```
  if (Boolean expression) statement
  ```

- If you want to execute one statement when an expression evaluates to any integer other than 0, and another when the expression evaluates to 0, **then** use an `if-else` statement:

  ```
  if (Boolean expression)
      if-true statement
  else
      if-false statement
  ```

- If you want to execute a group of statements in an `if` or `if-else` statement, **then** use braces to combine those statements into a single compound statement.

- If you want to use nested `if-else` statements, **then** use braces to clarify your grouping intention.

- If you want the value of an expression to be the value of one of two embedded expressions, **and** you want the choice to be determined by the value of a Boolean expression, **then** instantiate the following pattern:

  ```
  Boolean expression
      ?
      if-true expression : if-false expression
  ```

11 HOW TO COMBINE BOOLEAN EXPRESSIONS

176 In this section, you learn how to combine Boolean expressions to form larger Boolean expressions.

177 Roughly, the **and** operator, **&&**, and the **or** operator, ¦¦, do what they sound like they should do. The **and** operator returns 1 if *both* of its operands evaluate to any integer other than 0. The **or** operator returns 1 if *either* of its operands evaluates to an integer other than 0.

178 Recall that C treats 0 as false and any integer other than 0 as true. That is why you see the contorted expression, *any integer other than* 0, instead of just 1.

179 The following expression, for example, evaluates to 1 only if the value of the `ratio` variable is between 10 and 30:

```
10 < ratio && ratio < 30
```

Accordingly, the `printf` statement embedded in the following `if` statement is evaluated only if the value of the `ratio` variable is in the 10-to-30 range.

```
if (10 < ratio && ratio < 30)
  printf ("It is in the normal range.\n");
```

180 The evaluation of **&&** and ¦¦ expressions is complicated by the fact that some subexpressions may not be evaluated at all.

In **&&** expressions, the left-side operand is evaluated first: If the value of the left-side operand is 0, the right-side operand is ignored completely, and the value of the **&&** expression is 0.

If both operands evaluate to some integer other than 0, the value of the **&&** expression is 1.

In ¦¦ expressions, the left-side operand also is evaluated first: If the left-side operand evaluates to some integer other than 0, the right-side operand is ignored completely, and the value of the ¦¦ expression is 1; if both operands evaluate to 0, the value of the ¦¦ expression is 0.

181 Two ampersands, **&&**, and two vertical bars, ¦¦, are used for *and* and *or*, because & and ¦ are reserved for operations on bits, rather than on integers. Operations on bits are explained in Section 30

182 C, as a rule, does not specify the order of operand evaluation. Thus, **&&** and ¦¦ are exceptions to the general rule. The other exceptions are the conditional operator, about which you learned in Segment 169, and the comma operator, about which you learn in Segment 204.

It is possible to use && instead of an `if` statement by exploiting the property that the right-side operand of an && expression is evaluated only if the value of the left-side operand is not 0. Thus, the following two expressions are equivalent:

```
if (ratio > 30) printf ("It is expensive!\n");
```

```
(ratio > 30) && printf ("It is expensive!\n");
```

Similarly, it is possible to use ¦¦ instead of an `if-else` statement by exploiting the property that the right-side operand of an ¦¦ expression is evaluated only if the left-side operand evaluates to 0. Thus, the following two expressions are equivalent:

```
if (ratio > 30) ; else printf ("It is NOT expensive!\n");
```

```
(ratio > 30) ¦¦ printf ("It is NOT expensive!\n");
```

Note, however, that many programmers object to the use of && and ¦¦ operators to allow or block evaluation. They argue that, when an && or ¦¦ operator is included in an expression, anyone who looks at the expression—other than the original programmer—naturally expects the value produced by the expression to be used. If the value is not used, the person who looks at the program might wonder whether the original programmer left out a portion of the program unintentionally.

Accordingly, some C compilers complain about using an && or ¦¦ expression whenever the value of the expression is not actually put to use.

Write a function that transforms a jockey's weight into one of three integers: if the weight is more than, say, 120, the value returned by the function is to be -1; if the weight is more than 110, the value returned is to be 1; otherwise, the value returned is to be 0. Then, write another function that transforms a race horse's post position into one of three integers: if the post position is 6 or more, the value returned is to be -1; if it is 3 or less, the value returned is to be +1; otherwise, the value returned is to be 0.

Write a program that accepts two numbers—a jockey weight and a post position—and displays "The horse appears to be well situated," if both the jockey's weight and the horse's post position are low.

- If you want to combine two predicate expressions, **and** the result is to be 1 if the values of *both* expressions are other than 0, **then** use **&&**.

- If you want to combine two predicate expressions, **and** the result is to be 1 if the value of *either* expression is other than 0, **then** use ¦¦.

- Both **&&** and ¦¦ evaluate their left operand before they evaluate their right operand. The right operand is not evaluated if the value of the left operand of an **&&** expression is 0 or if the value of the left operand of a ¦¦ expression is not 0.

12 HOW TO WRITE ITERATION STATEMENTS

188   In this section, you learn how to tell C to repeat a computation by using C's most common iteration statements, the `while` and `for` statements.

189   C's **iteration statements** enable functions to do computations over and over until a test has been satisfied. C's `while` statement, for example, consists of a Boolean expression, in parentheses, followed by an embedded statement:

```
while ( Boolean expression )
  embedded statement
```

The Boolean expression is evaluated, and if the Boolean expression evaluates to *any integer* other than 0, the embedded statement is evaluated as well; otherwise, C skips the embedded statement. In contrast to an `if` statement, however, the evaluate-Boolean-expression–evaluate-embedded-statement cycle continues as long as the Boolean expression evaluates to some integer other than 0.

190   For example, the following function fragment repeatedly decrements n by 1 until n is 0:

```
while (n != 0)
  n = n - 1;
```

Replacement of the single embedded statement, n = n - 1;, by a compound statement enables the `while` statement to do useful computation while counting down n to 0.

191   Suppose, for example, that you are asked to figure out the price that a stock will have if the price doubles monthly. Plainly, the price after *n* months is proportional to 2^n, thus requiring you to develop a function that computes the *n*th power of 2.

One way to do the computation is to count down the parameter, n, to 0, multiplying a variable, `result`, whose initial value is 1, by 2 each time that you decrement n:

```
int power_of_2 (int n) {
  int result = 1;              /* Initial value is 1       */
  while (n != 0) {
    result = 2 * result;       /* Multiplied by 2 n times */
    n = n - 1;
  }
  return result;
}
```

192   Note that the value of the Boolean expression, n != 0, is 0, meaning false, if and only if the value of n is 0. Accordingly, the following `while` statements are equivalent:

```
while (n != 0)
   ...

while (n)
   ...
```

Thus, testing n to see whether it is not 0 is viewed by some C programmers as a form of lily gilding; such programmers use n rather than n != 0.

Other C programmers much prefer n != 0, because they believe that it is important to maintain a visible distinction between 0 viewed as a number and 0 viewed as a truth value.

193 The defect of many while loops is that the details that govern the looping appear in three places: the place where the counting variable is initialized, the place where it is tested, and the place where it is reassigned. Such distribution makes the looping difficult to understand. Accordingly, you also need to know about the for statement:

```
for ( entry expression ;
      Boolean expression ;
      continuation expression )
   embedded statement
```

The entry expression is evaluated only once, when the for statement is entered. Once the entry expression is evaluated, the Boolean expression is evaluated, and if the result is not 0, the embedded statement is evaluated, followed by the continuation expression. Then, the Boolean-expression–embedded-statement–continuation-expression evaluation cycle continues until the Boolean expression eventually evaluates to 0.

194 Specialized to counting down a counter variable, the for statement becomes the counting for loop:

```
variable declaration
for ( counter-initialization expression ;
      counter-testing expression ;
      counter-reassignment expression )
   embedded statement
```

195 Now you can define the power_of_2 function using a for loop instead of a while loop. The initialization expression, counter = n, assigns the value of the parameter n to counter. Then, as long as the value of counter is not 0, the value of result, whose initial value is 1, is multiplied by 2 and the value of counter is decremented by 1.

```
int power_of_2 (int n) {
  int counter, result = 1;
  for (counter = n; counter; counter = counter - 1)
    result = 2 * result;
  return result;
}
```

Augmented assignment operators reassign a variable to a value that your program obtains by combining the variable's current value with an expression's value via addition, subtraction, multiplication, or division. The following diagram illustrates how assignment using an augmented assignment operator differs from ordinary assignment:

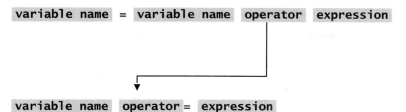

For example, you can rewrite `result = result * 2` in this way:

`result *= 2`

Even though this shorthand gives you a perfectly valid way to multiply and reassign, you may choose to write `result = result * 2`, which you see throughout this book, on the ground that `result = result * 2` stands out more clearly as a reassignment operation.

196
SIDE TRIP

Although augmented assignment operators are not used in this book, there are situations in which an expression written with an augmented assignment operator is arguably clearer than the corresponding expression without the augmented assignment operator. In Section 17, for example, you learn about C arrays; in particular, you learn that you can reassign an array element to twice its former value as follows:

`array name` [`index-producing expression`]
  = `array name` [`index-producing expression`] * 2

Alternatively, using an augmented assignment operator, you can write the reassignment expression as follows:

`array name` [`index-producing expression`] *= 2

Plainly, if the index-producing expression is complex, you should either compute the index separately, or you should use the augmented assignment operator to keep down size and to avoid a maintenance headache should the expression require modification.

197   In principle, you could rewrite `count = count - 1`, using an augmented assignment operator, as `count -= 1`. You are not likely to see such expressions, however, because C offers a still more concise shorthand for adding 1 to, or subtracting 1 from, a variable. To use the shorthand, you drop the equal sign altogether, along with the 1, and prefix the variable with the **increment operator, ++,** or the **decrement operator, --**. Thus, you replace `count = count - 1` by the following expression:

`--count`

Similarly, `++count` means increment the value of `count` by 1.

198   Using C's shorthand notations for variable reassignment, you can write the `power_of_2` function this way:

```
int power_of_2 (int n) {
  int counter, result = 1;
  for (counter = n; counter; --counter)
    result = result * 2;
  return result;
}
```

199   You can, in principle, embed expressions involving the increment operator, ++, or the decrement operator, --, in larger expressions, such as the following:

```
++x + x            /* Bad:  never do this */
```

In such an expression, the increment operator, ++, is said not only to produce a value, but also to have the **side effect** of incrementing x.

It is important that the C language does not prescribe the order in which operands are evaluated in arithmetic expressions. Thus, in the expression ++x + x, the left-side operand, ++x, may be evaluated either before or after the right-side operand, x, depending on the implementation.

Suppose, for example, that the initial value of x is 0. In an implementation that evaluates left-side first, the value of ++x + x will be 2; on the other hand, in an implementation that evaluates right-side first, the value of ++x + x will be 1.

Thus, the use of side-effect operators, such as ++ and --, can lead to mysterious portability problems.

Worse yet, a C compiler is free to compile some expressions for left-side-first evaluation and others for right-side-first evaluation. Thus, side-effect operands can cause plenty of trouble.

200   You can, in principle, position two plus signs or two minus signs as suffixes, rather than as
SIDE TRIP   prefixes. In either position, the plus signs or minus signs cause a variable's value to change, but if the incremented or decremented variable is embedded in a larger expression, the value handed over differs. If a variable is prefixed, the value handed over is the new, incremented value; if a variable is suffixed, the value handed over is the old, original value.

Suppose that the value of count is 3. Then, the value of the expression --count is 2, and the new value of count is 2. On the other hand, again supposing that the value of count is 3, the value of the expression count-- is 3, even though the new value of count is 2.

201   Consider, for example, the following oddball version of power_of_2, in which the decre-
SIDE TRIP   menting of the counter variable occurs in the Boolean expression, rather than in the normal continuation expression, which is rendered empty. The suffix form, counter--, must be used, rather than the prefix form, --counter, because decrementing is to be done after your program decides whether to go around the loop. Were you to use the prefix form, your program would fail to go around the loop enough times.

```
int power_of_2 (int n) {
  int counter, result = 1;
  for (counter = n; counter--;)
    result = 2 * result;
  return result;
}
```

202   There are many other ways to define power_of_2 using a for loop. Here is one in which the initialization of the result variable is included within the for statement, along with the initialization of the counter variable, the two being separated with a comma:

```
int power_of_2 (int n) {
  int counter, result;
  for (counter = n, result = 1; counter; --counter)
    result = result * 2;
  return result;
}
```

203   You can even, if you want, bring the reassignment of the result variable within the reassignment part of the for loop, joining it to the reassignment of the counter variable. The result is a for loop with an empty embedded statement, which, as you may recall from Segment 166, consists of a semicolon only:

```
int power_of_2 (int n) {
  int counter, result;
  for (counter = n, result = 1;         /* Initialization */
       counter;                         /* Test           */
       --counter, result = result * 2)  /* Reassignment   */
    ;                                   /* Empty statement */
  return result;
}
```

204   The initialization and reassignment portions of the for statement in Segment 203 both appear to consist of two separate expressions:

```
counter = n, result = 1
--counter, result = result * 2
```

However, both consist of just one expression, because the comma is viewed as just another operator—one on the lowest precedence level. The operands are evaluated left to right, and the value is the value of the right-side operand.

205   The definition of power_of_2 that appears in Segment 202 is the best of the lot in many respects: All initialization is done in the initialization part of the for statement, a simple test of a counter variable occurs in the testing part of the for statement, the counter variable is reassigned in the reassignment part of the for statement, and the computation of the result is separated from the reassignment part. The for statement is deployed straightforwardly; there are no parlor tricks.

Write an iterative program that accepts three positive integers: p, a principal amount, i, an interest rate, and n, a number of years, and computes the interest accumulated, assuming that the interest is compounded annually.

Write an iterative program that accepts a positive integer, n, and computes the factorial of n, written $n!$, where $n! = n \times n - 1 \times \ldots \times 1$.

- If you want to repeat a calculation for as long as a Boolean expression's value is not 0, then use a `while` loop:

  ```
  while ( Boolean expression )
     embedded statement
  ```

- If you want to repeat a calculation involving entry, Boolean, and continuation expressions, then use a `for` loop:

  ```
  for ( entry expression ;
       Boolean expression ;
       continuation expression )
     embedded statement
  ```

- If you want to repeat a calculation until a variable is counted down to 0, then use a counting `for` loop:

  ```
  variable declaration
  for ( counter-initialization expression ;
       counter-testing expression ;
       counter-reassignment expression )
     embedded statement
  ```

- If you want to increment or decrement the value of a variable by 1, then instantiate one of the following patterns:

  ```
  ++ variable name
  -- variable name
  ```

- If you want to change a variable's value by combining it with the value of an expression via addition, subtraction, multiplication, or division, then consider instantiating the following pattern:

  ```
  variable name  operator = expression
  ```

13 HOW TO WRITE ITERATIVE FILTERS

209 In this section, you learn how to use `while` loops and `for` loops to read data, processing each data item as it is encountered.

210 In Section 12, you learned about the `while` statement:

`while (` `Boolean expression` `)`
  `embedded statement`

The `while` reading pattern consists of a `while` statement with a read expression in the place reserved for a Boolean expression:

`while (` `read expression` `)`
  `embedded statement`

The value of a read expression, such as `scanf ("%lf%i", &price, &number)`, normally is the number of successfully assigned arguments.

Thus, the following `while` statement will continue looping, as you type numbers, because the value of the call to `scanf` is 2, rather than 0:

```
while (2 == scanf ("%lf%i", &price, &number)) {
  ...
}
```

When you decide to stop the loop, assuming that you are working with a typical version of the UNIX or DOS operating systems, you can arrange for the `scanf` call to stop reading before all variables are assigned, thus stopping the `while` loop, by typing the appropriate *keychord*.

You are said to type a **keychord** whenever you hold down one key while you press another. For example, if you are working with a typical version of UNIX, you tell the `scanf` function to stop reading by holding down the `control` key and pressing the `d` key, thereby typing the `control-d` keychord.

211 Unfortunately, the effects of various keychords vary with the operating system and with the way the parameters of the operating system are set. The keychords listed in the following table thus are only typical:

	UNIX	DOS
To stop a program	`control-c`	`control-c`
To stop reading	`control-d`	`control-z`

212 Thus, the following program computes trade values as you type price-per-share–number-of-shares pairs; it stops when you type the `control-d` keychord:

```
#include <stdio.h>
double trade_price (double p, int n) {
  return p * n;
}
main ( ) {
  double price;
  int number;
  while (2 == scanf ("%lf%i", &price, &number))
    printf ("The total price of the trade is %f.\n",
            trade_price (price, number));
}
```
———————————————— Sample Data ————————————————
2.5 500 7.5 500
———————————————————— Result ————————————————
The total price of the trade is 1250.000000.
The total price of the trade is 3750.000000.

213 Recall that, if you are using UNIX or DOS, you can redirect input from your keyboard to a
     file, enabling you to use the program in Segment 212 to find the trade prices of trades that
     you have described in a file. The only new fact you need to know is that read expressions
     stop, returning the number of values read so far, when the end of a file is encountered.

     Thus, to find the trade prices of some trades described in a file, you need only to type the
     following to your operating system, assuming that you have called your trade-analyzing
     program analyze_trades and that you have prepared a test file named test_data:

     analyze_trades < test_data

214 If you happen to be using UNIX or DOS, you may want to take advantage of the **output-
     redirection mechanism** that enables you to tell your program to send output to a file instead
     of displaying that output on your screen.

     Assuming that your program's name is analyze_trades, the following command line
     both redirects input from your keyboard to an input file and redirects output from your
     screen to a output file:

     analyze_trades < test_data > test_result

215 Just as there is a while reading pattern, there is also a for reading pattern. The following
     is the for reading pattern:

```
for ( initialization expression ;
      read expression ;
      reassignment expression )
   embedded statement
```

216 The for reading pattern is at work in the following amended version of the program in
     Segment 212:
```
```

```
#include <stdio.h>
double trade_price (double p, int n) {
  return p * n;
}
main ( ) {
  double price;
  int number;
  for (; 2 == scanf ("%lf%i", &price, &number);)
    printf ("The total price of the trade is %f.\n",
            trade_price (price, number));
}
```
——————————————— Sample Data ———————————————
2.5 300 7.5 300
——————————————— Result ———————————————
The total price of the trade is 750.000000.
The total price of the trade is 2250.000000.

217 An **iterative filter** is a program that transforms a sequence of inputs into a sequence of outputs. Thus, the programs in Segment 212 and Segment 216 are examples of iterative filters.

218 Amend the iterative filter in Segment 216 such that it produces numbered output lines,
PRACTICE such as the following:

```
1. The total price of the trade is 750.000000.
2. The total price of the trade is 2250.000000.
3. The total price of the trade is 2000.000000.
```

219 Consider the program in Segment 212. What will happen if it encounters the end of a file
PRACTICE after reading only one number? What will happen if you type control-d after providing only one number?

220
HIGHLIGHTS

- If you want to read data until you reach the end of a file, **then** instantiate a while-reading pattern:

```
while ( number of items to be read  ==  read expression )
  embedded statement
```

- If you want to read data until you reach the end of a file, **and** you want to keep track of how many data you read, **then** instantiate a for-reading pattern:

```
for ( initialization expression ;
      number of items to be read  ==  read expression ;
      reassignment expression )
  embedded statement
```

14 HOW TO WRITE RECURSIVE FUNCTIONS

221 In Section 12, you learned how to repeat a computation by using iteration statements. In this section, you learn how to perform a computation over and over by using recursive function calls.

The reason for introducing recursion at this point is to create a natural context for discussing function prototypes, which are introduced in Section 15. If you are already comfortable with recursive programs, you can skip ahead to that section.

222 If you are not yet familiar with recursion, it is best to see how recursion works through an example involving a simple mathematical computation that you already know how to perform using iteration. Suppose, for example, that you want to write a function, recursive_power_of_2, that computes the *n*th power of 2 recursively.

223 To define recursive_power_of_2, you can take advantage of the power_of_2 function already provided in Section 12.

Given that power_of_2 exists, one way to define recursive_power_of_2 is to hand over the real work to power_of_2 as follows:

```
int recursive_power_of_2 (int n) {
  return power_of_2 (n);
}
```

Once you see that you can define recursive_power_of_2 in terms of power_of_2, you are ready to learn how gradually to turn recursive_power_of_2 into a recursive function that does not rely on power_of_2.

224 First, note that you can eliminate the need to call power_of_2 in the simple case in which the value of recursive_power_of_2's parameter is 0:

```
int recursive_power_of_2 (int n) {
  if (n == 0)
    return 1;
  else
    return power_of_2 (n);
}
```

225 Next, note that you can arrange for recursive_power_of_2 to hand over a little less work to power_of_2 by performing one of the multiplications by 2 in recursive_power_of_2 itself, and subtracting 1 from power_of_2's argument:

```
int recursive_power_of_2 (int n) {
  if (n == 0)
    return 1;
    else
    return 2 * power_of_2 (n - 1);
}
```

Clearly, `recursive_power_of_2` must work as long as one of the following two situations holds:

- The value of the parameter, n, is 0; in this situation, the `recursive_power_of_2` function returns 1.

- The value of n is not 0, but `power_of_2` is able to compute the power of 2 that is 1 less than the value of n.

226 Now for the recursion trick: You replace `power_of_2` in `recursive_power_of_2` by `recursive_power_of_2` itself:

```
int recursive_power_of_2 (int n) {
  if (n == 0)
     return 1;
     else return 2 * power_of_2 (n - 1) ;
}
```

```
int recursive_power_of_2 (int n) {
  if (n == 0)
     return 1;
     else return 2 * recursive_power_of_2 (n - 1) ;
}
```

The new version works for two reasons:

- If the value of the parameter, n, is 0, `recursive_power_of_2` returns 1.

- If the value of n is not 0, `recursive_power_of_2` asks itself to compute the power of 2 for a number that is 1 less than the value of n. Then, `recursive_power_of_2` may ask itself to compute the power of 2 for a number that is 2 less than the original value of n, and so on, until the `recursive_power_of_2` needs to deal with only 0.

When a function, such as `recursive_power_of_2`, is used in its own definition, the function is said to be **recursive**. When a function calls itself, the function is said to **recurse**.

Given a positive, integer argument, there is no danger that `recursive_power_of_2` will recurse forever—calling itself an infinite number of times—because eventually the argument is counted down to 0, which `recursive_power_of_2` handles directly, without further recursion.

227 There is also no danger that the values taken on by the parameter n will get in one another's way. Each time `recursive_power_of_2` is entered, C sets aside a private storage spot to hold the value of n for that entry:

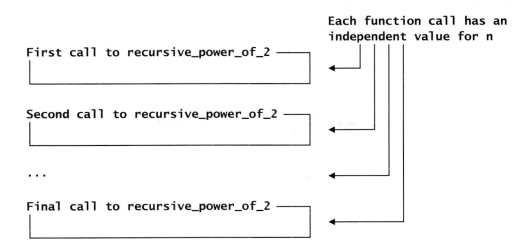

First call to recursive_power_of_2 ⎯

Second call to recursive_power_of_2 ⎯

...

Final call to recursive_power_of_2 ⎯

Each function call has an
independent value for n

228   Note that the simple case—the one for which the result is computed directly—is handled by the **base** part of the definition.

The harder case—the one in which the result is computed indirectly, by another problem being solved first—is handled by the **recursive** part of the definition.

229   You can experiment with recursive_power_of_2 in a program such as this:

```
#include <stdio.h>
/* Define recursive_power_of_2 function: */
int recursive_power_of_2 (int n) {
  if (n == 0)
    return 1;
  else
    return 2 * recursive_power_of_2 (n - 1);
}
/* Test recursive_power_of_2 function in main: */
main ( ) {
  printf ("The 0th power of 2 is %i.\n", recursive_power_of_2 (0));
  printf ("The 1st power of 2 is %i.\n", recursive_power_of_2 (1));
  printf ("The 2nd power of 2 is %i.\n", recursive_power_of_2 (2));
  printf ("The 3rd power of 2 is %i.\n", recursive_power_of_2 (3));
}
```

230   Here is a look at the four calls involved when the recursive_power_of_2 function is set to work on 3:

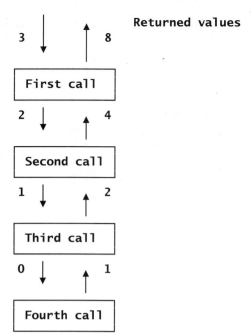

Arguments | Returned values

3 ↓ | ↑ 8

First call

2 ↓ | ↑ 4

Second call

1 ↓ | ↑ 2

Third call

0 ↓ | ↑ 1

Fourth call

231 The `recursive_power_of_2` function is an instance of the **recursive countdown pattern**:

```
int  function name  (int n) {
  if (n == 0)
    return  result for n equal 0 ;
  else
    return  combination operand
            combination operator
            function name  (n - 1);
}
```

232 As another, more interesting illustration of recursion, suppose that you are asked to figure out the number of such companies offering financial software packages if the number of companies begins multiplying like, say, rabbits.

Fortunately, Fibonacci figured out long ago how fast rabbits multiply, deriving a formula that gives the number of female rabbits after n months, under the following assumptions:

- Female rabbits mature 1 month after birth.

- Once they mature, female rabbits have one female child each month.

- At the beginning of the first month, there is one immature female rabbit.

- Rabbits live forever.

- There are always enough males on hand to impregnate all the mature females.

233 The following diagram shows the number of female rabbits at the end of every month for 6 months:

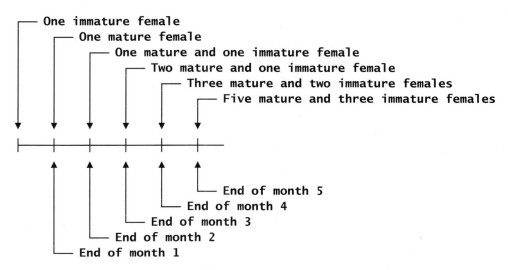

Clearly, the number of female rabbits at the end of the *n*th month is equal to the number of females at the end of the previous month plus the number of females that gave birth during the current month. But, of course, the number of females that gave birth during the current month is equal to the number of mature female rabbits at the end of the previous month, which is same as the total number of females at the end of the month before that. Thus, the following formula holds:

$$\text{Rabbits}(n) = \text{Rabbits}(n - 1) + \text{Rabbits}(n - 2)$$

234 Capturing the rabbit formula in the form of a C function, you have the following:

```
#include <stdio.h>
/* Define rabbits function */
int rabbits (int n) {
  if (n == 0 || n == 1)
    return 1;
  else return rabbits (n - 1) + rabbits (n - 2);
}
/* Test rabbits function */
main ( ) {
  printf ("At the end of month 1, there is %i.\n", rabbits (1));
  printf ("At the end of month 10, there are %i.\n", rabbits (10));
  printf ("At the end of month 20, there are %i.\n", rabbits (20));
}
```
————————————————— Result —————————————————
```
At the end of month 1, there is 1.
At the end of month 10, there are 89.
At the end of month 20, there are 10946.
```

235 Here is a look at the function `rabbits` at work on 3, the same argument previously used with `recursive_power_of_2`. The value returned is the number of rabbits at the end of the third month.

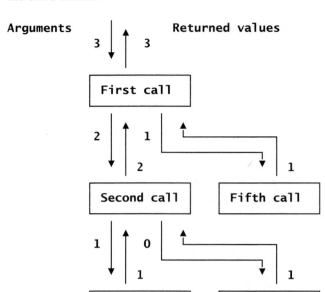

236
SIDE TRIP
Now you have seen two recursive definitions, one for `power_of_2` and one for `rabbits`. Many mathematically oriented programmers prefer such recursive definitions to iterative definitions, when both are possible, believing that there is inherent elegance in defining a function partly in terms of itself.

Other, practically oriented programmers dislike recursive definitions for one or both of two reasons: first, the recursive approach usually produces slower programs, because each function call takes time; and second, the recursive approach may have problems with large arguments, because the number of function calls in a recursive chain of calls is usually limited to a few hundred. Recursion aficionados counter by creating compilers that handle certain recursive functions in sophisticated ways that avoid such limits. These aficionados generally do not work on C compilers, however.

237
PRACTICE
Write a recursive program that accepts three positive integers: p, a principal amount, i, an interest rate, and n, a number of years, and computes the interest accumulated, assuming that the interest is compounded annually.

238
PRACTICE
Write a recursive program that accepts a positive integer, n, and computes the factorial of n, written $n!$, where $n! = n \times n - 1 \times \ldots \times 1$.

239
HIGHLIGHTS

- Recursive functions work by calling themselves to solve subproblems until the subproblems are simple enough for them to solve directly.

- The portion of a recursive function that handles the simplest cases is called the base part; the portion that transforms more complex cases is called the recursion part.

- **If** you want to solve a difficult problem, **then** try to break it up into simpler subproblems.

- **If** you are writing a recursive function, **then** your function must handle the simplest cases, **and** must break down every other case into the simplest cases.

- **If** your recursive function is to count down a number, **then** you may be able to instantiate the following pattern:

```
int function name (int n) {
  if (n == 0)
    return result for n equal 0 ;
  else
    return combination operand
           combination operator
           function name (n - 1);
}
```

15 HOW TO SOLVE DEFINITION ORDERING PROBLEMS WITH FUNCTION PROTOTYPES

240   You know that C ordinarily requires you to define functions before you use them. Sometimes, however, functions refer to one another, which means you must learn to use C's function prototype mechanism to solve ordering problems.

So that you see the need for function prototypes, you learn about a set of three cooperating functions that provide an alternative to the rabbit-computing function that was introduced in Section 14.

241   In Segment 232, you learned that the number of rabbits after more than 1 month is the sum of the number at the end of the previous month and the month before that. With only this information, you can rewrite the `rabbits` function in terms of two auxiliary functions, `previous_month` and `penultimate_month`:

```
int rabbits (int n) {
  if (n == 0 || n == 1)
    return 1;
  else return previous_month (n) + penultimate_month (n);
}
```

Then, realizing that `previous_month` must return the number of rabbits at the end of the previous month, you can see that you can define `previous_month` as follows:

```
int previous_month (int n) {return rabbits (n - 1);}
```

Analogous reasoning leads you to the following definition for `penultimate_month`:

```
int penultimate_month (int n) {return rabbits (n - 2);}
```

242   Although the `rabbits`, `previous_month`, and `penultimate_month` functions capture one line of reasoning about rabbits, the `previous_month` and `penultimate_month` functions are so short that most programmers would incorporate the expressions in those functions into the definition of `rabbits`, as shown in Segment 234. In this section, however, all three functions are retained, because, as separate functions, they provide a simple example of a situation for which you must use one or more function prototypes.

243   In principle, `rabbits`, `previous_month`, and `penultimate_month` should work fine together. However, if you just put them as is into a program, you soon discover that, no matter how you arrange the functions, at least one function is referred to before it is defined. In the following arrangement, for example, `rabbits` is referred to before it is defined.

```
int previous_month (int n) {return rabbits (n - 1);}
int penultimate_month (int n) {return rabbits (n - 2);}
int rabbits (int n) {
  if (n == 0 || n == 1)
    return 1;
  else return previous_month (n) + penultimate_month (n);
}
```

The C compiler cannot compile a program that includes these three functions defined in this order, because the C compiler does not know how to prepare calls to the `rabbits` function before the `rabbits` function is defined. Yet calls to the `rabbits` function occur in both `previous_month` and `penultimate_month`, both of which are defined before `rabbits` is defined.

244   The solution to the `rabbits` dilemma is to use a *function prototype*. A **function prototype** is like a function definition without parameter names or a body. By supplying a function prototype, you supply only what the C compiler needs to know about a function's parameter types and return type in order to prepare calls to the function. In the function prototype of `rabbits`, for example, the parameter name and the entire body disappear, leaving only the data-type declarations for the return value and the parameter:

```
int rabbits (int);
```

Because the body of the function is supplied later, a function prototype cannot refer to other functions, be they defined or not yet defined. Other definitions can refer to the function once its function prototype has been seen, however.

245   Accordingly, you can solve the `rabbits`, `previous_month`, and `penultimate_month` ordering problem this way:

- First, supply a function prototype for `rabbits`. Because the function prototype has no body, there are no references to `previous_month` or to `penultimate_month`.

- Next, supply definitions for `previous_month` and `penultimate_month`. Both refer to `rabbits`, but those references are now harmless, because the `rabbits` function prototype is in place.

- Finally, supply a definition for `rabbits`. This definition includes calls to other functions, `previous_month` and `penultimate_month`, but those calls are harmless, because both functions have been defined.

246   Thus, you can compile and run the following program:

```
#include <stdio.h>
/* Function prototype for rabbits function */
int rabbits (int);
/* Function definitions requiring rabbits function prototype */
int previous_month (int n) {return rabbits (n - 1);}
int penultimate_month (int n) {return rabbits (n - 2);}
/* Function definition for rabbits function */
int rabbits (int n) {
   if (n == 0 || n == 1)
      return 1;
   else return previous_month (n) + penultimate_month (n);
}
```

```
/* Test rabbits function */
main ( ) {
  printf ("At the end of month 1, there is %i.\n", rabbits (1));
  printf ("At the end of month 2, there are %i.\n", rabbits (2));
  printf ("At the end of month 3, there are %i.\n", rabbits (3));
}
```
─────────────────────────── Result ───────────────────────────
```
At the end of month 1, there is 1.
At the end of month 2, there are 2.
At the end of month 3, there are 3.
```
───

247 The following diagram shows `rabbits` and its two auxiliaries working to determine how many rabbits there are at the end of 3 months.

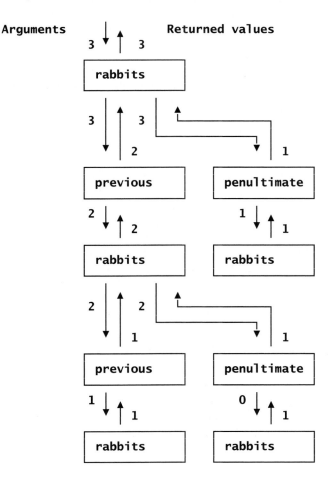

Each of the three cooperating functions can initiate a chain of calls that ends in a call to itself. Thus, the cooperating functions exhibit indirect, rather than direct, recursion.

The recursion bottoms out in calls to `rabbits` when the value of `n` is either 0 or 1. Thus, `rabbits` is not a particularly efficient function, because it twice computes the value of `rabbits (1)`.

248 You might think that the function prototype for a function that expects no arguments would look like this model:

return data type **function name** ( )

Alas, the use of a function prototype with no type specifiers is taken to mean that the C compiler should not check argument types or even the number of arguments appearing in function calls. Although such a function prototype is often used for functions that expect no arguments, such a function specification should be reserved, as described in Section 40, for functions that accept a variable number of arguments.

A clearer and safer way to specify a function prototype for a function that expects no arguments is to include only the special symbol `void` in the place normally reserved for parameter data types:

return data type **function name** (void)

By using such a specification, you tell the C compiler to complain if the function ever appears with one or more arguments. Nevertheless, many programmers sacrifice this benefit, using a function specification with no type specifiers, despite the inherent ambiguity.

249
SIDE TRIP
You may, if you want, include parameter names in function prototypes. For example, instead of `int rabbits (int);` you can write the following:

```
int rabbits (int n);
```

Although parameter names are optional, there are two advantages to including them. First, parameter names often provide a form of documentation; second, if you include parameter names in function prototypes, you can write the function prototype by copying from the function definition, without any error-prone removal of the parameter names.

250
SIDE TRIP
Some programmers supply function prototypes for all functions, thus stealing a march on the ordering problem. As you learn later, in Section 42, these function prototypes are often herded together into separate files called header files.

251
PRACTICE
Temporarily suspending disbelief, convert the program that you wrote in Segment 238 into a program consisting of three cooperating functions, `factorial`, `base`, and `recurse`. The factorial function is to look like this:

```
int factorial (n) {
  if (n == 0)
    return base ();
  else
    return recurse (n);
}
```

The `recurse` function is to call the `factorial` function, thus requiring you to use at least one function prototype.

- C generally requires you to define functions before you refer to them in other functions.

- You can, however, provide a function prototype, instead of a full definition. Once you have provided a function prototype, you can refer to the function.

- **If** you want to define cooperative, indirectly recursive functions, **then** you must provide at least one function prototype.

- **If** you need a function prototype, **then** instantiate the following pattern:

```
return data type  function name  (data type of parameter 1,
                                   ...
                                   data type of parameter n)
```

16 HOW TO CREATE STRUCTURES AND OBJECTS

253   To describe a stock trade, you think naturally in terms of the price per share of stock and number of shares traded.

Thus, the numbers that describe a trade constitute a natural bundle—a bundle of two numbers for each trade that belongs to the trade category.

In this section, you learn that C offers mechanisms that enable you to describe, construct, and manipulate bundles of descriptive data items that mirror real-world concepts such as *individual* and *category*.

254   C encourages you to define C **structures**, such as the trade structure, that correspond to naturally occurring categories. Once you have defined a structure, you can construct any number of **structure objects**, each of which corresponds to an individual.

When you define the `trade` structure, for example, you indicate that individual trades are associated with two numbers, one corresponding to the price per share and the other corresponding to the number of shares. Then, you can construct `trade` objects with particular prices and quantities.

Thus, the employment of structures enables you to create information bundles in your programs that describe naturally occurring individuals. Consequently, structures help you to produce clear, easy-to-understand programs.

255   The basic data types—such as character, integer, and floating-point number—are categories too. Thus, structures sometimes are called **user-defined data types**.

Analogously, individuals belonging to C's basic data types—such as characters, integers, and floating-point numbers—are objects. Thus, those individuals sometimes are called *data-type objects*.

256   In contrast to data-type objects, structure objects generally have multiple parts, which can be accessed separately. Accordingly, characters, integers, and floating-point numbers sometimes are called **atomic objects**, and structure objects sometimes are called **compound objects**.

Generally, you can refer to objects of all types by the word **object**, leaving it to the context to establish the precise kind of object you mean. Sometimes, you may want to be more precise by adding a specializing word, producing combinations such as structure object, data-type object, atomic object, and compound object.

257   When you define a structure, you tell C about the variables that describe the objects that belong to that structure.

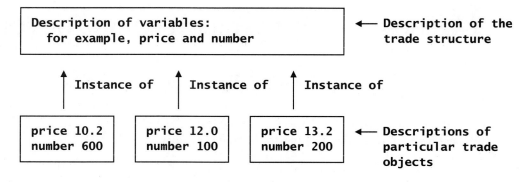

258 The following is a C definition of the `trade` structure; evidently, the individual chunks of memory that describe trades hold values for a floating-point number (namely, the price per share), and an integer (namely, the number of shares traded):

```
struct trade {
    double price;
    int number;
};
```

Here is what each part does:

```
struct          ← Tells C that a structure is to be defined
  trade         ← Tells C the name of the structure
    {           ← Marks the beginning of the body
  double price; ← Introduces floating point variable
  int number;   ← Introduces integer variable
}               ← Marks the end of the body
    ;           ← Marks the end of the structure definition
```

259 In Segment 129, you learned that a *declaration* is a program element that provides a compiler with information or advice, whereas a *definition* causes the compiler to allocate storage. Structure definitions do not cause storage to be allocated. Accordingly, some purists prefer to use the phrase **structure declaration**.

260 The variables that appear inside structure definitions—such as `price` and `number`—are called **structure variables**.

In other programming languages, structure variables are called **fields** or **slots**. The virtue of such alternative terms is that they encourage you to think of structure definitions as patterns and of structure objects as filled-in patterns. Bowing to convention, however, the term *structure variable* is used throughout the rest of this book.

261 Once the `trade` structure is defined, you can introduce a variable with `trade` as the variable's data type:

```
struct trade t;
```

The syntax is similar to the syntax that you use when you define a variable with `int` or `double` as that variable's data type, except that both the symbol `struct` and the name of the structure appear as the type specification.

262 Once you have created a `trade` object by defining a variable of the `trade` type, you can refer to that `trade` object's own `price` and `number` structure variables. To refer to a structure variable, you join the name of the `trade` variable, via the **structure-member operator**, a period, to the name of the structure variable in which you are interested. Thus, `t.price` produces the value of the `price` structure variable of the `trade` object named `t`.

Once you know how to refer to a `trade` object's structure variables, you are free to assign values to those structure variables and, subsequently, to retrieve those values.

263 In the following program, a `trade` object, `t`, is created; values are assigned to the price and number structure variables; and the `trade` object's price is computed by a function named `trade_price`.

```
#include <stdio.h>
struct trade {double price; int number;};
double trade_price (double p, int n) {return p * n;}
main ( ) {
  double price;
  int number;
  struct trade t;
  while (2 == scanf ("%lf%i", &price, &number)) {
    t.price = price;
    t.number = number;
    printf ("The total value of the trade is %f.\n",
            trade_price (t.price, t.number));
  }
}
```

———————————————— Sample Data ————————————————

`2.5 500 5.0 1000`

———————————————— Result ————————————————
```
The total value of the trade is 1250.000000.
The total value of the trade is 5000.000000.
```

264 Why, you might ask, do structure definitions end with a semicolon? After all, the final
SIDE TRIP brace makes it clear where the structure definition ends:

Semicolon

`struct trade {double price; int number;};`

One reason is that the semicolon syntax allows you to describe a structure and to define global variables using that structure in a single statement. In the following single statement, for example, the trade structure is defined and global variables t1 and t2 are defined to belong to the trade structure.

```
struct trade {double price; int number;} t1, t2;
```

Thus, the semicolon tells C where the list of defined variables ends.

265   In Segment 263, you saw trade_price defined as a function of two arguments:

```
double trade_price (double p, int n) {return p * n;}
```

Instead of handing two arguments to trade_price, you can redefine it to take just one argument, which you declare to be a trade object. If you choose this approach, you also need to change the body of trade_price: Instead of price and number parameters, the body must refer to the trade's price and number structure variables:

```
double trade_price (struct trade t) {return t.price * t.number;}
```

266   With trade_price redefined to operate on trade objects—instead of on a price and number combination—you can rewrite the program in Segment 263 as follows:

```
#include <stdio.h>
struct trade {double price; int number;};
double trade_price (struct trade t) {return t.price * t.number;}
main ( ) {
  double price;
  int number;
  struct trade t;
  while (2 == scanf ("%lf%i", &price, &number)) {
    t.price = price;
    t.number = number;
    printf ("The total value of the trade is %f.\n",
            trade_price (t));
  }
}
```
——————————————— Sample Data ———————————————
```
2.5 500
```
——————————————— Result ———————————————
```
The total value of the trade is 1250.000000.
```

267   A **call option** is an option to purchase a specified amount of a specified stock at a specified
PRACTICE   price at a specified due date—for example, to *buy* 100 shares of IBM for $25 per share on next May 1. Analogously, a **put option** is an option to sell a specified amount of a specified stock at a specified price at a specified due date—for example, to *sell* 100 shares of IBM for $25 per share on next May 1. Define call and put structures such that call and put objects have structure variables for the number of shares and price involved, as well as the due-date year and month.

- C structures correspond to categories, and C structure objects correspond to individuals.

- You can view structures as user-defined data types.

- Structure definitions contain structure variables.

- If you want to define a structure, **then** instantiate the following pattern:

```
struct structure name {
    structure variable declaration 1
    ...
    structure variable declaration n
};
```

- If you want to use a structure object's structure variable's value, **then** instantiate the following pattern:

```
structure object's name . structure variables's name
```

- If you want to assign a structure object's structure variables's value, **then** instantiate the following pattern:

```
structure object's name . structure variables's name
  = expression ;
```

17 HOW TO WORK WITH ARRAYS OF NUMBERS

269 In this section, you learn how to store numbers in arrays, and how to retrieve those numbers.

270 A one-dimensional **array** is a collection of places where objects are stored and retrieved using an integer **index**. Each object in an array is called an **element** of that array. In C, the first element is indexed by zero; hence, C is said to have zero-based arrays.

0	1	2	3	4	5	← Index

700	400	400	500	350

271 The number of bytes allocated for each place in an array is determined by the type of the objects to be stored. If an array is to hold integers of type short, for example, most implementations of C would allocate 2 bytes per integer:

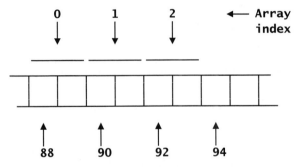

In this example, the first element of the array appears at memory address 88, the second appears at 90, and the third appears at 92.

272 Alternatively, if an array is to hold integers of type int, most implementations of C would allocate 4 bytes per integer:

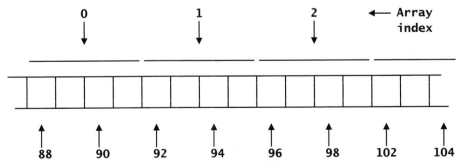

In this example, the first integer in the array appears at memory address 88, the second appears at 92, and the third appears at 96.

273 Note that a C array cannot hold integers of one type in some locations and integers of another type in other locations. All the objects in a C array must belong to the same data type.

274 To define an **array**, you need an array definition that tells C the name of the array, the type of objects that the array is to contain, the number of dimensions the array has, and the size of each dimension. The C compiler uses array definitions to calculate how much storage to allocate for the array.

The following array definition, for example, tells the C compiler to allocate memory for a one-dimensional array containing five numbers of type `double`, each of which represents the price per share of the stock involved in one of five stock trades:

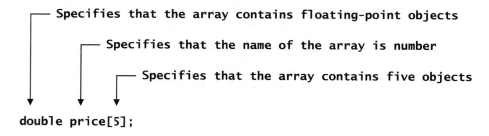

```
double price[5];
```

275 Thus, a one-dimensional global array definition looks like an ordinary global variable definition augmented by a bracketed number that specifies the array's size.

276 To use an array, once it is created, you need to know how to write into and read from the various array locations, each of which is identified by a numerical index.

277 Consider `price`, the one-dimensional array of floating-point numbers. To write data into `price`, you use assignment statements in which the array name and a bracketed integer index appear on the left side of an assignment statement, the place where you are accustomed to seeing variable names. The following expression, for example, inserts an integer into the place indexed by the value of `counter`.

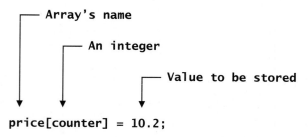

```
price[counter] = 10.2;
```

To read data from the `price` array, once the data have been written, you write an expression containing the array name and a bracketed integer index. The following expression, for example, yields the number stored in the place indexed by the value of `counter`:

```
price[counter]
```

278 The following is a program in which arrays of three floating-point numbers and three integers are defined; data are wired in via assignment statements, and later are accessed in a printf statement:

```c
#include <stdio.h>
/* Define trade_price */
double trade_price (double p, int n) {
  return p * n;
}
/* Define global arrays */
double price[3];
int number[3];
main ( ) {
  /* Wire in sample data */
  price[0] = 10.2; /* Store floating-point price in place 0 */
  price[1] = 12.0; /* Store floating-point price in place 1 */
  price[2] = 13.2; /* Store floating-point price in place 2 */
  number[0] = 600; /* Store integer number in place 0 */
  number[1] = 100; /* Store integer number in place 1 */
  number[2] = 200; /* Store integer number in place 2 */
  /* Display products */
  printf ("The trade prices are %f, %f, and %f.\n",
          trade_price (price[0], number[0]),
          trade_price (price[1], number[1]),
          trade_price (price[2], number[2]));
}
```

———————————————— Result ————————————————
The trade prices are 6120.000000, 1200.000000, and 2640.000000.

279 You can also use a read statement to assign a value to an array location directly, without using a variable as an intermediary:

scanf ("%lf", & array name [index])

280 Now suppose that you want to fill an array using data in a file. You probably do not know exactly how many objects you need to store. Accordingly, you need an approach to dealing with uncertainty.

One approach, about which you learn in Section 18, is to limit wasted memory by allocating memory for objects at run time. In this section, you learn about a simpler approach: You define an object array that is sure to be large enough to hold all the objects you can possibly encounter. Then, you proceed to fill that array using a while reading or for reading pattern.

In the following program, for example, you create two arrays, each of which can hold up to 100 integers representing the prices per share and the numbers of shares involved in a group of trades. Then, you fill part or all of that array with floating-point numbers and integers using a for reading pattern in which the value of the limit variable is counted up to the total number of price–number pairs. Finally, you use another `for` loop to add up the products of the numbers:

```c
#include <stdio.h>
/* Define trade_price */
double trade_price (double p, int n) {
  return p * n;
}
/* Define global arrays */
double price[100];
int number[100];
main ( ) {
  /* Declare various variables */
  int limit, counter;
  double sum = 0.0;
  /* Read numbers and stuff them into arrays */
  for (limit = 0;
       2 == scanf ("%lf%i", &price[limit], &number[limit]);
       ++limit)
    ;
  /* Add all products of corresponding elements in the two arrays */
  for (counter = 0; counter < limit; ++counter)
    sum = sum + trade_price (price[counter], number[counter]);
  /* Display sum */
  printf ("The total value of the %i trades is %f.\n",
                                     limit,        sum);
}
```

―――――――――――――― Sample Data ――――――――
10.2   600   12.0   100   13.2   200
―――――――――――――― Result ――――――――――――
The total value of the 3 trades is 9960.000000.

281   Of course, the program could be written with just one `for` loop, and with no array, but retaining data in an array makes it easy to perform a variety of computations without rereading the file.

282   You easily can define arrays with more than one dimension. Suppose, for example, that you want to store the high, low, and close of the Dow Jones Industrial Average for, say, 100 days. You can easily arrange to define a suitable array with three rows:

0	1	2		← Index, the day
3552.2	3560.0	3540.0		← High
3539.2	3544.8	3530.6		← Low
3550.5	3557.7	3530.6		← Close

To define such an array, you simply include a bracketed dimension size for each dimension. For example, to define a 3 by 100 array of floating-point numbers, each describing a Dow Jones Industrial Average, you write the following statement:

```
double djia[3][100];
```

283 To access an element of a multidimensional array, you specify each index in its own pair of brackets. For example, to access the closing price on the second day, you write the following:

```
    ┌── Row index, closing price (0 is the low, 1 is the high)
    ▼
djia[2][1];
    ▲
    └── Column index, second day (0 would be first day)
```

284 Note that all numbers in an array, no matter what the number of dimensions, must be of the same type. You cannot, for example, have a row of `double` type data followed by a row of `int` type data.

285
PRACTICE
You are said to practice **defensive programming** when you add tests to ensure that expected actions actually happen. For example, you should test array insertions to ensure that the indices are all within bounds. Add such a defensive-programming test to the program in Segment 280.

286
PRACTICE
Write a program that reads up to 100 lines of high–low–close price data. Your program is to write those data into a 3 by 100 array, and then to compute and display the averages of the high, the low, and the closing prices.

287
HIGHLIGHTS

- If you want to create a one-dimensional array, **then** instantiate the following pattern:

  ```
  data type  array name  [maximum number of items];
  ```

- If you have an array, **and** you want to write values into the array, **then** instantiate an assignment-statement pattern or a read-statement pattern (integer version shown):

  ```
  array name [index] = expression;
  scanf ("···%i···", ···, &array name [index], ···)
  ```

- If you have a value stored in an array, **and** you want to read that value, **then** instantiate the following pattern:

  ```
  array name [index]
  ```

18 HOW TO WORK WITH ARRAYS OF STRUCTURE OBJECTS

288   You can use arrays to store not only numbers but also structure objects. In this section, you learn how to create, write into, and read from an array of structure objects representing stock trades.

289   The following is a one-dimensional array with three places for storing `trade` objects, each of which includes, say, the price per share and the number of shares:

0	1	2	← Index
trade object	trade object	trade object	

290   The number of bytes allocated for each place in an array is determined by the objects to be stored. Suppose, for example, that you define the `trade` structure like this:

struct trade {double price; int number;};

Then, if an array is to hold `trade` objects, each of which contains a floating-point number of type `double` for the `trade` object's price and an integer of type `int` for the trade's number, each place will consist of 12 bytes in most implementations:

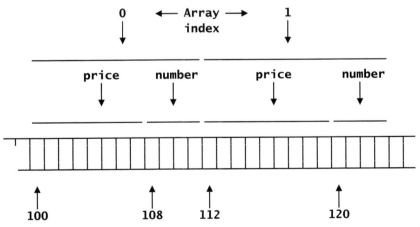

In this example, the first trade is described by the 12 bytes at memory addresses 100 through 111. Of these 12 bytes, the first 8 bytes contain a floating-point number that represents the trade's price, and the final 4 bytes contain an integer that represents the number of shares in the trade. The second trade is described by the 12 bytes starting at memory address 112.

291   To define a one-dimensional trade array, you must define the `trade` structure first; then, you can write an array definition, as you would to define any array.

The following statement, for example, is an array definition that tells C to allocate memory for a one-dimensional array, named trades, containing three trade objects:

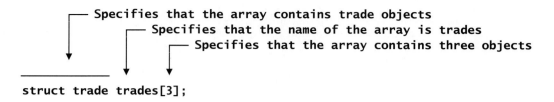

```
struct trade trades[3];
```

Thus, an array definition for structure objects looks like an ordinary array definition, except that the symbol struct, with a structure name, such as trade, appears instead of the name of a built-in type, such as int.

292   To write into the trades array, you can use assignment statements in which the array name, a bracketed integer index, and the structure-variable's name appear on the left side:

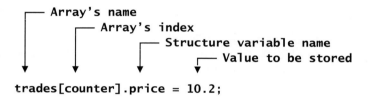

```
trades[counter].price = 10.2;
```

To read data from the trades array, once the data have been inserted, you simply write an expression containing the array name, a bracketed integer index, and the structure-variable's name. The following expression, for example, yields the price of the trade stored in the place indexed by the value of counter.

```
trades[counter].price
```

293   The following program creates an array of three trades, wires in data via assignment statements, and accesses the data in a printf statement:

```
#include <stdio.h>
/* Define the trade structure */
struct trade {double price; int number;};
/* Define trade_price */
double trade_price (struct trade t) {
  return t.price * t.number;
}
/* Define trade array */
struct trade trades[3];
```

```
main ( ) {
  /* Wire in sample data */
  trades[0].price = 10.2; trades[0].number = 600;
  trades[1].price = 12.0; trades[1].number = 100;
  trades[2].price = 13.2; trades[2].number = 200;
  /* Display products */
  printf ("The trade prices are, %f, %f, and %f.\n",
          trade_price (trades[0]),
          trade_price (trades[1]),
          trade_price (trades[2]));
}
```

—————————————————— Result ——————————————————

The trade prices are, 6120.000000, 1200.000000, and 2640.000000.

294 Similarly, in the following program, you create an array that can hold up to 100 trades. Then, you fill part or all of it using a for reading pattern, and you use another for loop to add up the trade prices:

```
#include <stdio.h>
/* Define the trade structure */
struct trade {double price; int number;};
/* Define trade_price */
double trade_price (struct trade t) {
  return t.price * t.number;
}
/* Define trade array */
struct trade trades[100];
main ( ) {
  /* Declare various variables */
  int limit, counter, number;
  double price, sum = 0.0;
  /* Read numbers and stuff them into array */
  for (limit = 0; 2 == scanf ("%lf%i", &price, &number); ++limit) {
    trades[limit].price = price;
    trades[limit].number = number;
  }
  /* Add all products */
  for (counter = 0; counter < limit; ++counter)
    sum = sum + trade_price(trades[counter]);
  printf ("The total value of the %i trades is %f.\n",
                                  limit,        sum);
}
```

295 Alternatively, you can have the read expression place numbers directly in the trade structure variables, rather than indirectly through price and number variables:

```
#include <stdio.h>
/* Define the trade structure */
struct trade {double price; int number;};
/* Define trade_price */
double trade_price (struct trade t) {
  return t.price * t.number;
}
/* Define trade array */
struct trade trades[100];
main ( ) {
  /* Declare various variables */
  int limit, counter;
  double sum = 0.0;
  /* Read numbers and stuff them into array */
  for (limit = 0;
       2 == scanf ("%lf%i",
                   &trades[limit].price,
                   &trades[limit].number);
       ++limit)
    ;
  /* Add all products */
  for (counter = 0; counter < limit; ++counter)
    sum = sum + trade_price(trades[counter]);
  printf ("The total value of the %i trades is %f.\n",
                          limit,        sum);
}
```

```
――――――――――― Sample Data ―――――――――――
10.2    600
12.0    100
13.2    200
――――――――――――― Result ―――――――――――――
The total value of the 3 trades is 9960.000000.
```

296

PRACTICE

Define a structure named hlc, for *high*, *low*, *close*, that has three structure variables, high, low, and close.

Use your structure in a program that reads up to 100 lines of high–low–close price data. Your program is to write those data into an array of 100 hlc structures, and then to compute and display the averages of the high, the low, and the closing prices.

297

HIGHLIGHTS

- If you want to create a one-dimensional array of structure objects, **then** instantiate the following pattern:

```
struct  structure name  array name  [ maximum number of items ];
```

- **If** you have an array of structure objects, **and** you want to write values into the array, **then** instantiate an assignment-statement pattern or a read-statement pattern (integer version shown):

```
array name [ index ]. structure-variable name = expression ;
scanf ("···%i···",
        ···,
        & array name [ index ]. structure-variable name ,
        ···);
```

- **If** you have a value stored in a structure variable in an array of structure objects, **and** you want to read that value, **then** read the value by instantiating the following pattern:

```
array name [ index ]. structure variable name
```

19 HOW TO USE POINTER PARAMETERS TO AVOID STRUCTURE COPYING

298   In this section, you start to learn about pointers. Pointers are extremely important for several reasons. First, pointer parameters enable you to circumvent C's call-by-value convention by which parameters are copied into at call time and out of at return time. Second, pointers provide an alternate way to access array elements. Third, pointers make it possible for your programs to ask for more memory only when those programs need more memory, thus reducing your need to estimate how much memory is likely to be necessary.

In this section and in Section 20, you learn how to use pointers in the first way, to circumvent C's call-by-value convention.

299   In Section 18, you learned about a program that sums the trade prices in an array of `trade` objects using a function, `trade_price`, that has a `trade` parameter.

300   Recall that C ordinarily reserves a memory chunk for each parameter whenever a function is called. Evaluated arguments are copied into those reserved memory chunks.

For example, when the `trade_price` function—as defined, for example, in Segment 294— is called, a `trade` object from the `trades` array is copied into the memory chunk reserved for `trade_price`'s t parameter. The following illustrates the first call to `trade_price`:

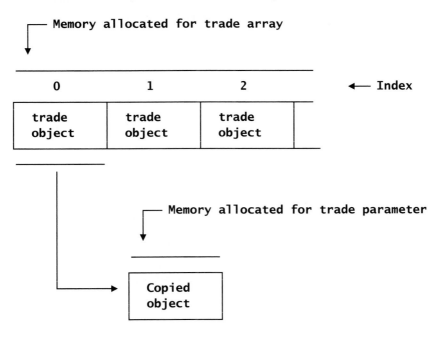

301   It is important to know that you can define `trade_price` in another way that avoids copying `trade` objects. One reason to avoid such copying is that copying a large structure takes time. If you want to write the fastest possible program, you may want to avoid the copying involved when handing a large structure object to a function in the ordinary way.

302   To learn how to avoid copying any sort of object when you call a function, you need to learn about pointers. Then, you can learn about address arguments and pointer parameters.

A **pointer** is a chunk of memory that holds the address of an object. A **pointer name** identifies a chunk of memory containing the address of an object.

303   In the following, for example, a 2-byte pointer variable identifies a chunk of memory that contains the address of an integer object:

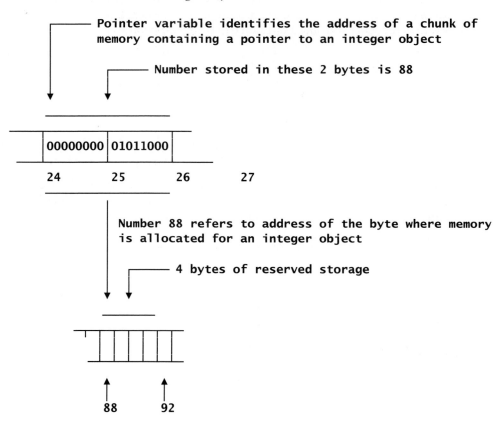

304   You define pointer variables just as you define other variables, except that an asterisk appears in the definition when you define a pointer variable:

```
int i;         /* Allocate space for an integer, i */
int *iptr;     /* Allocate space for a pointer to an integer, iptr */
```

Thereafter, iptr, without an asterisk, identifies the location of an address; *iptr, with an asterisk, identifies the location of the integer identified by the address.

305   To establish a proper value for a pointer variable, you need to know about the **address-of operator, &**. Whenever an expression identifies a value-holding chunk of memory, then operating on that expression with the address-of operator returns the address of that chunk of memory.

If i identifies a chunk of memory allocated to hold the value of an integer object, then &i is the address of that chunk of memory. In the following illustration, the value of i is 1943. inasmuch as the binary number 11110010111, rendered in ordinary decimal notation, is 1943. The value of &i, the address of the chunk of memory holding 1943, is 88 in decimal:

i

00000000	00000000	00000111	10010111		

    88   89   90   91   ← Addresses

306   Accordingly, if you want to have the pointer variable, iptr, point to the memory allocated for the ordinary variable, i, you can write the following assignment statement:

```
iptr = &i;
```

The result, viewed from the memory perspective, is that 88, the address of i, is deposited in the chunk of memory reserved for the pointer, iptr:

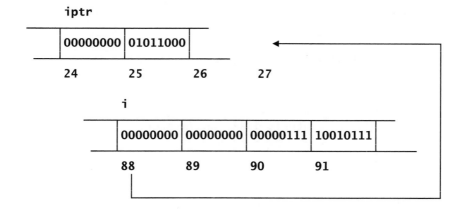

307   Note that allocating space for a pointer variable does not allocate space for the corresponding object. To set up an integer pointer and a corresponding integer object, you need two space-allocating statements and one assignment statement:

```
int i;          /* Allocate space for an integer, i */
int *iptr;      /* Allocate space for a pointer to an integer, iptr */
iptr = &i;      /* Assign iptr to the address of i */
```

308   In general, the amount of memory consumed by a pointer is determined by the designers of your C compiler. The programs in this book were tested using an implementation in which all pointers consist of 4 bytes, enabling the addressing of 2^{32} memory locations.

You need not know how much memory is consumed by a pointer, however, because the correct amount is determined by the C compiler.

309   Although pointers are usually longer, short, 2-byte pointers are used in the illustrations in this book so as to keep the size of the illustrations manageable.

310   Given that iptr is a pointer variable, the chunk of memory allocated for iptr contains the address of a chunk of memory allocated for an integer.

Thereafter, iptr, without an asterisk, refers to the location of an address; *iptr, with an asterisk, refers to the location of the integer identified by the address:

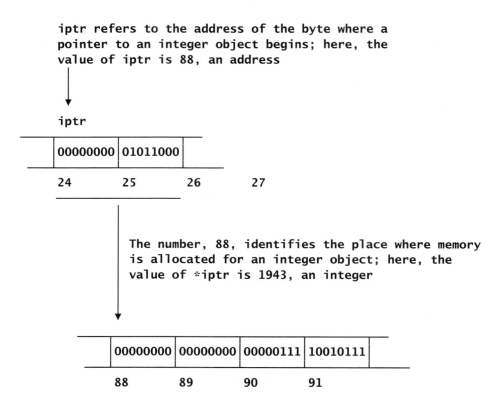

311   Thus, iptr identifies *a location that contains an address that refers to* a location in memory that contains an integer, whereas *iptr identifies a location in memory that contains an integer.

Because the asterisk has the effect of removing the italicized part of the preceding sentence—the part containing the words *refers to*—the asterisk is often called the **dereferencing** operator.

312   Of course, a pointer variable also can identify a chunk of memory that contains the address of a structure object, such as a trade:

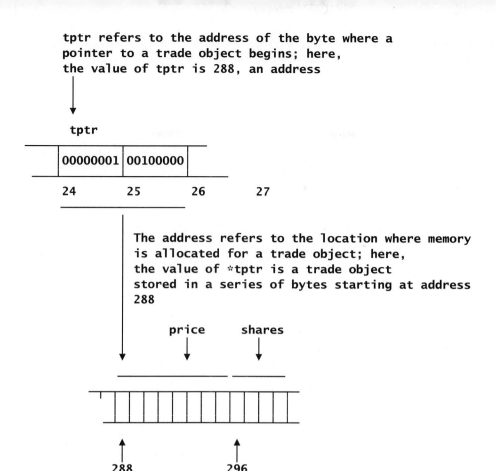

tptr refers to the address of the byte where a
pointer to a trade object begins; here,
the value of tptr is 288, an address

tptr

00000001	00100000

24   25   26   27

The address refers to the location where memory
is allocated for a trade object; here,
the value of *tptr is a trade object
stored in a series of bytes starting at address
288

price   shares

288   296

313 What you have learned about defining integer pointers applies to defining structure-object pointers as well:

```
struct trade t;       /* Allocate space for a trade */
struct trade *tptr;   /* Allocate space for a pointer to a trade */
```

The definition, struct trade *tptr; makes tptr a pointer variable, and the chunk of memory allocated for tptr contains the address of a chunk of memory allocated for a trade object.

Thereafter, tptr, without a dereferencing asterisk, refers to the location of the address; *tptr, with a dereferencing asterisk, refers to the location of the trade object identified by the address. Said more concisely, tptr's value is an address, whereas *tptr's value is a trade object.

314 Note that, when you define a pointer variable in your program, the C compiler allocates only the small amount of memory required to hold an address. Then, later on, you can arrange for that address to be the address of a chunk of memory that is allocated for an object at run time.

315   If you want to have the pointer variable, `tptr`, point to the memory allocated for the
ordinary `trade` variable, `t`, you can write the following assignment statement:

```
tptr = &t;
```

316   It is important to know that you can specify that a parameter is to be a **pointer parameter,**
rather than an ordinary parameter. Then, as you soon see, you can arrange for your pointer
parameter to point to an appropriate object through the parameter assignment process that
occurs when a function is called.

Just as an asterisk transforms an ordinary variable into a pointer variable, an asterisk
transforms an ordinary parameter into a pointer parameter. In the following illustration,
you see that `trade_price` function's previous parameter, `t`, has been converted into a
pointer parameter, `tptr`:

```
double trade_price (struct trade *tptr) {···}
```

Because of the asterisk, the value of `tptr` must be the address of trade structure, rather
than a trade structure.

317   In the version of `trade_price` shown in Segment 295, the object handed over was a `trade`
object taken from the `trades` array:

```
trade_price(trades[counter])
```

In accordance with normal C argument-to-parameter rules, the `trade` object was copied.

Now, however, with `trade_price` defined with a pointer parameter, `tptr`, the object
handed over must be an address of a `trade` object. Accordingly, you need to use the
address-of operator, **&,** which obtains the address of an object in memory:

```
          ┌── Address-of operator produces an address
          │
          ▼
trade_price(&trades[counter])
```

318   From the memory point of view, the modification of the parameter specification, to include
an asterisk, together with the modification of the argument, to include the address-of
operator, has a substantial effect; only the address of a structure is copied into the memory
reserved for the pointer parameter:

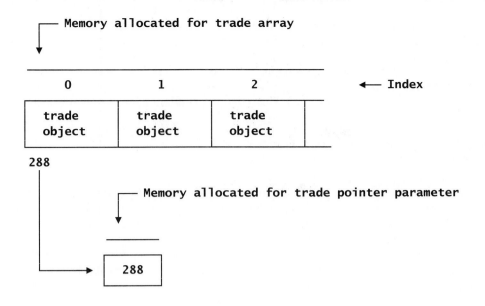

Without the modification, the entire structure is copied into the memory reserved for the structure parameter:

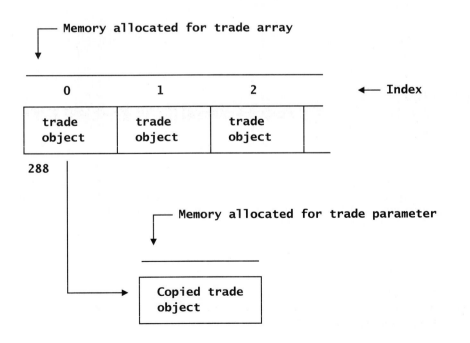

319 Having converted `trade_price`'s ordinary trade structure parameter, `t`, into a `trade` pointer parameter, `tptr`, your program must, of course, dereference `tptr` inside the `trade_price` function to identify a particular trade structure object in the `trades` array. Accordingly, instead of expressions, such as `t.price`, that read structure variables in a `trade` copy, you need expressions that read structure variables in a `trade` object identified by a dereferenced pointer. The redefined `trade_price` function is as follows:

```
double trade_price (struct trade *tptr) {
  return (*tptr).price * (*tptr).shares}
```

Note that you must enclose `*tptr` in parentheses to refer to the price of the `trade` object to which `tptr` points, because the structure-member operator, the period, has precedence higher than that of the dereferencing operator, the asterisk. Accordingly, a version without parentheses, `*tptr.price`, is equivalent to `*(tptr.price)`, which means *produce the object pointed to by a pointer stored, peculiarly, in the price member variable of a pointer to a trade object.* What you want, of course, is the version that means *produce the value stored in the price member variable of the dereferenced pointer to a trade object.*

320 Actually, few C programmers would write `(*tptr).price` to access the value of the `price` structure variable. Instead, most would take advantage of the **structure-pointer operator**, `->`, which you can think of as a shorthand that takes the place of both the dereferencing operator and the structure-member operator. The following, therefore, are equivalent:

	Equivalent	
`(*tptr).price`	←————————————→	`tptr -> price`

Thus, the structure-pointer operator takes the place of two other operators and eliminates the need for precedence-defeating parentheses:

```
double trade_price (struct trade *tptr) {
  return (tptr -> price) * (tptr -> shares);
}
```

321 You can use the member-pointer operator not only to read the value in a structure variable, but also to write into the memory reserved for a structure variable. Thus, the following writes `12.2` into the memory reserved for the `price` structure variable of a trade structure:

```
tptr -> price = 12.2;
```

322 The following is a revised version of the `analyze_trades` program shown in Segment 295. This version uses a `trade` pointer parameter in the `trade_price` function:

```
#include <stdio.h>
/* Define the trade structure */
struct trade {double price; int number;};
/* Define value-computing function */
double trade_price (struct trade *tptr) {
  return tptr -> price * tptr -> number;
}
/* Define trade array */
struct trade trades[100];
main ( ) {
  /* Declare various variables */
  int limit, counter;
  double sum = 0.0;
  /* Read numbers and stuff them into array */
  for (limit = 0;
       2 == scanf ("%lf%i",
                   &trades[limit].price,
                   &trades[limit].number);
       ++limit)
    ;
  /* Display value of shares traded */
  for (counter = 0; counter < limit; ++counter)
    sum = sum + trade_price(&trades[counter]);
  printf ("The total value of the %i trades is %f.\n",
                                    limit,        sum);
}
```
——————————— Sample Data ———————————
```
10.2    600
12.0    100
13.2    200
```
——————————— Result ———————————
The total value of the 3 trades is 9960.000000.

323
PRACTICE

Define a function, bigger_trade, that takes two trade-pointer arguments. It is to return a pointer to the trade object with the higher trade price.

Then, modify the program in Segment 322 such that it displays the value of the biggest trade.

324
HIGHLIGHTS

- A pointer variable's value is the address of a memory chunk.

- If you want to define a pointer variable, **then** proceed as though defining an ordinary variable, and then add an asterisk, *, in front of the name of the variable.

- If you want to know the address of a chunk of memory, **then** use the address-of operator, &, in front of the name of that memory location.

- If you want to access a structure variable in a structure object, **and** you have a pointer to that structure object, **then** instantiate one of the following patterns:

```
(*pointer name).structure variable name   /* Ok. */
pointer name -> structure variable name   /* Better. */
```

- If you want to write a value for a structure variable into a structure object, **and** you have a pointer to that structure object, **then** instantiate one of the following patterns:

```
/* Ok: */
(*pointer name).structure variable name = expression
/* Better: */
pointer name -> structure variable name = expression
```

20 HOW TO USE POINTER PARAMETERS TO ALTER VALUES

325   You have learned that C's call-by-value convention creates a wall around functions, pre-
       venting inside changes from inadvertently affecting computations done outside. Some-
       times, you may want to circumvent the effect of the call-by-value convention by using a
       pointer parameter to get your hands on an otherwise inaccessible object.

326   In Section 19, you learned about a version of `analyze_trades` in which a subfunction
       works on a `trade` object handed over to the subfunction by way of a pointer parameter.
       The value returned by the subfunction is the product of the values in the `price` and `number`
       structure variables:

```
          ┌── A value of type double is returned
          │
          ▼
double trade_price (struct trade *tptr) {
  return tptr -> price * tptr -> number;
}
```

327   Now consider the following, revised version of the `trade_price` function. Conspicuously,
       no value is returned. Equally conspicuously, a second parameter appears, `result`, a pointer
       to a floating-point number:

```
          ┌── No value is returned                      ┌── Extra parameter
          │                                             │
          ▼                                             ▼
void trade_price (struct trade *tptr, double *result) {
  *result = tptr -> price * tptr -> number;
}
```

Because `result` is a pointer parameter, its value must be the address of a chunk of memory
allocated before `result` is called. The assignment statement writes the product of the
`price` and `number` structure variables into that chunk of memory.

Thus, the computation performed in the `trade_price` function is passed out via the memory chunk identified by a dereferenced pointer, rather than via a normal return value. Put
to use, this version of the `trade_price` function appears in the following revised version
of the `analyze_trades` program; note the introduction of the floating-point variable,
`trade_price_result`, which provides the chunk of memory that the `result` pointer
parameter identifies:

```
#include <stdio.h>
/* Define the trade structure */
struct trade {double price; int number;};
/* Define value-computing function */
void trade_price (struct trade *tptr, double *result) {
  *result = tptr -> price * tptr -> number;
}
/* Define trade array */
struct trade trades[100];
main ( ) {
  /* Declare various variables */
  int limit, counter;
  double trade_price_result, sum = 0;
  /* Read numbers and stuff them into array */
  for (limit = 0;
       2 == scanf ("%lf%i",
                   &trades[limit].price,
                   &trades[limit].number);
       ++limit)
    ;
  /* Display value of shares traded */
  for (counter = 0; counter < limit; ++counter) {
    trade_price (&trades[counter], &trade_price_result);
    sum = sum + trade_price_result;
  }
  printf ("The total value of the %i trades is %f.\n",
                                    limit,        sum);
}
```

————————————————— Sample Data —————————————————

```
10.2    600
12.0    100
13.2    200
```

——————————————————— Result ———————————————————
The total value of the 3 trades is 9960.000000.

328 Now compare the two approaches to computing the trade value. The first approach uses an ordinary return value:

```
double trade_price (struct trade *tptr) {
  return tptr -> price * tptr -> number;
}
...
for (counter = 0; counter < limit; ++counter)
  sum = sum + trade_price(&trades[counter]);
```

The second approach uses a pointer parameter in combination with the address of a variable's value:

```
void trade_price (struct trade *tptr, double *result) {
  *result = tptr -> price * tptr -> number;
}
...
for (counter = 0; counter < limit; ++counter) {
  trade_price (&trades[counter], &trade_price_result);
  sum = sum + trade_price_result;
}
```

329   You normally should not pass information into or out of a function using a pointer parameter. Occasionally, however, the pointer-parameter mechanism for passing information into or out of a function is extremely useful.

First, you already know that it can be time consuming to copy a structure object when a function is called. It also can be time consuming to copy a structure object when a function returns. The pointer-parameter mechanism for passing information avoids both copying operations.

Second, the pointer-parameter mechanism for passing information out of a function allows you to get more than one value out of the function. You can get one value out for every pointer parameter, because each supplies access to a memory chunk reserved outside the function.

330   The scanf function is an example of a function that needs to return multiple values. Accordingly, the address-of operator, &, appears frequently in scanf calls. Those address-of operators enable the scanf function to gain access, via pointers, to the memory locations that are to receive values. Thus, scanf uses pointers to get more than one value out of a single scanf call.

331   Here, by way of summary, is where you are:

- You know that you ordinarily use call-by-value parameters. C always allocates a chunk of memory for each call-by-value parameter and C always arranges for an argument value to be copied into that chunk. The rationale is that you want to isolate each function's parameters from other parameters, local variables, and global variables that happen to have the same name.

- You know that you can use pointer parameters to circumvent C's isolation of function parameters. Changes made by way of dereferenced pointer parameters alter the information in the memory chunks supplied as arguments.

332   You can place the asterisk in pointer-variable definitions or pointer-parameter declarations just after the data type, just before the variable or parameter, or with space in between. Thus, all the following produce the same result:

```
struct trade *tptr;
struct trade* tptr;
struct trade * tptr;
```

Some programmers prefer to join the asterisk to the variable as a prefix, because that approach places the asterisk in the same position when the pointer is introduced and when the pointer is used. Others prefer to join the asterisk to the data type as a suffix, because they see the asterisk as a data-type modifier. Few like to put the asterisk in between, with spaces on both sides, because that looks too much like multiplication.

333 Revise the `bigger_trade`, which you were asked to define in Segment 323, such that it
PRACTICE takes a third argument by which it is to return a pointer to the `trade` object with the higher trade price.

Then, modify the program you were asked to define in Segment 323 such that it uses your new definition of `bigger_trade`.

334
HIGHLIGHTS

- C ordinarily uses call-by-value parameters.

- **If** you want to circumvent the isolating effect of C's call-by-value convention, **then** use a pointer parameter.

- **If** you want a variable to be a pointer variable, rather than an ordinary variable, **then** add an asterisk to the variable's type specification:

  `data type` `* variable name` ;

- **If** you want to define a parameter to be a pointer parameter, rather than an ordinary call-by-value parameter, **then** add an asterisk to the parameter type specification in the parameter list:

  `data type` `function name`
    (··· , `data type` `* parameter name` , ···)

21 HOW TO ACCESS ARRAY ELEMENTS USING POINTERS

335 In Section 19, you started to learn about pointers. You learned, in particular, that pointer parameters enable you to circumvent C's call-by-value convention by which parameters are copied into at call time and out of at return time. In this section, you learn that pointers also provide an alternate way—often a more concise way—to access array elements.

336 Recall that you can use the address-of operator on array locations. For example, suppose that number is the name of an integer array whose first element resides at memory location 88:

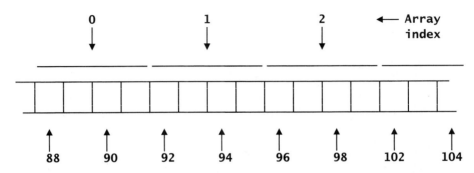

Then, &number[0] returns 88, the address of the first element, and &number[1] returns 92, the address of the second element, and so on.

337 Accordingly, you can arrange for the value of nptr—a pointer variable declared using the statement int *nptr;—to be the address of the first element in the number array:

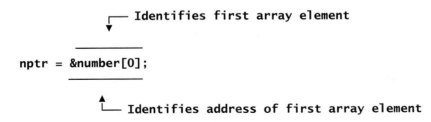

338 Once nptr is assigned, you can dereference it to get back to the array element:

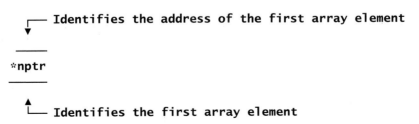

339 Viewed from the memory perspective, the result of the statement, nptr = &number[0];, is that 88, which is the address of number[0], is deposited in the chunk of memory reserved for the pointer, nptr:

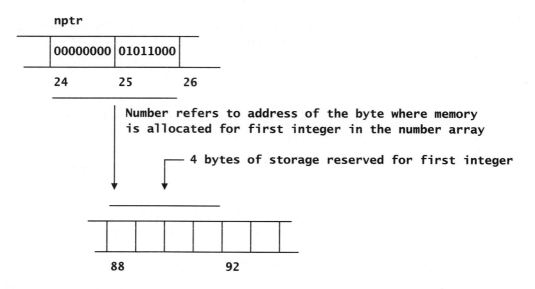

340 Now note the following carefully: Although the value of nptr is 88, when you evaluate the expression nptr + 1, the result is 92, rather than 89! Thus, nptr + 1 is the address of the second element in the array:

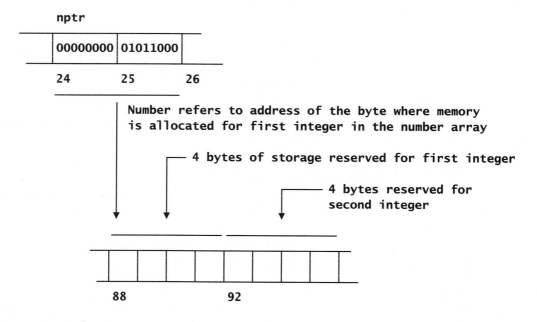

341 Evidently, C does arithmetic on pointers in a special way:

- Adding an integer to the value of a pointer variable produces an address that is the sum of the original value plus the product of the integer and the number of bytes occupied by the objects identified by the pointer.

342 Concretely, suppose that you define `nptr` to be a pointer variable that points to integers, and that you define `number` to be an array of integers:

```
int *nptr;
int number[100];
```

Then, you can arrange for `nptr`'s value to be the address of the first element in the array:

```
nptr = &number[0];
```

Once you have thus assigned a value to nptr, you can produce the address of other array elements by addition:

```
nptr + 0        /* Address of the first element */
nptr + 1        /* Address of the second element */
...
nptr + n - 1    /* Address of the nth element */
```

And once you know how to produce addresses, you know how to produce the elements themselves via the dereferencing operator:

```
*(nptr + 0)     /* Identifies the first element */
*(nptr + 1)     /* Identifies the second element */
...
*(nptr + n - 1) /* Identifies the nth element */
```

343 The incrementing and decrementing operators, ++ and --, also behave in a special way when used with pointers. They do not add 1; instead, they increment the pointer by the number of bytes occupied by the objects identified by the pointer. In a typical implementation, incrementing a character pointer would increment the address by 1, because a character occupies 1 byte. Incrementing an integer pointer, however, would increment the address by 4, assuming an integer occupies 4 bytes in the implementation. Incrementing a trade pointer would increment the address by 12, assuming `trade` objects consist of an 8-byte floating-point number and a 4-byte integer.

Suppose, once again, that you assign the address of the first element in an integer array to a pointer variable:

```
nptr = &number[0];
```

Then, you can reassign the pointer such that it points to the addresses of other array elements:

```
nptr        /* Pointer identifies the address of the first element */
++nptr      /* Pointer identifies the address of the second element */
++nptr      /* Pointer identifies the address of the third element */
```

344   If `number` is the name of an array, then the value of `number`, without any brackets, is the address of the first element in the array. Thus, the value of `number` and the value of `&number[0]` are the same. Accordingly, most seasoned C programmers never write `nptr = &number[0]`; instead, they write the following:

```
nptr = number;
```

345   Because the value of `number` is the address of the first element in the `number` array, `number` is viewed as a pointer. Accordingly, you can produce the addresses of other array elements using `number` in addition expressions:

```
number + 0          /* Address of the first element */
number + 1          /* Address of the second element */
...
number + n - 1      /* Address of the nth element */
```

Once you know how to produce addresses from `number`, you know how to produce the elements themselves via the dereferencing operator:

```
*(number + 0)       /* Identifies the first element */
*(number + 1)       /* Identifies the second element */
...
*(number + n - 1)   /* Identifies the nth element */
```

Thus, `*(number + n)` identifies the same element as `number[n]`. The bracket notation is just a shorthand for the addition-cum-dereferencing combination.

346   Given that `number` is the name of an array, you know that `number` itself is a pointer to the first element. However, you can neither assign a new value to `number`, nor increment or decrement `number`. Thus, `number` is a **constant pointer**.

347   Now suppose that `nptr1` and `nptr2` are both pointers into an array. You can subtract one from the other to establish how many array elements lie between the two addresses specified by the two pointers:

```
nptr2 - nptr1;  /* The number of elements between the two addresses */
```

Of course, it makes no sense to do such a subtraction if `nptr1` and `nptr2` are pointers into different arrays. Also, it makes no sense to add the two pointers whether or not they point into just one array:

```
nptr2 + nptr1;  /* ??? */
```

348   At this point, you know that pointer variables and pointer arithmetic provide an alternate notation for going after array elements. As an illustration, consider the `for` statement that appears in the version of the `analyze_trades` program in Segment 322:

```
for (counter = 0; counter < limit; ++counter)
  sum = sum + trade_price(&trades[counter]);
```

Note that a call to `trade_price` resides in the `for` statement. The argument, provided by `&trades[counter]` is the address of an element in the trades array.

You know, however, that you can provide the same address using pointer arithmetic: `trades + counter` is the same address as `&trades[counter]`. Accordingly, you can substitute the following for the `for` statement in Segment 322:

```
for (counter = 0; counter < limit; ++counter)
    sum = sum + trade_price(trades + counter);
```

349 You also know that you can increment pointer variables. Suppose that you define a `trade` pointer as follows:

```
struct trade tptr;
```

Then, you can initialize and increment the pointer, along with the counter, such that the pointer identifies successive addresses of the elements in the array:

```
for (counter = 0, tptr = trades; counter < limit; ++counter, ++tptr)
    sum = sum + trade_price(tptr);
```

350 You can hand an array to a function by passing the name of the array as an argument.

Suppose, for example, that you want to define a function, `sum_trade_prices`, to be used as follows:

```
                              ┌──── An array name, a pointer
                              ▼
sum = sum_trade_prices (trades, limit)
                                  ▲
                                  └──── Number of trades in array
```

To define `sum_trade_prices`, you declare that the first argument is a pointer to a `trade` object. That tells the C compiler what it needs to know to increment the corresponding parameter appropriately inside `sum_trade_prices`:

```
double sum_trade_prices (struct trade *p, int counter) {
    double result = 0;
    int i;
    for (i = 0; i < counter; i++, p++)
        result = result + trade_price (p);
    return result;
}
```

351 Dealing with arrays that have more than one dimension is more complicated, because the array declaration must include enough information about the array for the C compiler to compile array references correctly.

352 In Segment 282, you learned about a 3 by 100 multidimensional array of numbers declared by the following statement:

```
double djia[3][100];
```

353   Now, suppose that you want to define a function, mean_djia, that is to accept djia as
an argument, along with a day-specifying column number. The mean_djia function is to
find the average of the high and low of the Dow–Jones Industrial Average on that day by
computing one-half of the sum of the numbers in the first and second rows. For example,
the following is to produce the average of the high and low on the third day:

```
mean_djia (djia, 2)
```

To define mean_djia, you must include dimension information in the array specification
as follows:

```
double mean_djia (double array[3][100], day) {
   return 0.5 * (array[0][day] + array[1][day]);
}
```

The declaration, double array[3][100], tells the C compiler all there is to know about
the array argument.

354   Actually, when you declare an array parameter, you do not need to supply dimension
<small>SIDE TRIP</small> information for the first dimension:

┌── First dimension's size omitted
▼

```
double mean_djia (double array[ ][100], day) {
   return 0.5 * (array[0][day] + array[1][day]);
}
```

To see why you can omit the first dimension's size, you need to know that the objects stored
in two-dimensional arrays are placed sequentially in memory. In C, the storage is by rows:

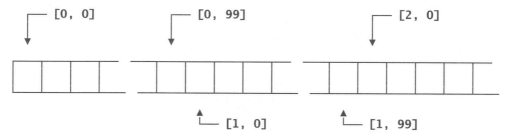

You do not need to indicate the number of rows in the array-parameter declaration, because
the C compiler needs to know only how many columns are stored in the array for each
row to find the place in memory corresponding to any index pair.

355   Write a program to compute the average of the means of the highs and lows accumulated
<small>PRACTICE</small> in an array named djia, as described in Segment 282. Use the mean_djia function defined
in Segment 352.

Define `closing_djia`, patterned on the `mean_djia` function defined in Segment 352. The `closing_djia` function is to find the closing Dow–Jones Industrial Average for a certain day in an array named `djia`, as described in Segment 282.

Then, write a program to compute the average of the closing Dow–Jones Industrial Averages.

- An array name, without brackets, is really a constant pointer to the first element in the array.

- **If** you want the address of an array element, **then** you can add the element's index to the value assigned to the array's name.

- **If** you want to march a pointer along an array, **then** define a pointer variable of the appropriate type, **and** assign the pointer initially to the value assigned to the array's name, **and then** increment the pointer.

- **If** you want to read the value of an array element, **then** you can use ordinary bracket notation by instantiating the following pattern:

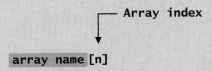

- **If** you want to read the value of an array element, **then** you can dereference an array pointer by instantiating the following pattern:

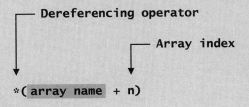

22 HOW TO CREATE NEW STRUCTURE OBJECTS AT RUN TIME

358 Ordinarily, whenever you define a global variable, the C compiler allocates the memory required to hold an object corresponding to the variable's type, be it a built-in type, such as int, or a user-defined structure, such as `trade`. In this section, you learn about an alternative whereby C allocates only a small amount of memory for a pointer at compile time, deferring until run time the allocation of memory for an object.

In Section 23, you learn that run-time allocation enables you to reduce the memory consumed by your program when the number of objects that your program encounters is smaller than your worst-case estimate of that number.

359 When you define a pointer variable in your program, the C compiler allocates only the small amount of memory required to hold an address. Then, later on, you can arrange for that address to be the address of a chunk of memory that is allocated for an object at run time.

360 Each C program has access to a large chunk of memory called the **free store**. The `malloc` function, for *m*emory *alloc*ate, removes a specified number of contiguous memory bytes from the free store.

361 To determine how many bytes of memory you need to store an object of a particular type, you deploy the `sizeof` operator using the object's type as the argument. Thus, `sizeof (int)` returns 4 in most implementations, because int objects occupy 4 bytes. Similarly, `sizeof (trade struct)` returns the number of bytes occupied by a `trade` object, which is likely to be 12, assuming that a `trade` object contains exactly one floating-point number representing the price per share traded and one integer representing the number of shares traded.

362 Combining `malloc` with `sizeof`, you can remove the required number of bytes from the free store for an object whose size you do not know. The following, for example, removes a chunk of memory from the free store that is just the right size for holding `trade` objects; the value returned is the address of that chunk:

```
malloc (sizeof (struct trade))
```

363 Now suppose that you want to assign a `trade` pointer to the address of a chunk of memory removed from the free store for a `trade` object. Suppose `tptr` is the pointer and `malloc (sizeof (trade struct))` is the expression producing the address of the memory chunk. You might think that the following would assign the proper value to `tptr`:

```
tptr = malloc (sizeof (struct trade));   /* DEFECTIVE */
```

The statement looks like it should work. After all, `tptr` is a variable whose value is supposed to be an address, and `malloc` is a function that is supposed to return an address. The problem is that the address returned by `malloc` is not the same as the type declared for `tptr`. Accordingly, C requires you to **cast** the value returned by `malloc`, thus converting that value into the type required for assignment to the `tptr` object pointer.

364   From the data-type perspective, `malloc` generates a pointer that is said to be of type `void*`. Such `void*` pointers have the property that they can be cast into pointers of any type.

To cast the result of a call to `malloc` into a form suitable for assignment to a `trade` object, you preface the call to `malloc` by a parentheses-enclosed specification of the appropriate pointer data type.

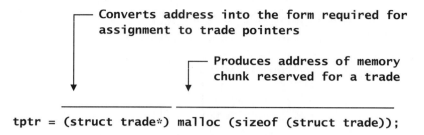

Converts address into the form required for
assignment to trade pointers

Produces address of memory
chunk reserved for a trade

```
tptr = (struct trade*) malloc (sizeof (struct trade));
```

Note that the specification of the data type includes an asterisk—the data type is to be a pointer to a `trade` object, rather than a `trade` object.

Also, remember that `malloc`-containing statements require the C compiler to create executable code that allocates memory for a `trade` object at run time, rather than at compile time.

365   The concept of pointer casting is related to the concept of number casting. In Segment 73, you learned that you can call for an explicit conversion of a number belonging to one type into a number belonging to another type, as in the following example:

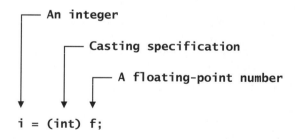

An integer

Casting specification

A floating-point number

```
i = (int) f;
```

366   In Segment 263, you saw a program in which memory for a single trade object is allocated when the program is compiled. The following alternative version demonstrates the use of a pointer variable, the `sizeof` function, `malloc` function, and pointer casting.

Note that no memory is allocated for any `trade` object at compile time. Instead, memory is allocated at compile time for a `trade` pointer. Then, at run time, memory for a single `trade` object is allocated by the `malloc` function, and that memory is referenced via the `trade` pointer.

```
#include <stdio.h>
struct trade {double price; int number;};
double trade_price (struct trade *t) {return t -> price * t -> number;}
main ( ) {
  double price;
  int number;
  struct trade *tptr;
  tptr = (struct trade*) malloc (sizeof (struct trade));
  while (2 == scanf ("%lf%i", &price, &number)) {
    tptr -> price = price;
    tptr -> number = number;
    printf ("The total value of the trade is %f.\n",
            trade_price (tptr));
  }
  printf ("You seem to have finished.\n");
}
```

───────────────────────── Sample Data ─────────────────────────

```
10.2    600
12.0    100
13.2    200
```

───────────────────────── Result ─────────────────────────

```
The total value of the trade is 6120.000000.
The total value of the trade is 1200.000000.
The total value of the trade is 2640.000000.
You seem to have finished.
```

Note that the purpose of this version is to illustrate the run-time allocation concept; it has no memory-conserving advantage. In Section 23, you learn about a more complex program that does illustrate memory conservation.

367 What will happen if you run the following program? Explain your answer.

PRACTICE

```
#include <stdio.h>
const double pi = 3.14159;
struct trade {double price; int number;};
};
main ( ) {
  struct trade *tptr;
  while (1)
    tptr = (struct trade*) malloc (sizeof (struct trade));
}
```

368

HIGHLIGHTS

- An ordinary variable refers to the location of an object. A pointer variable refers to the address of the location of an object.

- Pointers generally take far less memory than do structure objects.

121

- If you want to define a pointer variable, **then** instantiate the following pattern:

  `data type` * `pointer name` ;

- If you want to allocate a chunk of memory to a structure object at run time, **and** you want to assign the address of that chunk of memory to a pointer variable, **then** instantiate the following pattern:

```
pointer name
  = ( data type *)
    malloc (sizeof (struct data type ));
```

23 HOW TO STORE POINTERS TO STRUCTURE OBJECTS

369   Frequently, it is difficult to predict exactly how many data you will encounter at run time. Hence, you may find yourself creating ridiculously large global arrays just to be sure that you do not run out of space. Such arrays can waste a lot of memory, particularly if they hold large structure objects.

Fortunately, you now know that you can arrange for the C compiler to allocate only pointers at compile time, deferring the allocation of memory for objects until later, at run time.

In this section, you learn that arrays of pointers waste much less space on excess array capacity than arrays of objects do.

370   Recall that you define an array of integers with a definition that looks like a variable definition with a bracketed number added:

```
int integers[100];
```

Similarly, you can define an array of pointers to integer objects by adding an asterisk before the array name: The following, for example, defines `integer_pointers` to be an array of 100 pointers to integers:

```
int *integer_pointers[100];
```

371   Similarly, you can define an array of `trade` objects:

```
struct trade trades[100];
```

And you can define an array of pointers to `trade` objects by adding an asterisk before the array name:

```
struct trade *trade_pointers[100];
```

372   Note that the pointer-declaring asterisk, *, takes precedence over the array-declaring brackets, [ ], in declarations. Thus, `*trade_pointers[100]` means *an array of 100 pointers to trades*, rather than *a pointer to an array of 100 trades*.

373   Now it is time to develop a program that uses an array of pointers to structure objects. The program is to be a modification of the following program that reads trade prices per share and numbers of shares, stuffs them into an array of `trade` objects, and displays their total trade price:

```c
#include <stdio.h>
/* Define the trade structure */
struct trade {double price; int number;};
/* Define value-computing function */
double trade_price (struct trade *tptr) {
  return tptr -> price * tptr -> number;
}
/* Define trade array */
struct trade trades[100];
main ( ) {
  /* Declare various variables */
  int limit, counter, number;
  double price, sum = 0.0;
  /* Read numbers and stuff them into array */
  for (limit = 0;
       2 == scanf ("%lf%i", &price, &number);
       ++limit) {
    trades[limit].price = price;
    trades[limit].number = number;
  }
  /* Display value of shares traded */
  for (counter = 0; counter < limit; ++counter)
    sum = sum + trade_price(&trades[counter]);
  printf ("The total value of the %i trades is %f.\n",
                              limit,        sum);
}
```

————————————— Sample Data ——————————————

10.2	600
12.0	100
13.2	200

————————————————— Result ————————————————

```
The total value of the 3 trades is 9960.000000.
```

The modified program does the same work, but differs in that memory is allocated for the pointers at compile time, leaving memory for the trade objects to be allocated at run time.

374 First, the original version defines an array of trade objects:

```c
struct trade trades[100];
```

The modified version defines an array of pointers to trade objects:

```c
struct trade *trade_pointers[100];
```

375 Next, the original program contains a for statement that does reading and writing:

```
for (limit = 0;
     2 == scanf ("%lf%i", &price, &number);
     ++limit) {
  trades[limit].price = price;
  trades[limit].number = number;
}
```

You need to add a statement that allocates new space for a `trade` object and deposits the address of the newly allocated space into the appropriate array location:

```
trade_pointers[limit] = (struct trade*) malloc (sizeof (struct trade));
```

Also, you need to modify the existing statements to dereference pointers:

```
trade_pointers[limit] -> price = price;
trade_pointers[limit] -> number = number;
```

The structure-pointer operators appear in the assignment statements, because you are working with an array of `trade` pointers, rather than of `trade` objects.

376   Finally, the original program contains a `for` loop that computes the sum of the prices of the `trade` objects; the argument handed to `trade_price` is the address of an array item:

```
for (counter = 0; counter < limit; ++counter)
  sum = sum + trade_price (&trades[counter]);
                          ──────────────────
                                 ▲
                                 └── An address
```

The `for` loop in the modified program is nearly identical; the address-of operator disappears, however, because array items are the addresses of objects, rather than objects themselves:

```
for (counter = 0; counter < limit; ++counter)
  sum = sum + trade_price (trade_pointers[counter]);
                          ────────────────────────
                                    ▲
                                    └── Also an address
```

377   Combining the pieces, you have the following program:

```c
#include <stdio.h>
/* Define the trade structure */
struct trade {double price; int number;};
/* Define value-computing function */
double trade_price (struct trade *tptr) {
  return tptr -> price * tptr -> number;
}
/* Define trade array */
struct trade *trade_pointers[100];
main ( ) {
  /* Declare various variables */
  int limit, counter, number;
  double price, sum = 0.0;
  /* Read numbers and stuff them into array */
  for (limit = 0;
       2 == scanf ("%lf%i", &price, &number);
       ++limit) {
    trade_pointers[limit]
      = (struct trade*) malloc (sizeof (struct trade));
    trade_pointers[limit] -> price = price;
    trade_pointers[limit] -> number = number;
  }
  /* Display value of shares traded */
  for (counter = 0; counter < limit; ++counter)
    sum = sum + trade_price(trade_pointers[counter]);
  printf ("The total value of the %i trades is %f.\n",
                          limit,        sum);
}
```

————————————————— Sample Data —————————————————

```
10.2    600
12.0    100
13.2    200
```

————————————————— Result —————————————————

```
The total value of the 3 trades is 9960.000000.
```

378 Now consider the memory consumed by the old and new versions of the total-value–computing programs. The old version, using an array of 100 trades, each of which consumes, say, 12 bytes, uses 1200 bytes no matter how many trades are read from a file. The new version, using an array of 100 pointers—each of which consumes, say, 4 bytes—uses 400 bytes for pointers plus 12 bytes for each trade read from a file.

If 100 trades are read from a data—the worst case—the total memory consumed by the new version, the one that uses pointers, is 1600 bytes, which is more than the 1200 required by the old version. On the other hand, if only 10 trades are read, the total memory consumed by the new version is only $400 + 10 \times 12 = 560$, which is less than the 1200 required by the old version.

Thus, you can save a great deal of memory if the expected number of structure objects is much less than the worst-case number of structure objects you need. Your saving increases as the size of each structure object grows relative to the size of each pointer.

379
SIDE TRIP Later, in Section 37, you learn about `free`, a function that does the opposite of `malloc`: Instead of allocating a chunk of memory from the free store for an object, `free` returns the memory allocated to an object to the free store. You will see that you need to use `free` whenever you write a program that repeatedly reassigns one or more pointers to objects created at run time using `malloc`.

380
PRACTICE Use the `sizeof` operator to determine the number of bytes occupied on your computer by a `call` object, such as the one you were asked to define in Segment 267 and by a pointer to a `call` object.

381
PRACTICE Suppose that you want to be able to store information, on average, about 10 `trade` objects, but that you must be prepared, in the worst case, to handle 1000. In the average case, how much memory will you save by using an array of pointers to `trade` objects, created at run time, as compared to using an array of `trade` objects.

382
HIGHLIGHTS

- **If** you must be prepared to store a large number of structure objects in the worst case, **and** the expected number of structure objects is much smaller **and** you want to conserve memory, **then** define an array of pointers to structure objects instead of an array of structure objects.

- **If** you want to create a one-dimensional array of structure-object pointers, **then** instantiate the following pattern:

```
struct structure name *array name [number of objects];
```

- If you want to allocate a chunk of memory to a structure object at run time, **and** you want to refer to the address of that chunk of memory in a pointer array, **then** instantiate the following pattern:

```
array name [index]
  = (struct data type *)
    malloc (sizeof (struct data type));
```

- **If** you want to write a value for a structure variable in a structure object, **and** you have an array that contains a pointer to that structure object, **then** instantiate one of the following patterns:

```
/* OK: */
(*array name [index]).structure variable's name = expression;
/* Better: */
array name [index] -> structure variable's name = expression;
```

- **If** you want to access a structure variable in a structure object, **and** you have an array that contains a pointer to that structure object, **then** instantiate one of the following patterns:

```
/* Ok: */
(* array name [ index ]). structure-variable name
/* Better: */
array name [ index ] -> structure-variable name
```

24 HOW TO DEFINE CONSTRUCTOR, READER, AND WRITER FUNCTIONS

383 In this section, you learn that constructors are functions that enable you to initialize the structure variables in new structure objects. You also learn that reader and writer functions can help you to refer to structure-variable values and to assign values to structure variables subsequent to initialization.

384 In Section 22, you learned how to obtain an address for a chunk of memory allocated at run time:

```
(struct trade*) malloc (sizeof (struct trade))
```

Such an expression is a load to remember. Worse yet, you need to assign the address of the allocated chunk of memory to a pointer, and you have to assign the structure variables appropriately:

```
trade_pointers[limit] = (struct trade*) malloc (sizeof (struct trade));
trade_pointers[limit] -> price = price;
trade_pointers[limit] -> number = number;
```

Such allocation and assignment combinations are cumbersome and ugly.

385 Accordingly, you should hide the details of allocation and assignment in a function. You can, for example, define `construct_trade` so as to create a new trade and to assign values to both structure variables:

```
struct trade* construct_trade (double price, int number) {
  struct trade *tptr;
  tptr = (struct trade*) malloc (sizeof (struct trade));
  tptr -> price = price;
  tptr -> number = number;
  return tptr;
}
```

Once you have defined `construct_trade`, you can replace the three cumbersome lines of code in `main` with the following:

```
trade_pointers[limit] = construct_trade (price, number);
```

386 In the `analyze_trades` program, you gain little when you move details of data construction into `construct_trade`, because you have only moved three cumbersome lines from one place, in `main`, to another, in `construct_trade`. When you write a large program, however, you gain a great deal of clarity at each place where you create new `trade` objects.

387 Functions, such as `construct_trade`, that create new objects are called **constructors**. Naming the trade constructor `construct_trade` is a personal convention, rather than a C requirement. You can choose any name you like, but you should choose a name—such as `make_trade` or `initialize_trade`—that makes your function's purpose clear.

388   In the `analyze_trades` program, the `trade_price` function refers to structure variables in `trade` objects using the structure pointer operator, `->`:

```
double trade_price (struct trade *tptr) {
  return tptr -> price * tptr -> number;
}
```

Alternatively, you can refer to a structure variable's value indirectly by defining a function that returns the structure variable's value. In the following example, the definition for a function named `read_trade_price` indicates that `read_trade_price` returns the value of a `price` structure variable:

```
double read_trade_price (struct trade *tptr) {return tptr -> price;}
```

Accordingly, with `read_trade_price` defined, and `read_trade_number` is similarly defined, you have another way to refer to the values in the `price` and `number` structure variables in the `trade_price` function:

```
double trade_price (struct trade *tptr) {
  return read_trade_price (tptr) * read_trade_number (tptr);
}
```

389   A **reader** is a function that extracts information from an object. When you use readers, rather than accessing structure variables directly, you can include additional computation in a reader. For example, if you were concerned about how often your program accesses the `price` structure variables in trade structures, you could add a statement to the `read_trace_price` reader that announces each access:

```
double read_trade_price (struct trade *tptr) {
  printf ("Reading a trade price ...\n");
  return tptr -> price;
}
```

390   You also can assign a structure variable's value indirectly by defining a function that assigns a value. In the following, for example, the definition of the `write_trade_price` function indicates that `write_trade_price` assigns a value to the `price` structure variables:

```
void write_trade_price (double price, struct trade *tptr) {
  tptr -> price = price;
}
```

Inasmuch as the only purpose of the `write_trade_price` function is to assign a value to a structure variable, the `write_trade_price` function is marked `void`, indicating that no value is to be returned.

391   A **writer** is a function that inserts information into an object. When you use writers, rather than writing into structure variables directly, you can include additional computation in a writer. Earlier, in Segment 389, you saw how to add a statement to the `read_trade_price` reader that announces each access. The following provides the same enhancement to the `write_trade_price` writer:

130

```
void write_trade_price (double price, struct trade *tptr) {
  printf ("Writing a trade price ...\n");
  tptr -> price = price; }
```

392   The naming of the read_trade_price and write_trade_price functions, which include
      the read_ and write_ prefixes as well as the name of the structure, makes it clear that
      they are reader and writer functions for particular structures. Note that this use of prefixes
      is a personal convention, rather than a convention of C.

393   You may also want to use readers to provide access to **virtual structure variables** that
      exist only in the sense that their values can be computed from structure variables that do
      exist. For example, you can create a read_total_cost function, which seems to read the
      contents of a total_cost structure variable, but which actually works with the price
      and number structure variables:

```
double read_total_cost (struct trade *tptr) {
  return tptr -> price * tptr -> number;
}
```

394   The following, by way of summary, shows a complete set of trade constructors, readers,
      and writers in the context of a revised analyze_trades program. The writers, although
      defined, do not happen to be used:

```
#include <stdio.h>
/* Define the trade structure */
struct trade {double price; int number;};
/* Define constructor function */
struct trade* construct_trade (double price, int number) {
  struct trade *tptr;
  tptr = (struct trade*) malloc (sizeof (struct trade));
  tptr -> price = price;
  tptr -> number = number;
  return tptr;
}
/* Define readers */
double read_trade_price (struct trade *tptr) {return tptr -> price;}
int read_trade_number (struct trade *tptr) {return tptr -> number;}
/* Define writers */
void write_trade_price (double price, struct trade *tptr) {
  tptr -> price = price;
}
void write_trade_number (int number, struct trade *tptr) {
  tptr -> number = number;
}
/* Define value-computing function */
double trade_price (struct trade *tptr) {
  return read_trade_price (tptr) * read_trade_number (tptr);
}
```

```
/* Define trade array */
struct trade *trade_pointers[100];
main ( ) {
  /* Declare various variables */
  int limit, counter, number;
  double price, sum = 0.0;
  /* Read numbers and stuff them into array */
  for (limit = 0;
       2 == scanf ("%lf%i", &price, &number);
       ++limit)
    trade_pointers[limit] = construct_trade (price, number);
  /* Display value of shares traded */
  for (counter = 0; counter < limit; ++counter)
    sum = sum + trade_price(trade_pointers[counter]);
  printf ("The total value of the %i trades is %f.\n",
                                  limit,        sum);
}
```

————————————— Sample Data —————————————

10.2	600
12.0	100
13.2	200

——————————————— Result ———————————————
The total value of the 3 trades is 9960.000000.

395
PRACTICE
Rewrite the writers shown in Segment 394 such that they return 1 if the new value is different from the old value, and return 0 otherwise.

396
PRACTICE
Rewrite the readers shown in Segment 394 such that they display the number of times that they have been called.

397
PRACTICE
Rewrite the constructor shown in Segment 394 such that it keeps track of how much memory it has consumed. Write a companion function, display_bytes_consumed, that displays the number of bytes consumed.

398
HIGHLIGHTS

- Constructors perform computations, such as memory allocation and structure-variable assignment, that you want to occur when you create a structure object.

- Reader and writer member functions provide an indirect route to structure-variable reference and assignment.

132

- If you want to define a constructor for structures created at run time, **then** use the following pattern:

```
struct structure name *
  construct_ structure name ( first structure-variable type
                              first structure-variable value ,
                              ...) {
    struct structure name *ptr;
    ptr =
      (struct structure name *)
        malloc (sizeof (struct structure name ));
    ptr -> first structure-variable name
      = first structure-variable value ;
    ...
    return ptr;
}
```

- If **you want to use a constructor**, then **instantiate the following pattern:**

```
pointer =
  constructor name ( first structure-variable value , ...);
```

- If you want to refer to a structure variable's value using a reader, **then** instantiate the following pattern:

```
reader function ( pointer to structure object );
```

- If you want to assign a structure variable's value using a writer, **then** instantiate the following pattern:

```
writer function ( expression , pointer to structure object );
```

25 HOW TO BENEFIT FROM DATA ABSTRACTION

399 You now know how to use constructor, reader, and writer member functions. Moreover, you have seen how readers and writers make it easy to add computation at the point where information is read from or written into structure variables, and you have seen how to define readers for virtual structure variables. In this section, you learn more about the virtues of constructors, readers, and writers, and how such member functions help you to practice data abstraction.

400 At this point, two readers, `read_trade_price` and `read_trade_size`, and one nonreader, `trade_price`, all exhibit a parameter that is assigned to a `trade` object's address.

As you learned in Segment 393, you can, if you like, replace the `trade_price` nonreader by a readerlike function named `read_total_cost`:

```
double read_total_cost (struct trade *tptr) {
  return tptr -> price * tptr -> number;
}
```

401 Suppose that you develop a big program around trade structures only to discover that you are more often interested in total trade costs than in prices per share. For efficiency, you might want to switch from a `price` structure variable to a `total_cost` structure variable, so that multiplication is not needed when you want a `total_cost` delivered.

If you work with the information in `trade` objects using constructors, readers, and writers exclusively, you need only to change the definitions of those constructors, readers, and writers to work with a `total_cost` structure variable instead of a `price` structure variable. Instead of computing `total_cost` from `price` and `number` values, you compute `price` from `total_cost` and `number` values:

```
struct trade {double total_cost; int number;};

struct trade* construct_trade (double price, int number) {
  struct trade *tptr;
  tptr = (struct trade*) malloc (sizeof (struct trade));
  tptr -> total_cost = price * number;
  tptr -> number = number;
  return tptr;
}

double read_trade_price (struct trade *tptr) {
  return (tptr -> total_cost) / (tptr -> number);
}

int read_trade_number (struct trade *tptr) {
  return tptr -> number;
}
```

```
double read_total_cost (struct trade *tptr) {
  return tptr -> total_cost;
}

void write_trade_price (double price, struct trade *tptr) {
  tptr -> total_cost = price * tptr -> number;
}

void write_trade_number (int number, struct trade *tptr) {
  tptr -> number = number;
}

void write_total_cost (double total_cost, struct trade *tptr) {
  tptr -> total_cost = total_cost;
}
```

402   To understand the advantage of working with constructors, readers, and writers, suppose that your program has a statement that reads the price of a particular trade, T27. If you work with readers, you need to make no change to that statement to accommodate the switch from a price-based structure definition to a total-cost–based structure definition:

     ··· **read_trade_price (T27)** ···

On the other hand, if you do not work with the structure variables in trade objects using constructors, readers, and writers only, you have to go through your entire program, modifying myriad statements:

     ··· **T27.price** ···

     ··· **T27.total_cost / T27.number** ···

Thus, constructors, readers, and writers isolate you from the effects of your efficiency-motivated switch from a price-based structure definition to a total-cost–based structure definition.

403   In general, constructors, readers, and writers isolate you from the details of how a structure is implemented. Once you have written those functions, you can forget about how they refer to and assign values; none of the detail, such as whether you have a price or a total_cost structure variables, clutters the programs that use trade objects.

Collectively, constructors, readers, and writers are called **access functions**. Whenever you refer to the value of a variable or assign a value to a variable, you are said **to access** that variable.

404   When you move representation detail into a set of access functions, you are said to be practicing **data abstraction**, and you are said to be hiding behind a **data abstraction barrier** the details of how data are represented.

Good programmers carefully design into their programs appropriate access functions to create data-abstraction barriers.

405   The virtues of data abstraction parallel those of function abstraction. One of those virtues is that *you can push details out of sight and out of mind*, making your functions easier to read and enabling you to concentrate on high-level steps.

Another virtue of data abstraction is that *you can find easily the places where data are delivered and assigned*, thus making your functions easier to debug.

406   Still another virtue of data abstraction is that *you can augment what you can do with a structure*. You can, for example, add extra, information-displaying statements to your readers and writers, as you saw in Section 24.

407   Another virtue of data abstraction is that *you can easily improve how data are stored*. In this section, you have seen an example in which there is an efficiency-motivated switch from a price-based structure definition to a total-cost-based structure definition. The switch makes your code more efficient, reducing the number of multiplications required, should you have a need to work more with total costs than with prices.

408   Most good programmers provide readers and writers for some structure variables, but not for others. The choice, to a large extent, is a matter of taste and style. Until you have developed your own sense of taste and style, you should rely on the following heuristic:

- Whenever the detailed implementation of a structure may change, provide structure-variable readers and writers to insulate your structure-using functions from the potential change.

409   Of course, as you learn about C in this book, you need to see more examples of important C functions and operators, such as `malloc` and `->`. Accordingly, constructors, readers, and writers—which tend to hide such functions and operators—are not employed as liberally in this book as they should be in your programs.

410   Devise a structure, `deposit`, for a bank deposit for which interest is compounded annually.
PRACTICE   Include structure variables for the account number (an integer), the annual interest rate, and the amount of the deposit. Define readers and writers for all structure variables. Also include a reader and writer for a virtual monthly interest rate that is $\frac{1}{12}$ of the annual interest rate.

411   Revise the structure that you were asked to devise in Segment 410 such that it contains a
PRACTICE   structure variable for the monthly interest rate, rather than the annual interest rate. Revise all readers and writers as necessary to accommodate the change.

412   Now assume you have learned that interest is actually compounded monthly, which makes
PRACTICE   the equivalent annual interest rate different from 12 times the monthly interest rate. Revise the readers and writers that you were asked to devise in Segment 411 to accommodate monthly compounding. You will need to include the line `#include <math.h>` in your program, because that line allows you to use the library function, `pow`. The `pow` function takes two arguments, x and y, both of type `double`, and computes x^y.

- Constructors, readers, and writers are called access functions. When you move references and assignments into access functions, you are practicing data abstraction.

- Data abstraction has many virtues, including the following:

  - You can push details out of sight and out of mind.

  - You can easily find the places where data are delivered and assigned.

  - You can easily augment what a structure provides.

  - You can easily improve how data are stored.

- **If** you anticipate that the detailed definition of a structure may change, **then** you should provide access functions for the structure variables to isolate the effects of the potential changes.

26 HOW TO WRITE MULTIWAY CONDITIONAL STATEMENTS

414   The `analyze_trades` program shown, for example, in Segment 377, is a keystone program, because it brings together many concepts, including C's mechanisms for reading, displaying, testing, conditional execution, iteration, and pointer dereferencing.

Now you are ready to tackle still more C mechanisms through further modifications to the `analyze_trades` program. In this section, for example, you learn how to use `switch` statements when you want your program to decide which of many alternative statements to execute.

415   Imagine that your brokerage company has modified trade files such that each trade is described by an industry-encoding digit as well as by the price per share and number of shares traded. Here, for example, is a sample file:

```
0   3.3   300
1   2.5   400
5   9.9   100
5  10.1   500
2   5.0   200
```

Further imagine that you want to use the industry code to pick out trades of interest, ignoring the rest.

416   You can write a simple program to pick out just the right trades by inspecting the industry codes, doing nothing if the code is not the one you want. Suppose, for example, that you want to analyze only those trades with industry code 1 or 5, ignore those trades with industry code 0, 2, 3, or 4, and issue a warning for any other code. You need only to include the following in your program:

```
...
/* Read trade information */
for (limit = 0; 3 == scanf ("%i%lf%i", &industry, &price, &number);)
  if (industry == 1 || industry == 5) {
    trade_pointers[limit] =
      (struct trade*) malloc (sizeof (struct trade));
    trade_pointers[limit] -> price = price;
    trade_pointers[limit] -> number = number;
    ++limit;
  }
  else if (industry == 0 || industry == 2
                          || industry == 3
                          || industry == 4)
    ;
  else printf ("Industry code %i is unknown!\n", industry);
...
```

139

Note that `++limit` has moved from the `for` statement to the `if` statement, because you add elements to the array only when you see a trade with an industry code of 1 or 5.

417   Although there is nothing wrong with the program fragment in Segment 416, you can rewrite it, with a gain in elegance and clarity, by substituting what is called a `switch` statement for the `if--else--if--else` combination.

The purpose of a `switch` statement is to execute a particular sequence of statements according to the value of an expression that produces a number belonging to any of the integral types. Then, in most `switch` statements, integer constants and corresponding statement sequences are sandwiched between a `case` symbols on one end and a `break` statements on the other, with a colon separating the constant integer and the statement sequence:

```
switch ( integer-producing expression ) {
  case integer constant 1 : statements for integer 1 break;
  case integer constant 2 : statements for integer 2 break;
  ...
  default: default statements
}
```

When such a switch statement is encountered, the integer-producing expression is evaluated. The value is compared with the integer constants found following the `case` symbols. As soon as there is a match, evaluation of the following statements begins; evaluation continues up to the first `break` statement encountered.

The line beginning with the `default` symbol is optional. If the expression produces an integer that fails to match any of the `case` integer constants, the statements following the `default` symbol are executed.

If there is no match and no `default` symbol, no statements are executed.

418   The following `switch` statement pattern contains no `break` statements. Thus, once execution begins, all subsequent statements up to the end of the `switch` statement are executed.

```
switch ( integer-producing expression ) {
  case integer constant 1 : statements for integer 1
  case integer constant 2 : statements for integer 2
  ...
  default: default statements
}
```

In general, when there is no `break` statement to terminate the execution of a sequence of statements, execution is said to **fall through** to the next sequence of statements, where execution continues, once again, in search of a `break` statement.

The reason for the fall-through feature is that you occasionally want to perform the same action in response to any of several conditions. Note carefully, however, that an inadvertently forgotten `break` is a common error.

419   Rewriting the code fragment shown in Segment 416, using a `switch` statement, improves clarity:

```
switch (industry) {
  case 1: case 5:
    trade_pointers[limit]
      = (struct trade*) malloc (sizeof (struct trade));
    trade_pointers[limit] -> price = price;
    trade_pointers[limit] -> number = number;
    ++limit;
    break;
  case 0: case 2: case 3: case 4: break;
  default: printf ("Industry code %i is unknown!\n", industry);
}
```

If the industry code is 1, execution begins just after case 1. Because there are no statements before case 5, you might think that nothing would happen, but *no statements* implies no break statement, so execution falls through to the several statements, terminated by a break statement, following case 5.

Thus, trades with an industry code of 1 or 5 lead to the execution of the same statements. Codes 0, 2, 3, and 4 all lead to the execution of no statements. Other codes lead to a warning.

420 As it stands, the switch statement in the analyze_trades program displays a message when it encounters an unknown industry code. You may choose to have the program take more drastic action, however, such as terminating whenever it encounters an unknown industry code. To arrange for an orderly termination, you need to inform the C compiler that you intend to make use of the exit function by including the following line in your program:

```
#include <stdlib.h>
```

Then, you can insert a call to the exit function after the warning is displayed:

```
switch (industry) {
  case 1: case 5:
    ...
  case 0: case 2: case 3: case 4: break;
  default: printf ("Industry code %i is unknown!\n", industry);
          exit (0);
}
```

Note that exit expects an integer argument. That integer argument generally should be 0, thereby indicating that your program's termination is not to evoke a special reaction from your operating system.

421 Here is the revised program; any unrecognized industry code leads to immediate termination:

```c
#include <stdio.h>
/* Define the trade apparatus */
struct trade {double price; int number;};
double trade_price (struct trade *x) {return x -> price * x -> number;}
/* Define trade array */
struct trade *trade_pointers[100];
main ( ) {
  /* Declare various variables */
  int limit, counter, industry, number;
  double price, sum = 0.0;
  /* Read trade information */
  for (limit = 0; 3 == scanf ("%i%f%i", &industry, &price, &number);)
    switch (industry) {
      case 1: case 5:
        trade_pointers[limit]
          = (struct trade*) malloc (sizeof (struct trade));
        trade_pointers[limit] -> price = price;
        trade_pointers[limit] -> number = number;
        ++limit;
        break;
      case 0: case 2: case 3: case 4: break;
      default: printf ("Industry code %i is unknown!\n", industry);
               exit (0);
    }
  /* Compute cost */
  for (counter = 0; counter < limit; ++counter)
    sum = sum + trade_price (trade_pointers[counter]);
  printf ("The total cost of %i selected trades is %f.\n",
                           limit,                  sum);
}
```

──────────────── Sample Data ────────────────
```
0   3.3   300
1   2.5   400
5   9.9   100
5 10.1   100
2   5.0   200
7   5.0   200
```
──────────────── Result ────────────────
Industry code 7 is unknown!

422 If your program is activated by another program, rather than by your typing of a command
SIDE TRIP line to the operating-system, then exit's argument is returned to the calling program. It is
up to you and to the author of that calling program to negotiate what the calling program
is to do with the returned value.

423 Whenever you use the return function inside main, the effect is as though you had used
SIDE TRIP exit with the same argument supplied to return. If main has neither a return statement
nor an exit statement, the main statement is compiled as though the final statement were

`return 0;`, which is equivalent to `exit 0;`.

424
SIDE TRIP Incorporating the line `#include <stdlib.h>` in your program not only provides you with the function prototype for `exit`, but also provides you with a variety of diverse macros, structure definitions, and function prototypes for introducing, for example, sorting and random-number generation into your programs.

425
PRACTICE Write a program that accepts two numbers, representing a year and a month, and displays the number of days in that month. Use a `switch` statement, and be sure to exploit the fall-through feature. Note that leap years occur in years divisible by 4, except for centenary years that are not divisible by 400.

426
PRACTICE Amend the `analyze_trades` program such that it announces an error if you supply it with more than 100 trades.

427
HIGHLIGHTS
- If you want a program to decide which of many alternative sequences of statements to evaluate, **then** instantiate the following pattern:

```
switch ( integer-producing expression ) {
   case integer constant 1 : statements for integer 1 break;
   case integer constant 2 : statements for integer 2 break;
   ...
   default: default statements
}
```

- In `switch` statements, you may omit the symbol `default:` and the default statements.

- In `switch` statements, the integer-producing expression can produce a value belonging to any of the integral data types.

- In `switch` statements, once embedded statement execution begins, execution continues up to the first embedded `break` statement or the end of the `switch` statement, whichever comes first. Bugs emerge when you forget to pair `case` symbols with `break` statements.

- If you want a program to stop, because an error has occurred, **then** tell C you intend to make use of the standard library, **and then** insert an exit statement:

```
#include <stdlib.h>
...
exit (0);
```

27 HOW TO USE ENUMERATIONS TO IMPROVE READABILITY

428   In this section, you learn how to make your programs easier to understand by replacing integer codes by mnemonic symbols.

429   At this point, you have seen a `switch` statement that analyzes integer industry codes and creates appropriate `trade` objects:

```
switch (industry) {
  case 1: case 5:
    trade_pointers[limit]
      = (struct trade*) malloc (sizeof (struct trade));
    trade_pointers[limit] -> price = price;
    trade_pointers[limit] -> number = number;
    ++limit;
    break;
  case 0: case 2: case 3: case 4: break;
  default: printf ("Industry code %i is unknown!\n", industry);
           exit (0);
}
```

Although this `switch` statement works fine, it is difficult to remember which number goes with which industry. In general, it is difficult to maintain a program that is littered with such nonmnemonic encoding.

430   In principle, you could replace industry-encoding integers with macros. Then, you would need only to maintain the correct correspondence between the industry codes and the corresponding industries in just one place. Elsewhere, you have the mnemonic power of the macro's name working for you.

For example, you could define macros as follows near the beginning of your program:

```
#define FOOD          0
#define TRUCKING      1
#define COMPUTERS     2
#define METALS        3
#define HEALTH        4
#define AIRLINE       5
```

431   Although there is nothing wrong with defining macros, many experienced C programmers would be more likely to use an **enumeration declaration**, as in the following example:

```
enum {food, trucking, computers, metals, health, airline};
```

Such a declaration identifies all the symbols in braces as enumeration constants, and assigns integer values to those constants. By default, the value of the first enumeration constant is 0; also by default, the value of each succeeding enumeration constant is 1 more than the previous value. Hence, the value of `food` is 0 and the value of `trucking` is 1.

432 Once you have introduced enumeration constants, you can improve the clarity of the switch statement by replacing the integers with those enumeration constants. Such replacement is illustrated in the following revised version of the analyze_trades program:

```
#include <stdio.h>
/* Define the trade apparatus */
struct trade {double price; int number;};
double trade_price (struct trade *x) {return x -> price * x -> number;}
/* Define enumeration constants, needed in switch statement */
enum {food, trucking, computers, metals, health, airline};
/* Define trade array */
struct trade *trade_pointers[100];
main ( ) {
  /* Declare various variables */
  int limit, counter, industry, number;
  double price, sum = 0.0;
  /* Read trade information and compute cost */
  for (limit = 0; 3 == scanf ("%i%lf%i", &industry, &price, &number);)
    switch (industry) {
      case trucking: case airline:
        trade_pointers[limit]
          = (struct trade*) malloc (sizeof (struct trade));
        trade_pointers[limit] -> price = price;
        trade_pointers[limit] -> number = number;
        ++limit;
        break;
      case food: case computers: case metals: case health:
        break;
      default: printf ("Industry code %i is unknown!\n", industry);
              exit (0);
    }
  for (counter = 0; counter < limit; ++counter)
    sum = sum + trade_price (trade_pointers[counter]);
  printf ("The total cost of %i selected trades is %f.\n",
                            limit,                    sum);
}
```

```
------------------------------- Sample Data -------------------------------
0   3.3   300
1   2.5   400
5   9.9   100
5  10.1   100
2   5.0   200
------------------------------- Result -------------------------------
The total cost of 3 selected trades is 3000.000000.
```

433 If you like, you can specify the value of particular enumeration constants by including integers in the enumeration declaration. In the following example, the value of the additional

`clothing` constant is 10, and, because the value of each succeeding constant lacking an expressed value is 1 more than that of the previous constant, the value of `travel` is 11.

```
enum {food, trucking, computers, metals, health, airline,
      clothing = 10, travel};
```

Note the contrast with the following, alternative declaration, for which the value assigned to `clothing` is 6 and the value assigned to `travel` is 7:

```
enum {food, trucking, computers, metals, health, airline,
      clothing, travel};
```

434
SIDE TRIP
A more general form of the enumeration declaration allows you to create **enumeration data types**. These new data types allow you, in turn, to create **enumeration variables**.

The following declaration, for example, makes `industry_code` an enumeration data type and assigns values to six enumeration constants:

```
enum industry_code
  {food, trucking, computers, metals, health, airline};
```

Subsequently, you can specify that particular variables are `industry_code` variables by using the two symbols `enum industry_code` as a data type. The following, for example, makes `c` a `industry_code` variable:

```
enum industry_code c;
```

435
SIDE TRIP
Whenever you assign an enumeration variable, the right side of the assignment expression should be an enumeration constant of the same type. The following, for example, is appropriate, given that `c` is a `industry_code` enumeration variable:

```
c = food;
```

Some compilers warn you if you assign any object other than an enumeration constant to an enumeration variable. Using one of these compilers, you will get a warning if you write the following assignment statement:

```
c = 0;
```

436
SIDE TRIP
You should use an enumeration variable whenever you decide that any value assigned to the variable must belong to a prescribed set of integers. Then, the C compiler can help you to enforce your decision.

437
PRACTICE
Amend the program that you were asked to write in Segment 425 by using the names of the months as enumeration constants in the switch statement.

438
HIGHLIGHTS

- If you want to make your programs easier to read, **then** replace integer constants with enumeration constants.

147

- If you want to create a set of enumeration constants, **and** you want those constants to have consecutive values beginning with 0, **then** instantiate the following pattern:

```
enum { first constant , second constant , ···};
```

- If you want to create a set of enumeration constants, **and** you want those constants to have specified values, **then** instantiate the following pattern:

```
enum { first constant = first value ,
       second constant = second value ,
       ...
};
```

28 HOW TO USE TYPE SYNONYMS TO IMPROVE READABILITY

439   In this section, you learn how to make your programs easier to understand by replacing type-defining symbols, such as `double`, with synonyms that suggest intended use, such as `Price_per_share_traded`.

440   At this point, the `analyze_trades` program contains many type declarations. Because the names of functions, arrays, and variables reflect a personal preference for spelled-out, mnemonic names, the purposes of the functions, arrays, and variables are relatively easy to infer. A `price` variable defined by `double price;` is the variable that carries price information, for example.

441   Some programmers believe you can be even clearer about purpose by using C's `typedef` mechanism, whereby you can create a synonym for a type-defining symbol. Suppose, for example, that you include the following `typedef` declaration in your program:

typedef double Price_per_share_traded;

Henceforth, you can use the symbol `Price_per_share_traded` in place of `double`, as in the following variable declaration:

Price_per_share_traded price;

The substitution of `Price_per_share_traded` for `double` makes no difference to the C compiler, because the C compiler takes both to specify only that `price` is a floating-point number. For you, however, the substitution makes it absolutely clear for what the value of `price` is to be used.

442   You can use `typedef` to create synonyms for structures as well as for the other data types. For example, if you have a structure named `trade`, you can make a synonym, `Trade_description`, as follows:

typedef struct trade Trade_description;

Note that when you use `typedef` synonyms for structures, the synonym name is all you need; you do not include the `struct` symbol:

Trade_description *trade_pointers[100];

443 Many programmers use `typedef` synonyms for user-defined structures, but not for the built-in data types. The following, for the sake of illustration, uses `typedef` synonyms for both:

```c
#include <stdio.h>
/* Define the trade apparatus */
struct trade {double price; int number;};
/* Define enumeration constants, needed in switch statement */
enum {food, trucking, computers, metals, health, airline};
/* Define types */
typedef struct trade Trade_description;
typedef int Industry_code;
typedef int Number_of_shares_traded;
typedef double Price_per_share_traded;
typedef double Total_cost_of_trade;
/* Define trade array */
Trade_description *trade_pointers[100];
/* Define price-computing function */
Total_cost_of_trade trade_price (Trade_description *x) {
  return x -> price * x -> number;
}
main ( ) {
  /* Declare various variables */
  int limit, counter;
  double sum = 0.0;
  Industry_code industry;
  Price_per_share_traded price;
  Number_of_shares_traded number;
  /* Read trade information and compute cost */
  for (limit = 0; 3 == scanf ("%i%lf%i", &industry, &price, &number);)
    switch (industry) {
      case trucking: case airline:
        trade_pointers[limit] =
          (Trade_description*) malloc (sizeof (Trade_description));
        trade_pointers[limit] -> price = price;
        trade_pointers[limit] -> number = number;
        ++limit;
        break;
      case food: case computers: case metals: case health:
        break;
      default: printf ("Industry code %i is unknown!\n", industry);
              exit (0);
    }
  for (counter = 0; counter < limit; ++counter)
    sum = sum + trade_price (trade_pointers[counter]);
  printf ("The total cost of %i selected trades is %f.\n",
                           limit,                    sum);
}
```

```
0  3.3   300
1  2.5   400
5  9.9   100
5 10.1   100
2  5.0   200
```

──────────── Result ────────────
The total cost of 3 selected trades is 3000.000000.

444
PRACTICE

Suppose that you consider the type name `int` to be objectionable, because you dislike abbreviations, and you consider the type name `double` unaesthetic, because you keep thinking "double what?" Show how you can arrange to replace instances of `int` with `Integer` and `double` with `Real`.

445
HIGHLIGHTS

- You can make programs easier to read by replacing type specifications with mnemonic synonyms.

- If you want to create a type synonym, **then** instantiate the following pattern:

  typedef `type specification` `synonym` **;**

29 HOW TO USE UNIONS TO CAPTURE CLASS DISTINCTIONS

446   You have learned that C's attention to type requires all array elements to be of the same type. Accordingly, you might wonder what you can do when your problem is to deal with array elements that are inherently of mixed type.

In this section, you learn that C's union data type provides one solution to the mixed type problem. You should know, however, that other languages, such as C++, offer more elegant solutions.

447   Suppose that you have a file that contains information about both stock trades and bond trades. Further suppose that trades are described in terms of the price per share, the number of shares traded, and the price–earnings ratio of the stock (an integer); bond trades are described in terms of the price per bond, the number of bonds traded, and the current yield of the bond (a floating point number). In both cases, the type of trade is marked by a leading integer, which is 0 for stock trades and 1 for bond trades:

```
0    3.3   300 10
0    2.5   400 15
1    9.9   100 4.5
1   10.1   100 6.2
0    5.0   200 12
...
```

448   You can image the definition of two structure types, one for stock trades and one for bond trades:

```
/* Preliminary versions /*
struct stock_trade {double price; int number; int pe_ratio;};
struct bond_trade {double price; int number; double yield;};
```

As defined, `bond_trade` objects require 4 bytes more than `stock_trade` objects, in most implementations, because the floating-point number, `yield`, consumes 8 bytes, whereas the integer, `pe_ratio`, consumes just 4 bytes.

449   Ordinarily, you cannot mix in the same array objects belonging to two different structure types, because C requires you to define arrays in terms of exactly one data type. The rationale is that the C compiler must allocate just the right amount of storage for each array element, which it cannot do if the element types are not known at compile time.

450   There is a way to wiggle out of C's prohibition of mixed objects, however. You can tell the C compiler to allocate memory chunks for array elements such that each chunk is large enough for the larger of `bond_trade` objects and `stock_trade` objects:

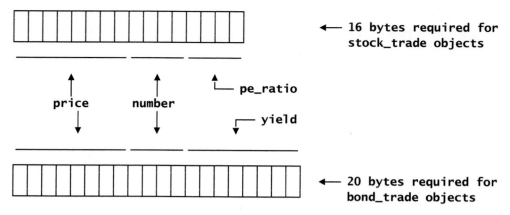

← 16 bytes required for
stock_trade objects

price   number   pe_ratio

yield

← 20 bytes required for
bond_trade objects

If you happen to put a stock_trade object in such a chunk, 4 bytes are left unused.

451 To tell C to allow enough space for the largest of several different object types, you must define a **union**. A union is similar to a structure in that a union is a user-defined data type that you define in terms of a collection of typed structure variables. Unlike a structure, however, a union accommodates only one object at any one time. When you create an object belonging to a union, the space reserved is just that required to hold an object of the largest type that appears in the specification, rather than that required to hold a collection of objects.

Suppose, for example, that you define a trade to be the union of a stock_trade and bond_trade. Then when you create a trade object, C reserves enough space to hold either a stock_trade or a bond_trade, but not both. The details of space allocation are, as usual, somewhat implementation dependent, but the following arrangement is likely:

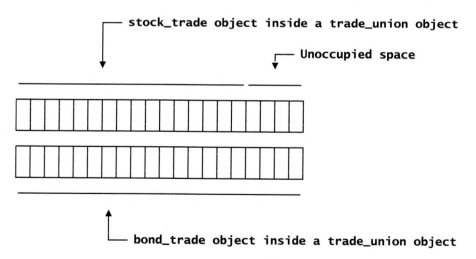

stock_trade object inside a trade_union object

Unoccupied space

bond_trade object inside a trade_union object

452 To define a union, you proceed as though you were defining a structure, except that you use the symbol union, rather than struct. In the following, for example, the trade union, as defined, contains either of two objects: a stock_trade object or a bond_trade object:

```
union trade {
  struct stock_trade stock;
  struct bond_trade bond;
};
```

453   Now suppose that `trade_union` is the name of a variable of type `trade`. Then, if the
memory chunk identified by `trade` is occupied by a `stock_trade` object, you access that
`stock_trade` object as though it were in a structure variable named `stock`:

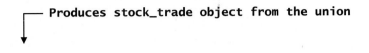

trade_union.stock

Then, if you want to get at the `stock_trade` object's price–earnings ratio, you go after
the value of the `pe_ratio` structure variable:

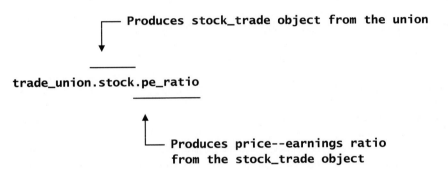

454   To create an array of union objects, you act as though you were creating an array of
structures, but you substitute the `union` symbol for the `struct` symbol:

union trade trades[100];

Similarly, you can create an array of pointers to union objects, which you subsequently
create at run time:

union trade *trade_pointers[100];

455   Unfortunately, you must keep track of what sort of object you have placed in the memory
chunk identified by a union variable or array element. There are no built-in C functions
that test for the type of item actually stored in such a memory chunk.

456   One simple way to keep track of what has gone into a union array element is to maintain
a parallel array of type-identifying integers.

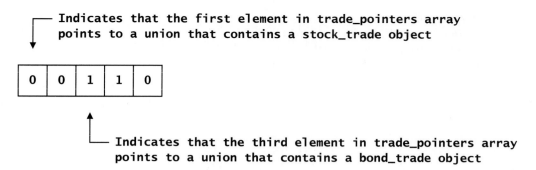

Indicates that the first element in trade_pointers array
points to a union that contains a stock_trade object

```
0 | 0 | 1 | 1 | 0
```

Indicates that the third element in trade_pointers array
points to a union that contains a bond_trade object

457 Maintaining parallel arrays, although simple, is awkward. It is safer and more elegant to package type information with the array elements. One way to do the packaging is to wrap a structure around both the trade-bearing union and a type-specifying integer:

```
struct tagged_trade {
  int code;
  union trade;
}
```

Then, you can define an array of tagged_trade objects:

```
struct tagged_trade *trade_pointers[100];
```

Given such an array, you determine type by extracting the value in the code structure variable, as in the following example, in which limit is an array index:

```
trade_pointers[limit] -> code
```

Once you know what sort of object is stored in the union, you can go after the values stored. The following example, which assumes that the trade is a stock_trade object, illustrates:

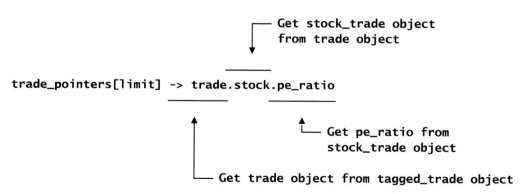

Get stock_trade object
from trade object

```
trade_pointers[limit] -> trade.stock.pe_ratio
```

Get pe_ratio from
stock_trade object

Get trade object from tagged_trade object

458 The following program exploits the tagged_trade structure. In contrast to previous versions of the analyze_trades program, this one computes average stock price/earnings ratios and average bond yields. Also, to keep the program more compact, information is transferred by scanf directly into the appropriate structures and unions, rather than through intermediate variables.

156

```c
#include <stdio.h>
/* Define the trade apparatus */
struct stock_trade {double price; int number; int pe_ratio;};
struct bond_trade {double price; int number; double yield;};
union trade {
  struct stock_trade stock;
  struct bond_trade bond;
};
struct tagged_trade {
  int code;
  union trade trade;
};
/* Define type codes */
enum {stock, bond};
/* Define trade array */
struct tagged_trade *trade_pointers[100];
main ( ) {
  /* Declare various variables */
  int limit, counter, trade_type, stock_count = 0, bond_count = 0;
  int pe_sum = 0;
  double yield_sum = 0.0;
  /* Read type code */
  for (limit = 0; 1 == scanf ("%i", &trade_type); ++limit) {
    /* Allocate space for structure */
    trade_pointers[limit] = (struct tagged_trade*)
                            malloc (sizeof (struct tagged_trade));
    trade_pointers[limit] -> code = trade_type;
    /* Read remaining information according to type */
    switch (trade_type) {
      case stock: scanf ("%lf%i%i",
                    &trade_pointers[limit] -> trade.stock.price,
                    &trade_pointers[limit] -> trade.stock.number,
                    &trade_pointers[limit] -> trade.stock.pe_ratio);
                  break;
      /* ... Similar code for bonds ... */
    }
  }
  /* Analyze array elements */
  for (counter = 0; counter < limit; ++counter)
    switch ((trade_pointers[counter] -> code)) {
      case stock:
        ++stock_count;
        pe_sum += trade_pointers[counter] -> trade.stock.pe_ratio;
        break;
      /* ... Similar code for bonds ... */
    }
  /* ... Continued on next page ...  ... */
```

```
/* Display report */
printf ("The average stock price/earnings ratio is %i.\n",
        pe_sum / stock_count);
printf ("The average bond yield is %f.\n",
        yield_sum / bond_count);
}
```

———————————————— Sample Data ————————————————

```
0    3.3   300 10
0    2.5   400 15
1    9.9   100 4.5
1   10.1   100 6.2
0    5.0   200 12
```

———————————————— Result ————————————————

```
The average stock price/earnings ratio is 12.
The average bond yield is 5.350000.
```

459   In the program shown in Segment 458, each tagged_trade structure object contains a trade union object, which contains either a stock_trade object or a bond_trade structure object. In the following, the trade union object contains a stock_trade object:

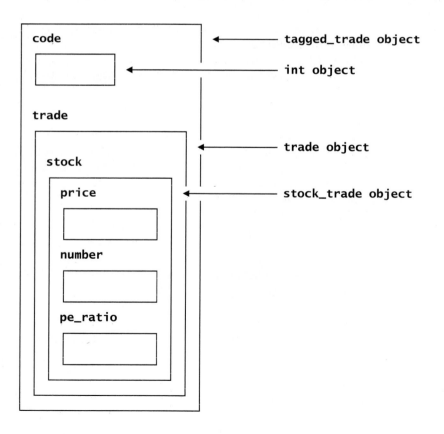

You may, if you wish, use macros to simplify expressions involving unions, structures, and structure variables. For example, suppose you define the macro PE_RATIO as follows:

```
#define PE_RATIO stock.pe_ratio
```

Then, you can replace the expression `trade_union.stock.pe_ratio` by an arguably simpler expression, `trade_union.PE_RATIO`.

If a company is losing money, then the notion of a price–earnings ratio makes no sense.

Modify the program shown in Segment 458 such that the appearance of 2 as the leading integer in a line of data indicates that there is to be no price earnings ratio, and that the data are to be used to construct an object of type `stock_trade_without_ratio`. Define `stock_trade_without_ratio` and include it in the definition of the `trade` union. Try your revised program on the following data.

```
0    3.3   300 10
2    2.5   400
1    9.9   100 4.5
1   10.1   100 6.2
0    5.0   200 12
2    9.1   100
```

- A union is a chunk of memory that is big enough to contain the largest of the union's specified object types.

- Unfortunately, C provides no way to test a union object to determine what it contains. You must keep track yourself using a parallel array or some other means.

- If an array element's type is not known at compile time, **then** you can combine the possible types into a union.

- If you want to define a union, **then** instantiate the following pattern:

```
union union name {
    union variable declaration 1
    ...
    union variable declaration n };
```

30 HOW TO USE BITS TO RECORD STATE INFORMATION

463   In this section, you learn about still another version of the `analyze_trades` program. This version keeps track of the state of the computation using individual bits as status-remembering switches. Through this version, you learn about status variables, masks, and logical operations on bits.

464   A **status register** is a collection of binary switches that either tells you about the state of an input–output device or allows you to tell an input–output device what to do or how to do what it does. When dealing with an input–output device, you frequently have occasion to transfer information back and forth between a status register and a **status variable** that you define so as to hold **status bits**.

465   You can think about status bits as though they were switches, each of which is either 0, representing off, or 1, representing on, thereby reflecting the off or on state of the switches in a device's status register.

466   You can also use status bits to reflect the state of any computational entity such as the state of a chunk of data or the state of a running program.

For example, you might want to use a status variable to keep track of several general characteristics of the data that the `analyze_trades` program has processed:

- Are there enough trade data?

- Are there too many trade data?

- Are any of the trade-price data corrupted?

- Are any of the trade-size data corrupted?

467   Of course, you do not have to use status bits to capture information about the state of a program, because you can use individual variables to record the same information. The extra memory required is not of practical significance.

Nevertheless, the example developed in this section involves a status variable that captures information about the state of a program. The example involves the state of a program—rather than input–output device control—because the details that govern the control of real input–output devices are intricate, highly device specific, and rarely a matter of concern to programmers new to C.

468   When you use a status variable, you must decide what each bit is to do. The following represents one way to pack state information into a 1-byte status variable for the `analyze_trades` program:

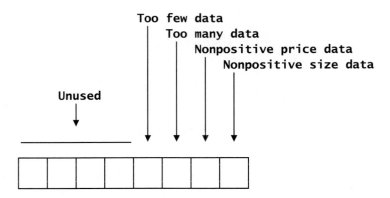

Too few data
Too many data
Nonpositive price data
Nonpositive size data

Unused

469 Note that the bits in a byte are usually spoken of as though numbered from the right, so the bit representing a binary 1 is bit 0 and the bit representing a binary 8 is bit 3.

```
7   6   5   4   3   2   1   0   ◄── Bit position
```

470 You define a status variable using one of the integral data types—one that is large enough to hold all the bits you need to represent state information. Note, however, that you add the keyword unsigned to the variable declaration. Otherwise, C assumes that 1 bit of the chunk of memory dedicated to the variable's value is to indicate whether the stored number is positive or negative:

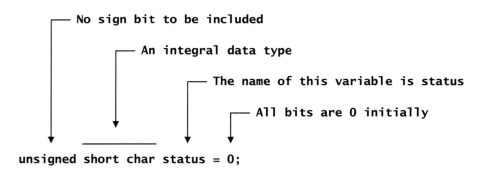

No sign bit to be included

An integral data type

The name of this variable is status

All bits are 0 initially

unsigned short char status = 0;

471 When you arrange for a particular bit to hold a binary 1, corresponding to an on switch, you are said to **set** the bit. When you arrange for a particular bit to hold a binary 0, corresponding to an off switch, you are said to **reset** the bit.

Now you need to know how to set a particular bit without altering any others. First, recall that, viewed as an integer, a byte with a single bit set can be interpreted as an integer that is a power of 2:

```
| 0 | 0 | 0 | 0 | 0 | 0 | 0 | 1 |   ← Corresponds to 1

| 0 | 0 | 0 | 0 | 0 | 0 | 1 | 0 |   ← Corresponds to 2

| 0 | 0 | 0 | 0 | 0 | 1 | 0 | 0 |   ← Corresponds to 4

| 0 | 0 | 0 | 0 | 1 | 0 | 0 | 0 |   ← Corresponds to 8
```

472   Next, you need to know about the **bitwise or operator**, ¦. Given 2 bytes as operands in a bitwise-or expression, the value produced is a byte whose bits are 1 in exactly those positions where one or both operands have a 1:

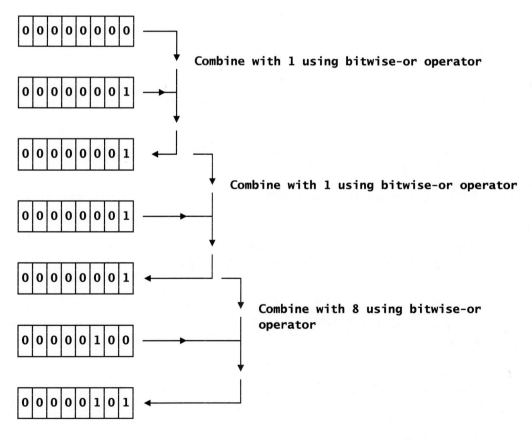

473   Note the difference between ¦ and ¦¦. The bitwise-or operator, ¦, treats an integer operand of any length as a set of independent entities, each of which can be 0 or 1. The ordinary-or operator, ¦¦, treats an integer operand as a whole: If its value is 0, the integer as a whole

represents false; if its value is not zero, with any number of bits set, the integer as a whole represents true.

474 Now you know that the powers of 2 correspond to single-bit-on numbers, and you know that the bitwise-or operator sets particular bits if either operand exhibits a 1 in the corresponding position. Accordingly, you know that, if you want to be sure that a particular bit in a status variable is set, you pick the power of 2 corresponding to that position, and then you use the bitwise-or operator to combine the value of the status variable with that power of 2.

For example, if you want to set bit 0 in the value of the status variable to 1, you combine the status variable's value with the integer 1, the zeroth power of 2, using the bitwise-or operator. If you want to set bit 2 to be 1, you combine the status variable's value with the integer 4:

```
status = status ¦ 1;      ←— Sets bit 0

status = status ¦ 4;      ←— Sets bit 2
```

475 You easily can forget which power of 2 corresponds to what position. Accordingly, it is a good idea to create an enumeration so that you do not have to remember the correspondence:

```
enum {bit0 = 1,  bit1 = 2,  bit2 = 4,  bit3 = 8
      bit4 = 16, bit5 = 32, bit6 = 64, bit7 = 128};
```

Alternatively, once you have decided what each bit position is to represent, you can compose an enumeration to reflect your decisions:

```
enum {bad_size_bit = 1, bad_price_bit  = 2,
      too_much_bit = 4, too_little_bit = 8};
```

476 Now that you know how to use the bitwise-or operator and powers of 2 to set particular bits, you can modify the analyze_trades program such that it includes a status variable, status:

```
#include <stdio.h>
/* Define the trade apparatus */
struct trade {double price; int number;};
/* Define trade array */
struct trade *trade_pointers[100];
/* Define enumeration constants for bit positions */
enum {bad_size_bit = 1, bad_price_bit  = 2,
      too_much_bit = 4, too_little_bit = 8};
```

```
main ( ) {
  /* Declare various variables */
  int limit, counter, number;
  double price, sum = 0.0;
  /* Declare status byte */
  unsigned char status = 0;
  /* Read trade information */
  for (limit = 0;
        2 == scanf ("%lf%i", &price, &number) && limit < 100;
        ++limit)
    if (price > 0.0 && number > 0) {
      trade_pointers[limit]
        = (struct trade*) malloc (sizeof (struct trade));
      trade_pointers[limit] -> price = price;
      trade_pointers[limit] -> number = number;
    }
    else {
     if (price <= 0.0) status = status | bad_price_bit;
     if (number <= 0) status = status | bad_size_bit;
    }
  if (limit < 10) status = status | too_little_bit;
  else if (limit == 100) status = status | too_much_bit;
  /* ... Analyze status variable ... */
}
```

477   Now that you know how to set the bits in a status variable, you need to learn how to analyze those bits. First, however, you need to know about the **bitwise-and operator, &.** Given 2 bytes as operands in a bitwise-and expression, the value produced is a byte whose bits are 1 in exactly those positions where both operands have a 1:

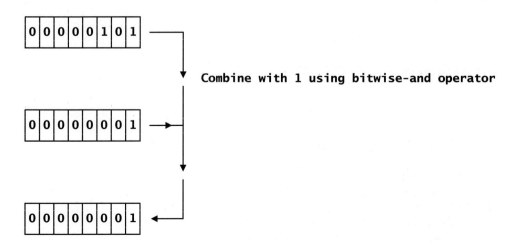

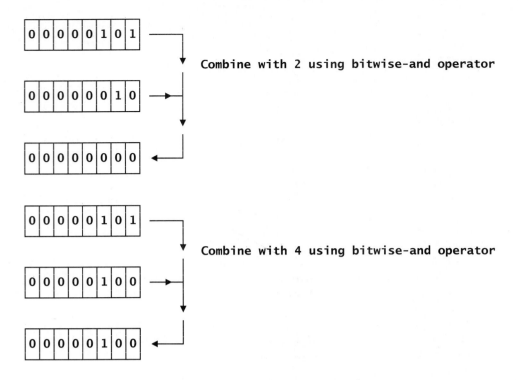

Combine with 2 using bitwise-and operator

Combine with 4 using bitwise-and operator

478 Thus, you can view one operand of the bitwise-and operation as a **mask**: The bits set to 1 in the mask pass along the bits set to 1 in the other operand, whereas the bits set to 0 in the mask filter out—or mask off—any corresponding bits set to 1 in the other operand.

Accordingly, to determine whether, say, the bad-price bit in the status variable is set, indicating that the `analyze_trades` program has encountered a 0 or negative price, you can mask off the other bits and determine whether the on bit gets through. If the on bit does get through, the result, viewed as an integer, is not zero, thus causing the statement embedded in the following if statement to be executed.

```
if (status & bad_price_bit)
   ...
```

Alternatively, you can use a mask with several bits set, as in the following example, which tests both bits that deal with the appearance of negative or zero numbers in the trade-describing file:

```
if (status & (bad_price_bit | bad_size_bit)
   ...
```

479 Once you know how to test the bits in the status variable, you can incorporate such tests in your programs:

```
#include <stdio.h>
/* Define the trade apparatus */
struct trade {double price; int number;};
struct trade *trade_pointers[100];
enum {bad_size_bit = 1, bad_price_bit  = 2,
      too_much_bit = 4, too_little_bit = 8};
main ( ) {
  /* Declare various variables */
  int limit, counter, number;
  double price, sum = 0.0;
  /* Declare status byte */
  unsigned char status = 0;
  /* Read trade information */
  for (limit = 0;
       2 == scanf ("%lf%i", &price, &number) && limit < 100;
       ++limit)
    if (price > 0.0 && number > 0) {
      trade_pointers[limit]
        = (struct trade*) malloc (sizeof (struct trade));
      trade_pointers[limit] -> price = price;
      trade_pointers[limit] -> number = number;
    }
    else {
      if (price <= 0.0) {status = status | bad_price_bit;}
      if (number <= 0) {status = status | bad_size_bit;}
    }
  if (limit < 10) status = status | too_little_bit;
  else if (limit == 100) status = status | too_much_bit;
  /* Check status variable */
  if (status & (bad_price_bit | bad_size_bit))
    printf ("Bad data were encountered and ignored.\n", status);
  if (status & (too_little_bit | too_much_bit))
    printf ("Wrong number of data were encountered.\n", status);
  /* ... Perform other computations ... */
}
```

――――――――――――― Sample Data ―――――――――――――

```
 3.3   300
 2.5   400
 9.9   100
10.1  -100
-5.0   200
```

―――――――――――――― Result ――――――――――――――

```
Bad data were encountered and ignored.
Wrong number of data were encountered.
```

480 Visually, the action of the `bad_price_bit | bad_size_bit` mask is to block passage:

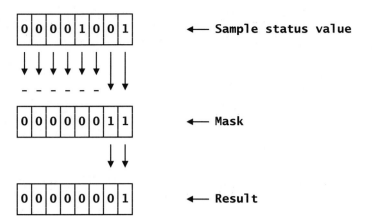

← Sample status value

← Mask

← Result

481 There are four other, occasionally useful, bitwise operators. The **bitwise-complement operator**, ~, converts 1s to 0s, and vice versa. Thus, if a certain mask, m, allows passage of bits 0 and 3, then ~m allows passage of all bits except bits 0 and 3:

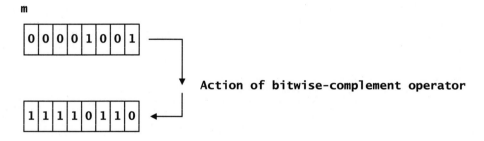

m

Action of bitwise-complement operator

482 The **shift operators**, << and >> move the bits in the left-side operand as far as specified by the right-side operand. For example, if m is a mask that allows passage of bits 0 and 3, you can shift the on bits two places to the left, creating a mask that allows passage of bits 2 and 5:

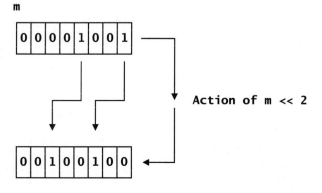

m

Action of m << 2

Similarly, you can shift the on bits two places to the right, losing the 0 bit, creating a mask that allows passage of bit 1 only:

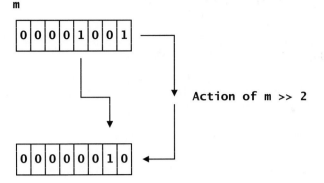

m

Action of m >> 2

483   Finally, there is the **xor operator**, ^. Given 2 bytes as operands in a xor expression, the value produced is a byte whose bits are 1 in exactly those positions where one of the two operands has a 1, but not both operands:

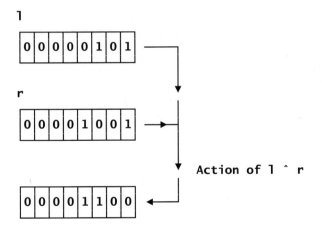

l

r

Action of l ^ r

484   When you design data chunks, you may want to include status bits in your chunks so as
SIDE TRIP   to have a place to describe whether a chunk has certain characteristics, such as *reliable* or *urgent*. By packing status bits 8 to the byte, you can conserve memory or cut down on communication time.

485   Explain how you can use the left-shift operator to create masks. Then, amend the pro-
PRACTICE   gram shown in Segment 479 such that `bad_size_bit`, `bad_price_bit`, `too_much_bit`, and `too_little_bit` are unsigned character variables that you set up using the left-shift operator.

486   Explain how you can use the **bitwise-augmented-or operator**, |=, to set a particular bit
PRACTICE   in a variable without disturbing the others. Then, explain how you can use the **bitwise-augmented-and operator**, &=, to reset a particular bit in a variable without disturbing the others.

- If you want to maintain state information in a status variable, **then** choose an integral data type of sufficient size, **and then** instantiate a pattern such as the following:

  ```
  unsigned char status variable name ;
  ```

- If you want to set a particular bit in a status variable, **then** combine the status variable with the corresponding power-of-2 integer using the bitwise or operator, ¦, **and then** assign the status variable to the result:

  ```
  status variable = status variable ¦ power of 2 ;
  ```

- If you want to test a particular bit in a status variable, **then** combine the status variable with the corresponding power-of-2 integer using the bitwise and operator, &, **and then** test the resulting value in an `if` statement.

  ```
  if ( status variable & power of 2 )
     ...
  ```

- Whenever you use the bitwise-and operator, &, you can treat one operand as a mask that lets through some bits of the other operand and that filters out others.

- If you want to test several bits in a status variable to see whether any are set, **then** combine the status variable with an appropriate multibit mask.

31 HOW TO WRITE FUNCTIONS THAT RETURN CHARACTER STRINGS

488   You have seen a variety of mechanisms that make programs easier to read and understand. Now you are ready to tackle still more C mechanisms, each of which helps you to make your programs read more elaborate files and display more elaborate reports. In this section, for example, you learn how you can return character strings from functions, and you learn how character strings are stored in your computer.

489   At this point, the `analyze_trades` program is reduced to displaying a straightforward report so as to provide a simpler base on which to build more C mechanisms. On the other hand, the trade structure is enriched to enable `trade` objects to retain an industry-encoding integer:

```
#include <stdio.h>
/* Define the trade apparatus */
struct trade {double price; int number; int industry;};
/* Define trade array */
struct trade *trade_pointers[100];
/* Define price-computing function */
double trade_price (struct trade *x) {
  return x -> price * x -> number;
}
main ( ) {
  /* Declare various variables */
  int limit, counter, number, industry;
  double price;
  /* Read trade information */
  for (limit = 0;
         3 == scanf ("%i%lf%i", &industry, &price, &number);
         ++limit) {
    trade_pointers[limit]
      = (struct trade*) malloc (sizeof (struct trade));
    trade_pointers[limit] -> price = price;
    trade_pointers[limit] -> number = number;
    trade_pointers[limit] -> industry = industry;
  }
  /* Display report */
  for (counter = 0; counter < limit; ++counter)
    printf ("%i %f %i %f\n",
              trade_pointers[counter] -> industry,
              trade_pointers[counter] -> price,
              trade_pointers[counter] -> number,
              trade_price(trade_pointers[counter]));
}
```

As you can see, the purpose of this `analyze_trades` program is to regurgitate the information supplied for each trade, with the addition of a trade-price column.

490　The first step toward improving the output would be to replace the industry codes with industry names, thus producing a report such as the following:

```
Food 3.300000 300 990.000000
Trucking 2.500000 400 1000.000000
Airline 9.900000 100 990.000000
Airline 10.100000 100 1010.000000
Computers 5.000000 200 1000.000000
```

One way to have analyze_trades do the required work is to introduce a function, display_industry_name, that displays an industry name when given a trade object, as determined by the enumeration constants for the various industries:

```
void display_industry_name (struct trade *t) {
  switch (t -> industry) {
    case trucking:     printf ("Trucking");     break;
    case computers:    printf ("Computers");    break;
    case metals:       printf ("Metals");       break;
    case health:       printf ("Health");       break;
    case airline:      printf ("Airline");      break;
    default:           printf ("Unknown");      break;
  }
}
```

Given display_industry_name, you could revise the information-displaying for statement as follows:

```
for (counter = 0; counter < limit; ++counter) {
  display_industry_name (trade_pointers[counter]);
  printf (" %f %i %f\n",
          trade_pointers[counter] -> price,
          trade_pointers[counter] -> number,
          trade_price(trade_pointers[counter]));
}
```

491　The problem with the display_industry_name approach is that some of the displaying is done inside a subfunction, and some is done with an explicit display statement. A more transparent, orthodox approach is to have a different function, industry_name, return a string, with all the displaying done in the explicit display statement:

```
/* Display report */
for (counter = 0; counter < limit; ++counter)
  printf ("%s %f %i %f\n",
          industry_name(trade_pointers[counter]),
          trade_pointers[counter] -> price,
          trade_pointers[counter] -> number,
          trade_price(trade_pointers[counter]));
```

492　Unfortunately, when you try to define industry_name, using display_industry_name as a model, you do not know what the return type should be:

```
what type here? industry_name (struct trade *t) {
   switch (t -> industry) {
      case food:          return "Food";        break;
      case trucking:      return "Trucking";    break;
      case computers:     return "Computers";   break;
      case metals:        return "Metals";      break;
      case health:        return "Health";      break;
      case airline:       return "Airline";     break;
      default:            return "Unknown";     break;
   }
}
```

Accordingly, it is time for you to learn about character strings.

493 When you delimit a sequence of characters by double-quotation marks, you are telling C to create an array in which the elements are the particular characters between the double-quotation marks. The following, for example, is what C stores on encountering "Food".

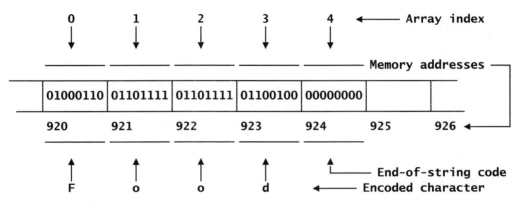

Note that the four characters in *Food* are actually stored in a five-element array in which the last element is filled by the **null character**, usually an all-zero byte, rather than by an actual character's code.

Character arrays terminated by null characters are called **character strings**, or, more succinctly, **strings**. Thus, "Food" is a notation for a string. Somewhat colloquially, most programmers say that "Food" is a string.

494 You frequently see the null character written as '\0' in string-manipulation programs. Thus, '\0' is a name for 0. By using '\0' to denote the null character, you identify the places where 0 is used as the special null character, rather than as an ordinary integer, and you increase program clarity.

495 Strings are terminated by null characters because string-manipulation functions—both those that are built in and those you may choose to define—generally have no way to know, in advance, how many characters there are in any given string. Those functions rely, instead, on null characters—serving as end-of-string markers—to tell them when to stop as they work their way through the characters.

173

In particular, the display function, `printf`, relies on null characters when it displays strings.

496 Whenever a string appears in an expression, the value of that string is a pointer to the first character in the corresponding character array. Thus, the following declaration creates a character-pointer variable and arranges for the initial value of that variable to point to the first character in the "Food" string:

```
char *character_pointer = "Food";
```

Such a character pointer declaration, with a string provided as the initial value, produces the following sort of arrangement in memory:

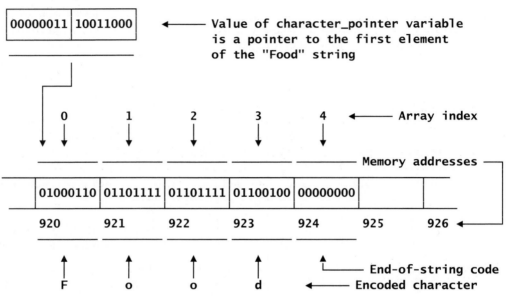

497 Thus, there is no such data type as a string. When you hand over a string to a function, you supply a character pointer that points to the first character in that string. When you want to return a string from a function, you really ask for a pointer to the first character in that string.

For example, when you define the `industry_name` function, you declare that it is to return a character pointer as follows:

```
char* industry_name (struct trade *t) {
  switch (t -> industry) {
    case food:          return "Food";          break;
    case trucking:      return "Trucking";      break;
    ...
  }
}
```

After you install the new `industry_name` function, you have the following version of the `analyze_trades` program:

```c
#include <stdio.h>
/* Define the trade apparatus */
struct trade {double price; int number; int industry;};
/* Define enumeration constants */
enum {food, trucking, computers, metals, health, airline};
/* Define trade array */
struct trade *trade_pointers[100];
/* Define price-computing function */
double trade_price (struct trade *x) {
  return x -> price * x -> number;
}
/* Define name-producing function */
char* industry_name (struct trade *t) {
  switch (t -> industry) {
    case food:         return "Food";         break;
    case trucking:     return "Trucking";     break;
    case computers:    return "Computers";    break;
    case metals:       return "Metals";       break;
    case health:       return "Health";       break;
    case airline:      return "Airline";      break;
    default:           return "Unknown";      break;
  }
}
main ( ) {
  /* Declare various variables */
  int limit, counter, number, industry;
  double price;
  /* Read trade information */
  for (limit = 0;
       3 == scanf ("%i%lf%i", &industry, &price, &number);
       ++limit) {
    trade_pointers[limit]
      = (struct trade*) malloc (sizeof (struct trade));
    trade_pointers[limit] -> industry = industry;
    trade_pointers[limit] -> price = price;
    trade_pointers[limit] -> number = number;
  }
  /* Display report */
  for (counter = 0; counter < limit; ++counter)
    printf ("%s %f %i %f\n",
            industry_name(trade_pointers[counter]),
            trade_pointers[counter] -> price,
            trade_pointers[counter] -> number,
            trade_price(trade_pointers[counter]));
}
```

Devise a function, size_description, that takes one argument, of type double, and returns a pointer to a character string that depends on the size of the argument: If the argument is more than 100000, the character string is to be noteworthy; if it is less than 1000, the character string is to be trifling; otherwise, the character string is to be empty. Use size_description to dress up the report produced by the program shown in Segment 498, such that an extra column appears, as in the following example:

```
Food 3.300000 300 990.000000 trifling
Trucking 2.500000 40000 100000.0000
Airline 9.900000 100 989.999939 trifling
Airline 10.100000 10000 101000.0061 noteworthy
Computers 5.000000 2000 10000.00000
```

- Character strings are stored as one-dimensional character arrays terminated by the null character.

- If you want to define a variable whose value is a constant string, **then** define a character-pointer variable by instantiating the following pattern:

  char * variable name = character string ;

- If a function is to return a string, **then** define its return type to be a character pointer by instantiating the following pattern:

  char* function name ···

32 HOW TO WRITE STATEMENTS THAT READ CHARACTER STRINGS

501 You learned a little about character strings in Section 31—you know how to display them, and you know how to have them handed to a function and returned from a function. In this section, you learn how to obtain character strings, and how to deposit them into an array in preparation for analysis.

502 You have learned about a program that presumes that trade data contain integers that encode industry types. Now suppose that you replace the industry-identifying digit by a string of characters that encodes all sorts of information about the trade.

The string itself has two parts, separated by a hyphen. The first part contains descriptive codes; the second part contains an abbreviated company name. The first character of the first part—F, T, C, M, H, or A—identifies the industry type:

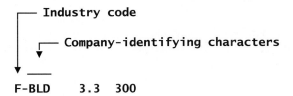

F-BLD   3.3   300

If there are extra characters in the first part, and if one of those extra characters is X, the company has just paid a dividend. Similarly, if one of those extra characters is B, the company is under bankruptcy protection.

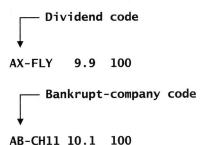

AX-FLY   9.9   100

┌── Bankrupt-company code
│
▼
AB-CH11 10.1   100

To read such descriptive strings, you must first create an **input buffer**—an array in which to store strings as they are read. You must be sure that the array that you create is long enough to hold all anticipated characters plus the required null character that serves as the end-of-string marker. For the information to be read by the `analyze_trades` program, 100 characters is far more than needed, but allocating an array of that size anticipates other uses for the array:

```
char input_buffer[100];
```

503 Next, you learned in Section 21 that, when you define an array, the array name becomes a constant, the value of which is a pointer to the first element of the array.

Thus, the input_buffer symbol is really a constant, and its value is a pointer to the first element of the input_buffer array:

input_buffer

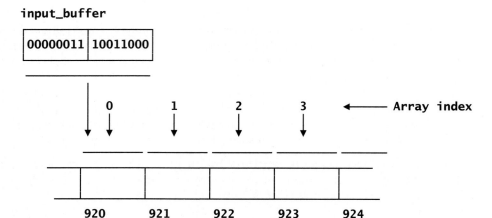

504 Happily, the read function, scanf, recognizes a %s read specification. On seeing %s, scanf reads a string from the input stream, up to the first **whitespace character**—space, tab, or carriage return. Then, scanf deposits that string into the memory chunk identified, as always, by an address.

Suppose, for example that the expression scanf ("%s", input_buffer) is evaluated, given that the next unread characters are C-IBM. The evaluation causes the first part of the input_buffer array to look like this:

input_buffer

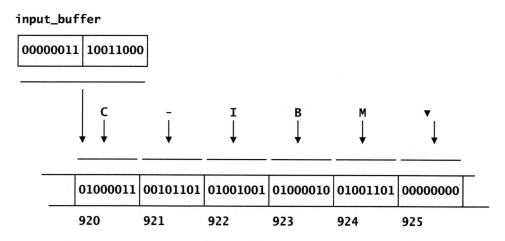

505 The second and subsequent arguments in a call to the scanf function usually are prefixed by the address-of operator, &, because scanf's parameters are pointer parameters. Note, however, that input_buffer is not prefixed by the address-of operator in the following call to the scanf function:

```
scanf ("%s", input_buffer)
```

There is no address-of operator, because `input_buffer` is the name of a character array, and the value returned by the name of a character array is an address already.

- A character-array name is really the name of a constant that points to the first element in the character array. A variable of the character-pointer type can point to any character in a character array.

- Wherever you see the phrase *name of character array* in a pattern, the phrase *variable of the character-pointer type* usually works, and vice versa. You cannot, however, reassign the name of a character array, because array names are constants.

- If you want to prepare to read a string, **then** you must create a character array large enough to hold the string.

- If you want to read a string from your keyboard, **and** you have created a character array to hold the string, **then** instantiate the following pattern:

```
scanf ("%s", input_buffer)
```

33 HOW TO DEPOSIT CHARACTER STRINGS INTO STRUCTURE OBJECTS

507   In Section 32, you learned how to obtain a trade-describing string. In this section, you learn how to move that string from a temporary buffer to a permanent location inside a structure object using functions provided by C's string-handling library.

508   If you want to store the appropriate trade-describing string with each new structure object, you need to create a character array to store that description. You cannot just use the `input_buffer` array, because that array is reused repeatedly, once for each trade-describing string read. Fortunately, you can allocate space for new arrays just as you can allocate space for new structure objects. In fact, you use the same operator, `malloc`. Thus, the following allocates enough bytes to hold the five characters in the string "C-IBM" plus a terminating null character:

```
malloc (6)
```

509   You must measure the length of the string lying in the `input_buffer` array so that you can reserve just the right number of bytes. To measure the length of a string, such as a trade-describing string, you can use a function supplied by C's string-handling library, which you announce your intention to use through the following declaration:

```
#include <string.h>
```

The string-handling function you need is `strlen` for *string length*:

```
strlen (input_buffer)
```

Because `strlen` returns the number of characters in a string, you need to add 1, to account for the null character, when you allocate space for a new array:

```
malloc (strlen (input_buffer) + 1)
```

510   You can keep a grip on the new character array using a member variable declared in the `trade` structure. That member variable must be a character pointer:

```
struct trade {
  double price;
  int number;
  char* description;
};
```

Note that the old structure variable that held an integer industry code has been dropped.

511   As you learned in Segment 364, `malloc` returns a pointer of type `void`. The `description` pointer is of type `char`. Accordingly, you must cast the pointer returned by `malloc`, producing a pointer of type `char`:

```
(char*) malloc (strlen (input_buffer) + 1);
```

512   Now, you have a character pointer to a chunk of memory big enough to hold the characters in the input buffer. Next, you must assign the member variable of the appropriate `trade` object to that character pointer:

```
trade_pointers[limit] -> description
  = (char*) malloc (strlen (input_buffer) + 1)
```

513   Finally, you copy the trade description into the new character array using `strcpy`, for *string copy*, another function from the string library. Note that the target array is the first argument and the source array is the second:

```
strcpy (trade_pointers[limit] -> description, input_buffer);
```

The effect of `strcpy` is to copy the trade description from the `input_buffer` array, which has to be large enough for trade descriptions of any conceivable length, into a new character array that is just big enough to hold the trade description actually observed:

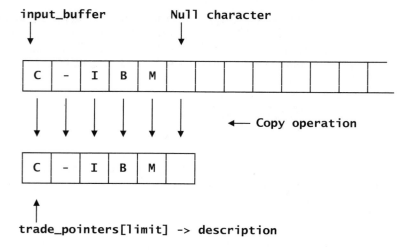

514   Here is the revised program, with an addition to the `printf` statement that displays the recorded trade description:

```
#include <stdio.h>
#include <string.h>
/* Define the trade apparatus */
struct trade {double price; int number; char *description;};
/* Define trade array and input buffer array*/
struct trade *trade_pointers[100];
char input_buffer[100];
/* Define price-computing function */
double trade_price (struct trade *x) {
  return x -> price * x -> number;
}
```

```
main ( ) {
  /* Declare various variables */
  int limit, counter, number;
  double price;
  /* Read trade information */
  for (limit = 0;
       3 == scanf ("%s%lf%i", input_buffer, &price, &number);
       ++limit) {
    trade_pointers[limit]
      = (struct trade*) malloc (sizeof (struct trade));
    trade_pointers[limit] -> price = price;
    trade_pointers[limit] -> number = number;
    trade_pointers[limit] -> description
      = (char*) malloc (strlen (input_buffer) + 1);
    strcpy (trade_pointers[limit] -> description, input_buffer);
  }
  /* Display report */
  for (counter = 0; counter < limit; ++counter)
    printf ("%s %f %i %f\n",
            trade_pointers[counter] -> description,
            trade_pointers[counter] -> price,
            trade_pointers[counter] -> number,
            trade_price(trade_pointers[counter]));
}
```

———————————————— Sample Data ————————————————

```
F-BLD    3.3   300
T-GG     2.5   400
AX-FLY   9.9   100
AB-CH11 10.1   100
C-IBM    5.0   200
```

———————————————— Result ————————————————

```
F-BLD 3.300000 300 990.000000
T-GG 2.500000 400 1000.000000
AX-FLY 9.900000 100 990.000000
AB-CH11 10.100000 100 1010.000000
C-IBM 5.000000 200 1000.000000
```

515 The read function, scanf, reads character sequences only up to the first whitespace character. Occasionally, you find it more convenient to read a whole line of characters using the gets function, where gets is an acronym for *get string*:

gets (name of character array)

The gets function reads the characters in the next line that you type and puts those characters into the array, without the end-of-line character, terminating those characters with the null character, \0. Thus, you can put the next line of keyboard input, or redirected input, into the input_buffer array with the following statement:

```
gets (input_buffer);
```

516   Although the `gets` function generally returns a pointer to the first character in the character array, should you redirect input to a file, and should the `gets` function encounter the end of a file, it returns the **null pointer**, which is a pointer to address zero.

You frequently see the null pointer written as NULL, a macro symbol. By using NULL, instead of 0, you identify those places where 0 is used as a special pointer, thereby increasing program clarity.

Thus, the following expression tests the result of a call to `gets` to ensure that the end of a file has not yet been encountered:

```
gets (input_buffer) != NULL
```

517   Once you have moved the next line into the `input_buffer` array, you can, if you want, treat `input_buffer` as a source of characters in place of your keyboard or a file. The appropriate function is `sscanf`, for string *scan f*ormatted. The `sscanf` function is just like the `scanf` function, except that there is an extra argument that identifies the character string to be read from.

Suppose, for example, that your input data may include occasional comments, marked by semicolons, as in the following example:

```
F-BLD     3.3   300              ; Merger likely
T-GG      2.5   400
AX-FLY    9.9   100
AB-CH11  10.1   100              ; Court action imminent
C-IBM     5.0   200
```

Once you have moved a line of text into the `input_buffer` array, you can use `sscanf` to pick up the description, price, and number of shares traded, placing the description in another buffer named `description_buffer`:

```
sscanf (input_buffer "%s%lf%i", description_buffer, &price, &number);
```

Thus, the description, price, and number of shares traded are read from the input buffer; the remaining comment, if any, is ignored.

518   In Segment 285, you learned that you are said to practice **defensive programming** when
PRACTICE   you add tests to ensure that expected actions actually happen. Add such a defensive-programming test to the program in Segment 514. To do this, you need to know that `malloc` returns the null pointer, NULL, if it fails to find a memory chunk of the size requested by your program.

519   Modify the program shown in Segment 514 such that it discards any semicolon-marked
PRACTICE   comments. Test your modified program on the data shown in Segment 517.

520

HIGHLIGHTS

- If you want to use C's string-handling functions, **then** include the following line in your program:

  ```
  #include <string.h>
  ```

- If you want to determine the number of characters in a character array, **and** you have included #include <string.h> in your program, **then** instantiate the following pattern:

  `strlen (`name of character array`)`

- If you want to allocate space for an array at run time **and** you want to assign the starting address of that space to a character-pointer variable, **then** instantiate the following pattern:

  ```
  character-pointer variable
    = (char*) malloc (strlen (buffer name) + 1);
  ```

- If you want to copy a string from one array into another, **and** you have included #include <string.h> in your program, **then** instantiate the following pattern:

  `strcpy (`name of target array`,` name of source array`);`

34 HOW TO TEST STRING CHARACTERS

521 In this section, you learn how to extract characters from strings, and you learn how to use such characters to determine what to do next.

522 At this point, you have learned to install descriptions, in the form of character strings, in the `description` structure variables of each `trade` object.

523 Recall that the `industry_name` function, as defined in Segment 498, takes an argument that is a trade pointer and returns the name of an industry:

```
char* industry_name (struct trade *t) {
  switch (t -> industry) {
    case food: return "Food"; break;
    ...
  }
}
```

Now you need to modify the `industry_name` function such that it uses the character string obtained from the `description` structure variable of a `trade` object.

524 Before you go on, recall that `switch` views characters as a type of integer. Accordingly, you can use a particular character in a character array in place of an integer:

```
char* industry_name (struct trade *t) {
  switch (t -> description[0]) {
    ...
  }
}
```

As long as you compare the first character in the description character array—the one encoding the industry type—with various characters, viewed as integers, `switch` works just fine.

525 In C, you obtain the integer corresponding to a specific character by surrounding that character with single-quotation marks. For example, C translates 'A' into 65; accordingly, 65 is said to be the **character code** for the character *A*.

526 Given a means to obtain specific character codes, you can replace industry-denoting enumeration constants in the `industry_name` function with specific character codes:

```
char* industry_name (struct trade *t) {
  switch (t -> description[0]) {
    case 'F': return "Food"; break;
    ...
  }
}
```

527 There is a better way to use character codes in switch statements, however. You can change the values of the type-defining enumeration constants. Previously, in Section 27, they were declared as follows, with C assigning food to 0, trucking to 1, and so on, by default:

```
enum {food, trucking, computers, metals, health, airline};
```

Recall, however, that you can supply particular integers instead. Further recall that C views characters as an integer data type. Thus, you can declare the type-defining enumeration constants as follows:

```
enum {food = 'F',
      trucking = 'T',
      computers = 'C',
      metals = 'M',
      health = 'H',
      airline = 'A'};
```

528 Having redefined the industry-defining enumeration constants, you need only to replace the conditional part of the switch statement; the rest remains the same as it was:

```
char* industry_name (struct trade *t) {
  switch (t -> description[0]) {
    case food: return "Food"; break;
      ...
  }
}
```

Thus, enumeration constants provide a form of detail-hiding data abstraction, and, as usual with data abstraction, the use of enumeration constants simplifies change.

529 If you like, you can write another simple function, company_name, that returns a pointer to the portion of the description that contains the company-identifying characters.

Because the company name occupies the final portion of the description string, there is no need to create a new character array. Instead, you can view the final portion of the description string as a substring.

Thus, the company_name function can do its job by locating the character in the description string immediately following the hyphen, whereupon the company_name function can return the address of that character. That address is the address of a substring containing the company-identifying characters. In the following, for example, company_name is to return 922:

188

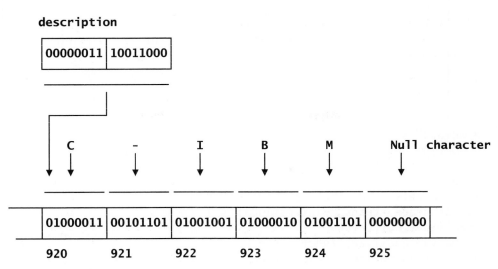

description

00000011	10011000

C   –   I   B   M   Null character

01000011	00101101	01001001	01000010	01001101	00000000
920	921	922	923	924	925

The following is one interesting way to implement company_name. Note that nothing needs to be initialized in the for statement; hence, nothing appears before the first semicolon. Also note that the iteration terminates when the cptr pointer points to the hyphen; hence, the pointer has to be incremented once after leaving the for loop so as to move the pointer forward to the first character in the company name:

```
char* company_name (struct trade *t) {
  char* cptr = t -> for;
  description (; CPTR[0] != '-'; ++cptr)
    ;
  return ++cptr;
}
```

530 The getchar function obtains integer-cast characters from keyboard input or input redirected from a file; the putchar function displays characters. If getchar encounters an error or the end of a file, it returns whatever value the macro EOF expands to, which is -1 in most implementations. The following program, an iterative filter, converts lower-case letters to upper-case letters, because each upper-case letter, viewed as an integer, is equally offset from the corresponding lower-case letter:

```
#include <stdio.h>
int transform_letter (int arg) {
  int offset = 'A' - 'a';
  if ((int) 'a' <= arg && arg <= (int) 'z')
    return arg + offset;
  else return arg;
}
main ( ) {
  int input;
  while (EOF != (input = getchar ( )))
    putchar (transform_letter (input));
}
```

Note that getchar casts input characters into integers of type int, thereby requiring a cast at the point where those characters are compared with character constants.

531 In summary, the following is the analyze_trades program, modified to use enumeration constants with character-code assignments.

```c
#include <stdio.h>
#include <string.h>
/* Define trade structure, industry enumeration, and arrays */
struct trade {double price; int number; char *description;};
enum {food = 'F', trucking = 'T', computers = 'C',
      metals = 'M', health = 'H', airline = 'A'};
struct trade *trade_pointers[100];
char input_buffer[100];
/* Define auxiliary functions */
double trade_price (struct trade *x) {
  return x -> price * x -> number;
}
char* industry_name (struct trade *t) {
  switch (t -> description[0]) {
    case food:          return "Food";        break;
    case trucking:      return "Trucking";    break;
    /* ... More cases ... */

    default:            return "Unknown";     break;
  }
}
char* company_name (struct trade *t) {
  char* cptr = t -> description;
  for (; cptr[0] != '-'; ++cptr) ;
  return ++cptr;
}
main ( ) {
  /* Declare various variables */
  int limit, counter, number;
  double price;
  /* Read trade information */
  for (limit = 0;
       3 == scanf ("%s%lf%i", input_buffer, &price, &number);
       ++limit) {
    trade_pointers[limit]
      = (struct trade*) malloc (sizeof (struct trade));
    trade_pointers[limit] -> price = price;
    trade_pointers[limit] -> number = number;
    trade_pointers[limit] -> description
      = (char*) malloc (strlen (input_buffer) + 1);
    strcpy (trade_pointers[limit] -> description, input_buffer);
  }
```

```
/* Display report */
for (counter = 0; counter < limit; ++counter)
  printf ("%s %s %f %i %f\n",
          industry_name(trade_pointers[counter]),
          company_name(trade_pointers[counter]),
          trade_pointers[counter] -> price,
          trade_pointers[counter] -> number,
          trade_price(trade_pointers[counter]));
}
```

──────────────── Sample Data ────────────────

```
F-BLD     3.3   300
T-GG      2.5   400
AX-FLY    9.9   100
AB-CH11  10.1   100
C-IBM     5.0   200
```

──────────────── Result ────────────────

```
Food BLD 3.300000 300 990.000000
Trucking GG 2.500000 400 1000.000000
Airline FLY 9.900000 100 990.000000
Airline CH11 10.100000 100 1010.000000
Computers IBM 5.000000 200 1000.000000
```

532

PRACTICE

Suppose that, incredibly, the trade-description standard changes. Now the line describing a stock includes information about the size of the company via a size-indicating character. Of these characters, L indicates that the company is one of the largest 500; M indicates that the company is one of the largest 1000, but is not one of the largest 500; S indicates that the company is not one of the largest 1000; and X indicates that the company's size is unknown:

```
  ┌── Size-indicating character
  │
  ↓
L-F-BLD     3.3   300
S-T-GG      2.5   400
M-AX-FLY    9.9   100
L-AB-CH11  10.1   100
L-C-IBM     5.0   200
```

Modify the program in Segment 531 to accommodate the changes. Be sure to change only the industry_name and company_name functions.

533

HIGHLIGHTS

- If you want to extract a character from a character array, **then** access that array as you would any other:

  `array name [ character's index ]`

- If you want to obtain the character code for a specific character, **then** surround that character with single-quotation marks.

- You can use character codes in switch statements.

- You can assign character codes to enumeration constants in enumeration statements.

35 HOW TO DO TABULAR PRINTING

534   C's display function, `printf`, provides you with a convenient, easy-to-use way to get information out of your programs. Read this section if you want to learn how to use `printf` to display in aligned columns.

535   At this point, you have seen many examples in which C's display function, `printf`, displays strings and numbers. Unfortunately, the report printed by the most recent version of `analyze_trades` is ragged looking:

```
Food BLD 3.300000 300 990.000000
Trucking GG 2.500000 400 1000.000000
Airline FLY 9.900000 100 989.999939
Airline CH11 10.100000 100 1010.000061
Computers IBM 5.000000 200 1000.000000
```

You would rather have the report look like this:

```
Food       BLD    3.3    300     990
Trucking    GG    2.5    400    1000
Airline    FLY    9.9    100     990
Airline   CH11   10.1    100    1010
Computers   IBM    5.0    200    1000
```

536   You can, if you want, display neater reports by telling `printf` how much space each argument should occupy. You supply this space information by adding a number to the print specification. The print specification %6s, for example, means display at least six characters using the corresponding argument value, a string, along with extra spaces, if necessary, on the left. Similarly, %8i means display at least eight characters using the corresponding argument value, an integer, along with spaces, if necessary, on the left.

Consider, for example, the following statement:

```
printf ("%6s%8i\n", "Food", 300);
```

The result includes the argument values, along with the spaces required to meet the stipulated minimum number of characters:

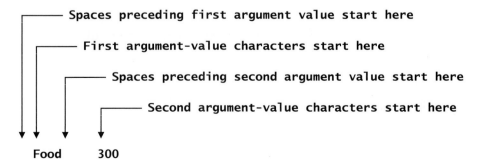

The stipulated minimum number of characters is called the **field width**. The spaces used to augment the space taken by the argument values are called **padding characters**.

537 If you like, you can tell C to put the padding on the right by adding a minus sign:

```
printf ("%-6s%-8i\n", "Food", 300);
```

The result is left justification, rather than right justification:

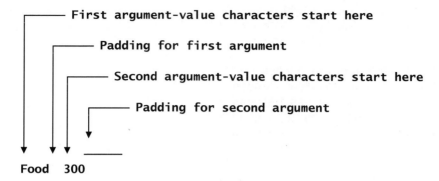

```
Food   300
```

538 You can, if you want, display a floating-point number without the fractional part by converting it to an integer using C's casting mechanism. All you need to do is to preface the number with (int), as in the following illustration:

```
printf ("%-6s%8i\n", "Food", (int) 4700.1287);
```

The result is as follows:

```
Food       4700
```

539 Alternatively, you can display handsome floating-point numbers, in columns, by including a field width, a period, and the number of digits that you want to appear to the right of the decimal point. Consider, for example, the following display statement:

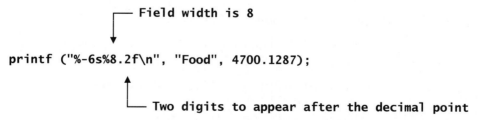

```
printf ("%-6s%8.2f\n", "Food", 4700.1287);
```

The result is as follows:

```
Food   4700.12
```

Note that the number displayed is truncated, rather than rounded.

540 The following version of the `analyze_trades` program uses string, integer, and floating-point print specifications to display the neater report shown early in this section.

```c
#include <stdio.h>
#include <string.h>
/* Define trade structure, industry enumeration, and arrays */
struct trade {double price; int number; char *description;};
enum {food = 'F', trucking = 'T', computers = 'C',
      metals = 'M', health = 'H', airline = 'A'};
struct trade *trade_pointers[100];
char input_buffer[100];
/* Define auxiliary functions */
double trade_price (struct trade *x) {
  return x -> price * x -> number;
}
char* industry_name (struct trade *t) {
  switch (t -> description[0]) {
    case food:          return "Food";       break;
    /* ... Other cases ... */
    default:            return "Unknown";     break;
  }
}
char* company_name (struct trade *t) {
  char* cptr = t -> description;
  for (; cptr[0] != '-'; ++cptr) ;
  return ++cptr;
}
main ( ) {
  /* Declare various variables */
  int limit, counter, number;
  double price, sum = 0.0;
  /* Read trade information */
  for (limit = 0;
       3 == scanf ("%s%lf%i", input_buffer, &price, &number);
       ++limit) {
    trade_pointers[limit]
      = (struct trade*) malloc (sizeof (struct trade));
    trade_pointers[limit] -> price = price;
    trade_pointers[limit] -> number = number;
    trade_pointers[limit] -> description
      = (char*) malloc (strlen (input_buffer) + 1);
    strcpy (trade_pointers[limit] -> description, input_buffer);
  }
  /* Display report */
  for (counter = 0; counter < limit; ++counter)
    printf ("%-10s %4s %5.1f %6i %9.0f\n",
            industry_name(trade_pointers[counter]),
            company_name(trade_pointers[counter]),
            trade_pointers[counter] -> price,
            trade_pointers[counter] -> number,
            trade_price(trade_pointers[counter]));
}
```

541   The %f print specification—along with those for integers, strings, and other data types—is explained more fully in Appendix A.

542   Revise the program shown in Segment 540 such that the report printed is as follows:

PRACTICE

```
*======*=========*=============*=========*========*=========*=======*
: Code : Status  : Industry    : Company : Price  : Shares  : Value :
*======*=========*=============*=========*========*=========*=======*
: F    :         | Food        :     BLD :  3.3 :      300 :    990 :
: T    :         | Trucking    :      GG :  2.5 :      400 :   1000 :
: A    : X       | Airline     :     FLY :  9.9 :      100 :    990 :
: A    : B       | Airline     :    CH11 : 10.1 :      100 :   1010 :
: C    :         | Computers   :     IBM :  5.0 :      200 :   1000 :
*======*=========*=============*=========*========*=========*=======*
```

543

HIGHLIGHTS

- If you want to specify a field width, **and** you want the displayed characters to be to the right of the padding, **then** include an integer between the percent sign and the character.

- If you want to specify a field width, **and** you want the displayed characters to be to the left of the padding, **then** include a negative integer between the percent sign and the character.

- If you want to control the number of digits displayed to the right of the decimal point in a floating-point number, **then** add a decimal point after the field width along with the number of digits desired to the right of the decimal point.

36 HOW TO READ FROM AND WRITE TO FILES

544   In this section, you learn how to access information in files directly, so that you do not have to depend on input–output redirection to get information in and out of files.

545   To read from a file or to write to a file, you must inform the C compiler that you plan to use C's standard file-handling functions. Those file-handling functions are in the same library as other input–output functions; accordingly, you include the following declaration in your program:

```
#include<stdio.h>
```

546   To read from a file, you first declare a **file pointer** using `FILE` as the data type:

FILE* `file-pointer name` **;**

You are probably wondering why the data type, `FILE`, is in upper-case characters, given that just about every other character string you have seen is in lower-case characters. `FILE` is upper-case, because `FILE` is really an implementation-dependent macro that defines a structure. As you have learned, most C programmers adhere to this convention: upper-case for macros.

547   Once you have declared a file pointer, you arrange for it to point to a file-describing structure that is created at run time by a function named **fopen**, an acronym for *file open*. Note that the call to **fopen** has two arguments: the first specifies the name of a file, and the second specifies whether the file is to be read from, written to, or appended to. Whenever the second argument is `"r"`, **fopen** prepares for reading:

`file-pointer name` **= fopen(** `file specification` **, "r");**

You do not need to know about the structure variables in the structure created by **fopen**, because your access to the structure variables is via access functions that know about them.

548   The following is an example in which the file pointer named `trade_source` is declared, and that file pointer is attached to a structure, via **fopen**, that names `"test.data"` as the file to be read from:

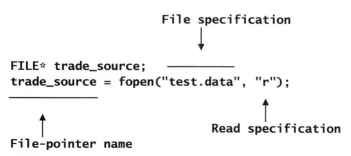

```
                              File specification
                                      |
                                      v
FILE* trade_source;        —————————
trade_source = fopen("test.data", "r");
————————————                     ^
       ^                         |
       |                  Read specification
File-pointer name
```

Thus, the file-opening ritual involves one statement that creates a pointer and another that attaches the pointer to a file-describing structure.

549 Once you open a file for input, you must switch from scanf to fscanf, an acronym for *file scan field*. The fscanf function takes an additional argument, a file pointer, and reads from the file associated with the file pointer instead of from your keyboard. Thus, unlike scanf, fscanf knows about the structure variables in the structures created by fopen, and fscanf uses that knowledge to get at the information in a file.

For example, the following statement tells C to read a floating-point price and an integer number from the file identified by the trade_source pointer:

```
fscanf (trade_source, "%f%i", &price, &number);
```

550 Generally, when you have a program attempt to open a file, you should also have that program check to see whether its attempt was successful. To arrange for such a check, you can take advantage of the fact that fopen returns a pointer to zero, also known as the **null pointer**, when it fails to open a file:

```
FILE* trade_source;
trade_source = fopen("test.data", "r");
/* Test for successful opening */
when (! trade_source) {
 printf ("The attempt to open the test.data file failed!\n");
 ...
}
```

Note that when you work on a pointer with the negation operation, the result is 0, of type int, if the pointer is the null pointer; otherwise, the result is 1, of type int.

551 To write to a file, you proceed as though you were reading from a file, except that you use "w" as the second argument of fopen, rather than "r".

```
FILE*  file-pointer name ;
file-pointer name  = fopen( file specification , "w");
```

The following is an example for which the file pointer is named analysis_target and the file specification is "test.result":

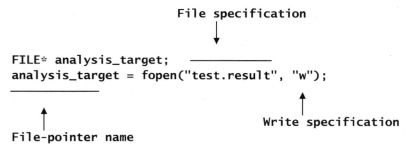

If you want to add data to a file that may exist already, you use "a" rather than "w". If the file does not exist, "a" acts like "w". If it does happen to exist, "a" tells C that you want your write statements to append data to the end of the existing file.

552　Once you open a file for output, you must switch from `printf` to `fprintf`, an acronym for *f*ile *print f*ield. The `fprintf` function takes an additional argument, a file pointer, and writes to the file associated with the file pointer instead of to your screen. Thus, the following statement tells C to write a result into the file identified by the `analysis_target` pointer:

```
fprintf (analysis_target,
        "The total value of the %i trades is %f.\n",
                              limit,         sum);
```

553　Once you have finished writing information into a file, you must **close** the file before you can open it for reading and further processing. The do-nothing, somewhat dangerous way to close your files is to wait until your program stops executing: At that point, your operating system is supposed to close all open files automatically. The safer way to close your files is to include an explicit file-closing statement, such as the following, which closes the output file associated with the `analysis_target` file pointer:

```
fclose (analysis_target);
```

554　It is good programming practice to close input files when you are finished reading from them, just as you should close output files when you are finished writing to them. You close input files with the same kind of statement you use to close output files:

```
fclose ( file pointer name );
```

555　Of course, `fscanf`, `fprintf`, and `fclose` must know about the structure variables in structures returned by calls to `fopen`. You yourself need to know nothing at all about those structure variables, because `fscanf`, `fprintf`, and `fclose` isolate you from them. Accordingly, the actual structure variables included may vary from implementation to implementation, as long as `fscanf`, `fprintf`, `fclose`—and other input–output functions— perform the right computations.

As you have learned, when you move the details of how information is stored behind a set of functions, you are said to be doing **data abstraction,** and you are said to be hiding the details of how a computation is done behind a **data-abstraction barrier.**

556　Collecting what you have just learned about file input and output, you easily can amend programs that read from your keyboard and display on your screen such that they read from a file and write to a file. The following program, for example, fills an array with `trade` objects using information from a file named `test.data`, and then writes the result of its analysis of those `trade` objects into a file named `test.result`:

```c
#include <stdio.h>
/* Define the trade structure */
struct trade {double price; int number;};
/* Define value-computing function */
double trade_price (struct trade *tptr) {
  return tptr -> price * tptr -> number;
}
/* Define trade array */
struct trade *trade_pointers[100];
main ( ) {
  /* Declare various variables */
  int limit, counter, number;
  double price, sum = 0;
  /* Define trade_source, a pointer to a file structure */
  FILE* trade_source;
  /* Define analysis_target, a pointer to a file structure */
  FILE* analysis_target;
  /* Prepare a file structure for reading */
  trade_source = fopen ("test.data", "r");
  /* Read numbers from the file and stuff them into array */
  for (limit = 0;
       2 == fscanf (trade_source, "%lf%i", &price, &number);
       ++limit) {
    trade_pointers[limit]
      = (struct trade*) malloc (sizeof (struct trade));
    trade_pointers[limit] -> price = price;
    trade_pointers[limit] -> number = number;
  }
  /* Close source file /*
  fclose (trade_source);
  /* Find value of shares traded */
  for (counter = 0; counter < limit; ++counter)
    sum = sum + trade_price(trade_pointers[counter]);
  /* Prepare a file structure for writing*/
  analysis_target = fopen("test.result", "w");
  /* Write value of shares traded */
  fprintf (analysis_target,
           "The total value of the %i trades is %f.\n",
                                    limit,         sum);
  /* Close target file */
  fclose (analysis_target);
}
```

557 At the moment, the `analyze_trades` program uses `test.data` and `test.result` as wired-in file names. In Section 39, you learn how to supply file names at run time.

For now, it is enough to know how to open files for reading and writing and how to close such files when you are finished with them. As you might expect, however, there is a great deal more that you can learn about file input and file output.

The analog to `gets` for reading a line directly from a file is `fgets`, an acronym for *f*ile *get string*:

```
fgets( name of character array ,
       maximum characters to be read + 1 ,
       file-pointer name )
```

Like `gets`, the `fgets` function generally returns a pointer to the first character in the character array, but should the `fgets` function encounter the end of a file, it returns `NULL`. Unlike `gets`, `fgets` stops when it either reaches the end of a line or has read the maximum number of characters. If `fgets` does reach the end of a line, `fgets` copies an end-of-line character into the array, just before the terminating `\0`, which appears in the character array no matter what.

Thus, you can read the next line of input from a file into the `input_buffer` array with the following statement:

```
                          ┌── You do not want more characters than
                          │   input_buffer can hold
                          ▼
fgets(input_buffer, 100, trade_source);
                         ▲
                         └── A file pointer, set up by FILE*
```

The analog to `getchar` for reading a character directly from a file is `fgetc`, an acronym for *f*ile *get c*haracter:

```
fgetc( file-pointer name )
```

The analog of `putchar` for writing a character directly into a file is `fputc`, an acronym for *f*ile *put c*haracter:

```
fputc( file-pointer name )
```

Write a program that transforms all the alphabetic characters in an input file into upper-case characters in an output file. Call the input file `lower.source`, and call the output file `upper.sink`. Base your program on the one shown in Segment 530.

- If you want to tell C that you intend to work with input or output files, **then** include the following line in your program:

  ```
  #include<stdio.h>
  ```

- If you want to open an input file, **then** instantiate the following pattern:

  ```
  FILE* file-pointer name ;
  file-pointer name = fopen( file specification , "r");
  ```

- If you want to open an output file, **then** instantiate the following pattern:

```
FILE* file-pointer name ;
file-pointer name = fopen( file specification , "w");
```

- If you want to read data from an open input file, **then** substitute `fscanf` for `scanf`, and add a file pointer as the first argument.

- If you want to write data into an open output file, **then** substitute `fprintf` for `printf`, and add a file pointer as the first argument.

- If you are finished with an input or output file, **then** you should close it by instantiating the following pattern:

```
fclose ( file-pointer name );
```

37 HOW TO RECLAIM MEMORY

562 At this point, the latest version of the `analyze_trades` program—the one shown in Segment 556—extracts trade information from a trade-describing file and displays a report. Along the way, the program creates new `trade` objects that are accessed through an array of pointers.

In this segment, you learn about still another version of `analyze_trades` that reads the trade-describing file, displays a report, waits a while, and then repeats the read–display–wait cycle ad infinitum.

You soon see that the modified program creates structure objects that become not only obsolete, but also inaccessible. That brings you to the heart of this section, where you learn how to reclaim the memory used for such structure objects.

563 Contemporary operating systems, such as UNIX, encourage you to run several programs at once, in the sense that your computer works on each for a while in a round robin.

Accordingly, you can imagine that you have a program, connected to a network, that periodically produces a new file full of trade information. You can further imagine that you would want the `analyze_trades` to unleash itself on the trade-information file every few minutes, so as to keep an up-to-date analysis on your screen.

564 Reexamine the version of the `analyze_trades` program shown in Segment 556. To convert that program into one that does periodic updates, you need only to put the reading and displaying statements in a special kind of `while` statement. To repeat a series of statements ad infinitum, you can insert them into a `while` loop in which the Boolean expression consists of just the number 1. Because 1 is not 0, the `while` loop will carry on until you type the `control-c` keychord—or the appropriate alternative recognized by your operating system:

```
while (1) {
  ...
}
```

565 So that your program will pause a little after each attack on the `test.data` file, you insert a call to the `sleep` function, which is found in C's standard library. The argument you supply to `sleep` is the number of seconds that you want your program to pause. In the following example, you ask for a 5-minute pause:

```
while (1) {
  ...
  sleep (300);
}
```

Whenever you use `sleep`, you must announce your intention by including the following line in your program:

```
#include <time.h>
```

566   The converted program, with 5-minute pauses, is as follows:

```c
#include <stdio.h>
#include <time.h>
/* Define the trade structure */
struct trade {double price; int number;};
/* Define value-computing function */
double trade_price (struct trade *tptr) {
  return tptr -> price * tptr -> number;
}
/* Define trade array */
struct trade *trade_pointers[100];
main ( ) {
  /* Declare various variables */
  int limit, counter, number;
  double price, sum;
  /* Declare trade_source, a pointer to a file-describing structure */
  FILE* trade_source;
  while (1) {
    /* Initialize sum */
    sum = 0.0;
    /* Prepare a file-describing structure for reading */
    trade_source = fopen ("test.data", "r");
    /* Read numbers from the file and stuff them into array */
    for (limit = 0;
         2 == fscanf (trade_source, "%f%i", &price, &number);
         ++limit) {
      trade_pointers[limit]
        = (struct trade*) malloc (sizeof (struct trade));
      trade_pointers[limit] -> price = price;
      trade_pointers[limit] -> number = number;
    }
    /* Close source file /*
    fclose (trade_source);
    /* Find value of shares traded */
    for (counter = 0; counter < limit; ++counter)
      sum = sum + trade_price(trade_pointers[counter]);
    /* Display value of shares traded */
    printf ("The total value of the %i trades is %.2f.\n",
                                    limit,        sum);
    sleep (300);
  }
}
```

567   At this point, your modified `analyze_trades` program is complete, and works fine, but if
you run it long enough, it will fill up your computer's memory with useless `trade` objects.
If you want to see why, note that, once one file has been analyzed—one that contains, say,
three trades—the memory involved in the analysis looks as follows:

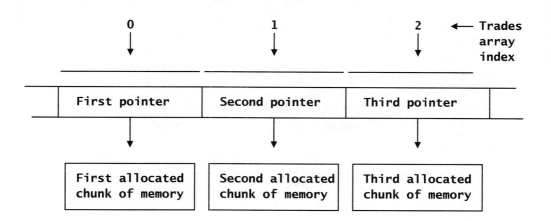

568   Now, as soon as `analyze_trades` works on the `test.data` file a second time, it allocates memory for three new `trade` objects in addition to the memory previously allocated for three other `trade` objects:

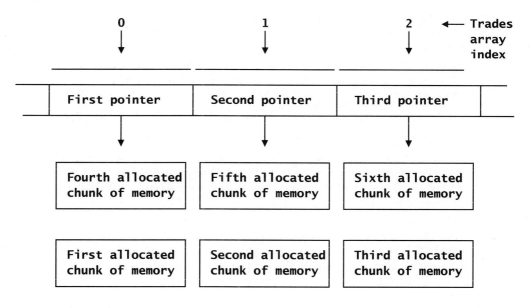

Now, however, there are no pointers to the first three of the memory chunks allocated at run time for `trade` objects. Accordingly, they are completely inaccessible.

569   Plainly, your program spins off inaccessible chunks of memory each time that it reads a file other than the first. If your program does nothing to reclaim those chunks, it will eventually run out of memory.

Whenever a chunk of memory becomes inaccessible, that chunk of memory is called **garbage**. Whenever a program creates garbage, the program has a **memory leak**.

570   Here are the conditions that lead to memory leaks:

- You define a pointer variable or a pointer array.

- You arrange for a pointer to point to a chunk of memory allocated by the `malloc` function at run time.

- You subsequently arrange for the pointer to point to a different chunk of memory, thereby rendering the previous chunk inaccessible.

571   The following is an assignment statement in the current version of `analyze_trades`:

```
trade_pointers[limit] = (struct trade*) malloc (sizeof (struct trade));
```

To prevent the memory leak, you use the `free` function before you reassign a pointer and lose your access to the memory you want to reclaim. You can, for example, deploy the `free` function just before the allocation of new objects:

```
...
free (trade_pointers[limit]);
trade_pointers[limit] = (struct trade*) malloc (sizeof (struct trade));
...
```

So situated, the `free` function reclaims memory previously allocated by the corresponding `malloc`. Once reclaimed, memory automatically becomes available for subsequent applications of `malloc`.

The first time that `analyze_trades` is called, the `trade_pointers` array contains pointers to 0, because the elements of global arrays are initialized to 0 by the C compiler. Fortunately, `free` does nothing when its argument is 0.

572   You might wonder why C does not reclaim memory automatically whenever a pointer is reassigned to a new object created by the `malloc` function. The rationale is that chunks of memory accessed through a pointer are often accessible through more than one pointer. Accordingly, C cannot assume that reassignment of a single pointer makes a chunk of memory inaccessible.

573   The fully converted `analyze_trades` program, with the memory leak removed, is as follows:

```c
#include <stdio.h>
/* Define the trade structure */
struct trade {double price; int number;};
/* Define value-computing function */
double trade_price (struct trade *tptr) {
  return tptr -> price * tptr -> number;
}
/* Define trade array */
struct trade *trade_pointers[100];
main ( ) {
  /* Declare various variables */
  int limit, counter, number;
  double price, sum;
  /* Declare trade_source, a pointer to a file-describing structure */
  FILE* trade_source;
  while (1) {
    /* Initialize sum */
    sum = 0.0;
    /* Prepare a file-describing structure for reading */
    trade_source = fopen ("test.data", "r");
    /* Read numbers from the file and stuff them into array */
    for (limit = 0;
         2 == fscanf (trade_source, "%f%i", &price, &number);
         ++limit) {
      free (trade_pointers[limit]);
      trade_pointers[limit]
        = (struct trade*) malloc (sizeof (struct trade));
      trade_pointers[limit] -> price = price;
      trade_pointers[limit] -> number = number;
    }
    /* Close source file /*
    fclose (trade_source);
    /* Find value of shares traded */
    for (counter = 0; counter < limit; ++counter)
      sum = sum + trade_price(trade_pointers[counter]);
    /* Display value of shares traded */
    printf ("The total value of the %i trades is %.2f.\n",
                                       limit,        sum);
  sleep (300);
  }
}
```

574   Note that the analyze_trades program contains a readily seen free–malloc pair.

Readily seen free–malloc pairs are indicative of good programming practice, because you can determine at a glance that memory allocated by a malloc call is eventually reclaimed by a free. Thus, you can determine at a glance that the call to malloc does not cause a memory leak.

The lack of such pairing is considered extremely bad, because it makes memory management much more difficult.

575 Although the revised `analyze_trades` function uses the `free` function to reclaim the memory consumed by obsolete and inaccessible structure objects, those objects themselves may contain pointers to character arrays created at run time. In an earlier version of `analyze_trades`, shown in Segment 514, you saw, for example, that it is possible to insert a pointer to a trade-describing string that occupies space allocated at run time.

To reclaim such memory, you need to place another call to `free` just before the structure-object-reclaiming `free`.

```
...
free (trade_pointers[limit] -> description);
free (trade_pointers[limit]);
...
```

576 Now, however, you must also be sure that `trade_pointers[limit]` contains a nonnull pointer before you try to access the string. The first time `analyze_trades` is called, the `trade_pointers` array contains null pointers, and you must not try to access a structure variables via a null pointer. Accordingly, you must test for the null pointer before deploying `free`.

```
...
if (! trade_pointers [limit]) {
  free (trade_pointers[limit] -> description);
  free (trade_pointers[limit]);
}
...
```

If your program fails to test for a null pointer, your program is likely to corrupt a memory location near zero, leading to a spectacular crash.

577 You can, of course, also test for the null pointer by using the inequality operator, rather than the negation operator:

```
...
if (trade_pointers [limit] != 0) {
  free (trade_pointers[limit] -> description);
  free (trade_pointers[limit]);
}
...
```

Note, however, that most programmers prefer to substitute NULL for 0, as in the following example:

```
...
if (trade_pointers [limit] != NULL) {
  free (trade_pointers[limit] -> description);
  free (trade_pointers[limit]);
}
...
```

As you learned in Segment 516, NULL is a macro symbol that is replaced by 0 during compilation. By using NULL instead of 0, you identify the places where 0 is used as a special pointer, rather than as an ordinary integer, thereby increasing program clarity.

578
PRACTICE

A destructor is a function that frees memory. Write a destructor, destroy_trade, that reclaims the memory consumed by a trade object, including the memory occupied by the characters associated with the description structure variable. Assume that the destructor's argument is to be a trade object pointer. Revise the program shown in Segment 573 such that it reads data that include information for a description structure variable and such that all instances of free appear only in destroy_trade.

579
HIGHLIGHTS

- Inaccessible memory is called garbage.

- Whenever a program creates garbage, the program is said to have a **memory leak**.

- If you want to plug a memory leak caused by reassigning a pointer, **then** instantiate one of the following patterns just before the pointer is reassigned:

  ```
  free (pointer to object);
  free (pointer to array);
  ```

- If you want to have your program pause for a specified number of seconds, **then** instantiate the following pattern:

  ```
  #include <time.h>
  ...
  sleep (seconds to pause);
  ```

38 HOW TO TELL TIME

580   In Section 37, you learned how to use the `sleep` function from the time library. In this section, you learn how to use other time-library functions to dress up your reports with lines such as the following:

At 8:38, the value of the ··· trades in the test.data file was ····.

581   To work with time, you use the `time` and `localtime` functions. The `time` function asks your operating system how many seconds have elapsed since the beginning of 1970, and the `localtime` function uses that number of seconds to fill structure variables in a time-structure object:

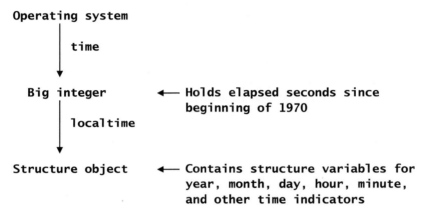

582   Because the `time` and `localtime` functions are a bit fussy about their arguments, you may find it wise to understand what they do once, and then to hide them in a function.

583   The `time` function has a pointer parameter of type `time_t`, where `time_t` in many implementations is defined via a `typedef` statement in the time library to be a synonym for `long`. The purpose of the `time` function is to set a `time_t`-type variable, one declared by you, to the number of elapsed seconds since the beginning of 1970.

```
/* Declare variable to hold clock ticks since 1970 */
time_t elapsed_seconds;
...
/* Fetch elapsed seconds from operating system */
time(&elapsed_seconds);
```

584   The `localtime` function also has a pointer parameter of type `time_t`, but the purpose of `localtime` is to analyze your `time_t` variable's value, rather than to assign a value to your `time_t` variable. In the following, for example, `localtime` is to analyze the number of elapsed seconds previously fetched from your operating system by the `time` function:

```
localtime (&elapsed_seconds);
```

585   The `localtime` function returns a pointer to a structure of type `tm`, which is defined in the time library. Accordingly, you need a pointer variable of that same `tm` type to hold on to the value returned by `localtime`:

```
/* Declare pointer to a tm object containing time information */
struct tm *time_structure_pointer;
...
/* Use elapsed seconds to update time-structure object */
time_structure_pointer = localtime (&elapsed_seconds);
```

586   The time-structure object itself has structure variables with difficult-to-remember names. You have no need to remember them, however, because you can extract values from those structure variables, and assign those values to global variables with fully spelled-out names, once and for all:

```
/* Extract useful information from the time structure */
year = 1900 + time_structure_pointer -> tm_year;
month = time_structure_pointer -> tm_mon;
day = time_structure_pointer -> tm_mday;
hour = time_structure_pointer -> tm_hour;
minute = time_structure_pointer -> tm_min;
```

587   Finally, you can hide all the detail in a function:

```
/* Define global time variables */
int year, month, day, hour, minute;
/* Define function to establish time-variable values */
void assign_time_variables ( ) {
  /* Declare variable to hold elapsed seconds since 1970 */
  time_t elapsed_seconds;
  /* Declare pointer to an object containing time information */
  struct tm *time_structure_pointer;
  /* Fetch elapsed seconds from operating system */
  time(&elapsed_seconds);
  /* Use elapsed seconds to update time-structure object */
  time_structure_pointer = localtime (&elapsed_seconds);
  /* Extract useful information from the time structure */
  year = 1900 + time_structure_pointer -> tm_year;
  month = time_structure_pointer -> tm_mon;
  day = time_structure_pointer -> tm_mday;
  hour = time_structure_pointer -> tm_hour;
  minute = time_structure_pointer -> tm_min;
}
```

588   Given `assign_time_variables`, you can display time messages as in the following example:

212

```
#include <stdio.h>
#include <time.h>
/* Define global time variables */
int year, month, day, hour, minute;
/* ... Define assign_time_variables ... */
main ( ) {
  assign_time_variables ( );
  printf ("At %i:%s%i, ...\n",
            hour,
               (minute < 10) ? "0" : "",
                  minute);
}
```

——————————————— Result ———————————————

```
At 9:09, ...
```

589   A more advanced way to display time information is to appeal to other time-library mechanisms that enable you to transform a time-structure pointer into displayed forms under
the direction of strings similar to those you find in printf statements. Here is an example
in which time specifications dictate that the hour, minute, and PM are to be displayed:

```
/* Declare variable to hold elapsed seconds since 1970 */
time_t elapsed_seconds;
/* Declare pointer to an object containing time information */
struct tm *time_structure_pointer;
/* Declare buffer to hold time string */
char *time_buffer[100];
...
/* Fetch elapsed seconds from operating system */
time(&elapsed_seconds);
/* Use elapsed seconds to update time structure object */
time_structure_pointer = localtime (&elapsed_seconds);
/* Use time-structure object to fill time buffer */
strftime (time_buffer, 100, "%I:%M %p", time_structure_pointer);
/* Use time buffer to display the time */
printf ("The time is %s.\n", time_buffer);
```

Executing all these statements displays a line such as the following:

```
The time is 12:17 PM.
```

The key statement, obscurely, is the one with strftime, which is an acronym for *string
format time*:

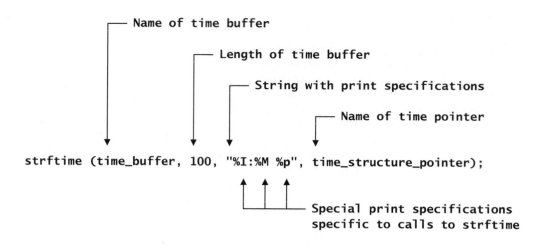

590 Other, occasionally useful time specifications for use in `strftime` are provided in Appendix D.

591
PRACTICE

Write a program that displays lines such as the following once each minute:

```
...
The time is 7:09 AM.
...
The time is 3:52 PM.
...
```

592
HIGHLIGHTS

- If you want to have your program report the time, **then** you must inform the C compiler that you plan to use functions in the time library:

  ```
  #include <time.h>
  ```

- If you want to have your program report the time, **then** you must declare variables for a number that records seconds and a structure that records miscellaneous time elements:

  ```
  time_t elapsed_seconds;
  struct tm *time_structure_pointer;
  ```

- If you want to have your program report the time, **then** you must use `time` and `localtime` to instantiate your seconds and time-structure variables:

  ```
  time(&elapsed_seconds);
  time_structure_pointer = localtime (&elapsed_seconds);
  ```

- **If** you want to have your program report the time, **then** you must dig the required time elements out of the time structure:

```
1900 + time_structure_pointer -> tm_year; /* The year */
time_structure_pointer -> tm_mon;   /* The month */
time_structure_pointer -> tm_mday;  /* The day of the month */
time_structure_pointer -> tm_hour;  /* The hour (0-23) */
time_structure_pointer -> tm_min;   /* The minute */
```

593 So far, you have learned how to create file pointers for wired-in files. In this section, you learn how to create file pointers for files specified at run time. You also learn how to deal with command-line arguments.

594 The version of the `analyze_trades` program in Segment 573 contains a wired-in character string supplied when the `analyze_trades` program was written. Generally, you want a way to have your program ask you for a file-specifying character string at run time. Then, once you have supplied that file-specifying character string, your program can read information from it.

You can, for example, include the following code, which leads to the insertion of a file-specifying character string into the `input_buffer` character array:

```
printf ("Please type the name of a trade file.\n");
scanf ("%s", input_buffer);
```

Next, you can use that file-specifying character string instead of wired-in character string:

```
analysis_target = fopen(input_buffer, "r");
```

595 Most programmers prefer to have their programs take a file name as a **command-line argument**, rather than via a `scanf` statement.

To handle command line arguments, you need to know that C allows you to include two parameters in the `main` function. If you include those two parameters, then the value of the first parameter is the number of white space-separated character strings on the command line. The value of the second parameter, exotically enough, is the name of an array of pointers to arrays. Each of those pointed-to arrays holds one of the space-separated character strings.

In Segment 612, you learn how to include the two parameters in the `main` function. In preparation, suppose that the name of the first parameter is `argument_count` and the name of the second parameter is `argument_array`. Further suppose that you type the following command line:

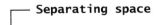

┌─ **Separating space**
│
▼

`analyze_trades test.data`

Then, as your program is entered, C assigns 2 to `argument_count`, and C assigns the address of an array of pointers to `argument_array`:

argument_array

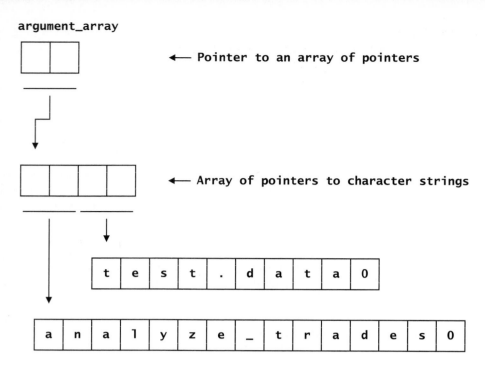

Thus, argument_array is the name of an array of pointers to character strings; the value of argument_array is the address of the first element in a pointer array. Alternatively, the value of argument_array[0], the first element in the array, is itself the address of a character string.

596   Now you can understand which data types you need for the argument_count parameter and the argument_array parameter. Specifying the data type for argument_count is straightforward, of course, as argument_count is just an integer:

main (int argument_count, ···) {···}

Specifying the data type for argument_array is a bit tricky, however. It would be wrong to specify char argument_array, for that would mean that argument_array is just a single character. It would be almost as wrong to specify char *argument_array, for that would mean that argument_array is just a pointer to a character. What you need is an extra asterisk, producing char **argument_array, for that must be a pointer to a pointer to a character. Inasmuch as each object pointed to can always be the first element in an array of such objects, you can also say that char **argument_array establishes that the value of argument_array is the address of an array of addresses of character strings.

597   Assembling the type specifications and parameters into main, you have the following demonstration program, which just displays the name of the program and the argument, which is presumed to be a file specification:

218

```
#include <stdio.h>
main (int argument_count, char **argument_array) {
  printf ("You have supplied %s to %s.\n",
                         argument_array[1],
                             argument_array[0]);
}
```

Accordingly, if the name of the demonstration program is `demonstration_program` and you type the command line `demonstration_program file_name.extension`, you obtain the following result:

You have supplied file_name.extension to demonstration_program.

598 Now you can combine what you know about command-line arguments with what you know about opening files so as to supply a file name to a program that actually reads from the file. For example, the following, revised version of `analyze_trades` works on a command-line argument, rather than on a wired-in file name:

```
#include <stdio.h>
/* Define the trade structure */
struct trade {double price; int number;};
/* Define value-computing function */
double trade_price (struct trade *tptr) {
  return tptr -> price * tptr -> number;
}
/* Define trade array */
struct trade *trade_pointers[100];
main (int argument_count, char **argument_array) {
  /* Declare various variables */
  int limit, counter, number;
  double price, sum = 0;
  /* Declare trade_source, a pointer to a file-describing structure */
  FILE* trade_source;
  /* Prepare a file-describing structure for reading */
  trade_source = fopen (argument_array[1], "r");
  /* Read numbers from the file and stuff them into array */
  for (limit = 0;
       2 == fscanf (trade_source, "%f%i", &price, &number);
       ++limit) {
    trade_pointers[limit]
      = (struct trade*) malloc (sizeof (struct trade));
    trade_pointers[limit] -> price = price;
    trade_pointers[limit] -> number = number;
  }
  /* Close source file */
  fclose (trade_source);
  /* ... Analyze data ... */
}
```

599 Actually, as a seasoned C programmer, you would add tests to the program to ensure that exactly one command-line argument has been supplied and to ensure that the command-line argument works as a file name. To check the number of arguments, you merely test argument_count, and exit if the number is wrong:

```
if (argument_count != 2) {
  printf ("Sorry, %s requires exactly one argument.\n",
              argument_array [0]);
  exit (0);
}
```

To check that the argument is a file name, you make sure that the pointer returned by fopen is not the NULL pointer, which would indicate that the file failed to open:

```
if (trade_source == NULL) {
  printf ("Sorry, %s is not a file name.\n",
              argument_array [1]);
  exit (0);
}
```

600 Combining the argument-testing statements into the analyze_trades program, you have the following:

```
#include <stdio.h>
/* Define the trade structure */
struct trade {double price; int number;};
/* Define value-computing function */
double trade_price (struct trade *tptr) {
   return tptr -> price * tptr -> number;
}
/* Define trade array */
struct trade *trade_pointers[100];
main (int argument_count, char **argument_array) {
  /* Declare various variables */
  int limit, counter, number;
  double price, sum = 0;
  /* Declare trade_source, a pointer to a file-describing structure */
  FILE* trade_source;
  /* Test argument count */
  if (argument_count != 2) {
    printf ("Sorry, %s requires exactly one argument.\n",
            argument_array [0]);
    exit (0);
  }
```

```
/* Prepare a file-describing structure for reading */
trade_source = fopen (argument_array[1], "r");
/* Make sure file opened properly */
if (trade_source == NULL) {
  printf ("Sorry, %s is not a file name.\n", argument_array [1]);
  exit (0);
}
/* Read numbers from the file and stuff them into array */
for (limit = 0;
     2 == fscanf (trade_source, "%f%i", &price, &number);
     ++limit) {
  trade_pointers[limit]
    = (struct trade*) malloc (sizeof (struct trade));
  trade_pointers[limit] -> price = price;
  trade_pointers[limit] -> number = number;
}
/* Close source file */
fclose (trade_source);
/* Find value of shares traded */
for (counter = 0; counter < limit; ++counter)
  sum = sum + trade_price(trade_pointers[counter]);
/* Display value of shares traded */
printf ("The total value of the %i trades is %f.\n",
                                    limit,        sum);

}
```

601   Now that you know how to supply a command-line file name, you probably want to know how to supply other command-line arguments as well. In particular, you probably will want to know how to supply and make use of command-line arguments that determine exactly what your program is to do, given several slightly different options.

Suppose, for example, that you want a version of `analyze_trades` that examines a specified trade file, computing either the average price-per-share paid, or the average number of shares traded, or both. Following the conventions of UNIX, you probably would want your program to accept an option-specifying character called a **flag**, marked as such by a hyphen. You would want your program to recognize the following indication that it is to compute average price:

          ┌─ **Indicates program is to compute average price**
          │
          ▼

analyze_trades -p test.data

Similarly, your program should recognize the following indication that it is to compute the average number of shares traded:

          ┌─ **Indicates program is to compute average number**
          │
          ▼

analyze_trades -n test.data

602   By convention, your `analyze_trades` program should take any one of the following to mean that both the average price and the average number of shares traded are to be computed:

```
analyze_trades -p -n test.data
analyze_trades -n -p test.data
analyze_trades -pn test.data
analyze_trades -np test.data
```

603   Thus, your program must be prepared to handle a variety of flag arrangements. Fortunately, you need to understand only once how to do what needs to be done; then, you can just copy your flag-analysis fragment from program to program.

604   Note that the flag arguments -p and -n leave you with a memory structure that looks like this:

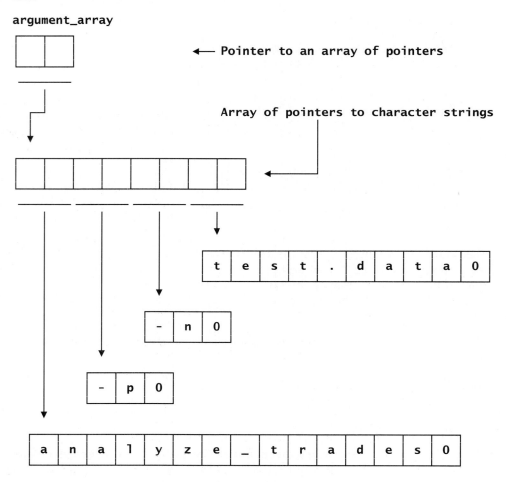

605   Evidently, you need to have your program do the following:

- Iterate over all command-line arguments that may contain flags.

- For each such argument, determine whether the first character indicates the presence of flags.

- For each flag-containing argument, iterate over all flag characters.

- For each flag character, set a variable value to indicate that the flag has been seen.

To accomplish this work, you can use a `for` statement to iterate over the appropriate command-line arguments, an `if` statement to test for flag-marking hyphens, another `for` statement to iterate over flag characters, and a `switch` statement to look for specific flags and to take appropriate variable-assignment actions.

606   More specifically, to iterate over the command-line arguments, you can use the following `for` statement, which increments a counter, `argument_counter`, and runs the loop for values of `argument_counter` ranging from 1 to 2 less than the value of `argument_count`:

```
for (argument_counter = 1;
     argument_counter < argument_count - 1;
     ++argument_counter)
  ...
```

You do not run the loop with `argument_counter` equal to 0, because the first character string is the name of the program, rather than a flag argument; similarly, you do not run the loop with `argument_counter` equal to 1 less than the value of `argument_count`, because the final argument is file-specifying character string, rather than a flag argument.

607   To check for flag-marking hyphens, you can use the following `if` statement:

```
if (argument_array[argument_counter][0] == '-')
  ...
```

To understand how this `if` statement does its job, you first note that the value of the expression `argument_array[argument_counter]` is the location of a pointer to a character array. Then, recall that you can place a bracketed integer, such as `[0]`, after such a pointer to select a particular character. Thus, `argument_array[argument_counter][0]` is the first character in the array identified by a particular pointer in the argument array.

608   To iterate over all flag characters, you can use the following `for` statement, which increments a counter, `string_counter`:

```
for (string_counter = 1;
     argument_array[argument_counter][string_counter];
     ++string_counter)
  ...
```

To understand how this `if` statement does its job, you first note that the value of the expression `argument_array[argument_counter][string_character]` is an ordinary character until you reach the end of the character string, whereupon the value is the null character, an all-0 byte, which terminates the iteration.

609   Finally, your program must examine the characters as encountered. Accordingly, you write a `switch` statement in which appropriately named variables are assigned:

```
switch (argument_array [argument_counter][string_counter]) {
  case 'p': mean_price_switch = 1; break;
  case 'n': mean_size_switch = 1; break;
  default: printf ("%c is not a recognized flag.\n",
                    argument_array [argument_counter][string_counter]);
          break;
}
```

The %c print specification causes a character to be inserted into the displayed string.

610   Once flags cause appropriate switches to be set, all your program needs to do is to test those switches when it is time to act. For example, the following statement displays the price per share, once `mean_price` is defined, as long as the value of the `mean_price_switch` is 1:

```
if (mean_price_switch == 1)
  printf ("The mean price per share of the trades is %.2f.\n",
          mean_price (trade_pointers, limit));
...
```

611   To define the `mean_price` function, note that you hand it an array of pointers to `trade` objects. The appropriate data type for the corresponding parameter cannot be, say, `struct trade *array`, for that would specify an array of `trade` objects, rather than pointers to `trade` objects. Accordingly, the correct specification must include two asterisks: `struct trade **array`. Also, as there is no end-of-array marker for arrays other than character arrays, you also must hand `mean_price` the length of the array:

```
double mean_price (struct trade **array, int length) {
  int counter; double sum = 0.0;
  for (counter = 0; counter < length; ++counter)
    sum = sum + array[counter] -> price;
  return sum / counter;
}
```

612   Assembling all these functions, iterations, tests, and appropriate variable definitions together, you have the following program:

```
#include <stdio.h>
/* Define the trade structure */
struct trade {double price; int number;};
/* Define auxiliary functions */
double mean_price (struct trade **array, int length) {
  int counter; double sum = 0.0;
  for (counter = 0; counter < length; ++counter)
    sum = sum + array[counter] -> price;
  return sum / counter;
}
```

224

```c
double mean_size (struct trade **array, int length) {
  int counter; double sum = 0.0;
  for (counter = 0; counter < length; ++counter)
    sum = sum + array[counter] -> number;
  return sum / counter;
}
/* Define trade array */
struct trade *trade_pointers[100];
main (int argument_count, char **argument_array) {
  /* Declare various variables */
  int limit, counter, number;
  double price;
  /* Declare trade_source, a pointer to a file-describing structure */
  FILE* trade_source;
  /* Declare variables for flag analysis */
  int argument_counter, string_counter;
  /* Define flag switches */
  int mean_price_switch = 0;
  int mean_size_switch = 0;
  /* ... Open file ... */
  /* Analyze flags */
  for (argument_counter = 1;
       argument_counter < argument_count - 1;
       ++argument_counter)
    if (argument_array [argument_counter][0] == '-')
      for (string_counter = 1;
           argument_array[argument_counter][string_counter];
           ++string_counter)
        switch (argument_array [argument_counter][string_counter]) {
          case 'p': mean_price_switch = 1; break;
          case 'n': mean_size_switch = 1; break;
          default:
            printf ("%c is not a recognized flag.\n",
                argument_array [argument_counter][string_counter]);
            break;
        }
  /* ... Process and close file ... */
  /* Perform actions as dictated by flag switches */
  if (mean_price_switch == 1)
    printf ("The mean price per share of the trades is %.2f.\n",
          mean_price (trade_pointers, limit));
  if (mean_size_switch == 1)
    printf ("The mean number of shares traded is %f.\n",
          mean_size (trade_pointers, limit));
}
```

613 Once you understand how the flag-processing fragment works, you can, of course, copy it into other programs with appropriate modifications.

Note, however, that other programmers may choose to use pointer arithmetic to implement flag processing, rather than array notation. Still others may choose to use a mixture of pointer arithmetic and array notation, deploying one to iterate over character strings and the other to iterate over the command-line arguments. The version you have learned about here represents a personal opinion about which approach is the easiest to understand.

614
PRACTICE

Revise the program shown in Segment 612 such that it accepts an additional flag, v, for *verbose*. If v is provided as a flag, the program is to perform as it does now. Otherwise, it is to suppress the full-sentence output and return numbers only: It returns a floating-point price if the p flag is provided, an integer number of shares if the n flag is provided, both numbers if both flags are provided, and nothing if neither flag is provided.

615
HIGHLIGHTS

- **If** you want to supply command-line arguments, **then** indicate that the main function is to have two parameters—one that holds a count of the space-separated command-line strings, and another that holds an array of pointers to those command-line strings:

```
main (int argument_count, char **argument_array) {···}
```

- **If** you want to include a command-line file name, which, by convention, should be the final command-line argument, **then** instantiate the following pattern:

```
main (int argument_count, char **argument_array) {
  ...
  /* Declare a pointer to a file-describing structure */
  FILE* file-pointer name ;
  ...
  /* Test argument count */
  if (argument_count < 2) {
    printf ("Sorry, %s requires at least one argument.\n",
                    argument_array [0]);
    exit (0);}
  /* Prepare a file-describing structure for reading */
  file-pointer name
    = fopen (argument_array[argument_count - 1], "r");
  /* Make sure file opened properly */
  if ( file-pointer name  == NULL) {
    printf ("Sorry, %s is not a file name.\n",
                    argument_array [argument_count -1]);
    exit (0);}
  ...
  statements that read information from the specified file
```

- **If** you want to include command-line flags, which, by convention, should be marked with hyphens, as well as with a file name, **then** instantiate and supplement the following pattern for a single flag:

```
main (int argument_count, char **argument_array) {
  ...
  /* Declare flag switches */
  int flag_switch = 0;
  ...
/* ... Set up file pointer ... */
 /* Analyze flags */
 for (argument_counter = 1;
      argument_counter < argument_count - 1;
      ++argument_counter)
   if (argument_array [argument_counter][0] == '-')
     for (string_counter = 1;
          argument_array[argument_counter][string_counter];
          ++string_counter)
       switch (argument_array [argument_counter][string_counter])
         {
         case 'flag character to be recognized':
           flag_switch = 1;
           break;
         default:
           printf ("%c is not a recognized flag.\n",
               argument_array [argument_counter][string_counter]);
           break;
         }
```

40 HOW TO DEFINE FUNCTIONS WITH A VARIABLE NUMBER OF ARGUMENTS

616 Several popular functions take a variable number of arguments, such as `printf`, `scanf`, `fprintf`, and `fscanf`. This section explains how to define such functions.

617 When you define a function that takes a variable number of arguments, you generally provide the following instructions to the C compiler:

- You inform the C compiler that a function is to take a variable number of arguments.

- You use a C mechanism that establishes where argument values are located in memory.

- You use a C mechanism that obtains argument values from those locations, and you write statements that assign those argument values to variables.

- You use a C mechanism that performs some clean-up operations.

618 Suppose, for example, that you decide to write a function that constructs trades, similar to the one defined in Segment 385:

```
/* Define trade structure */
struct trade {
    double price;
    int number;
};
/* Define constructor for trade structures */
struct trade* construct_trade (double price, int number) {
  struct trade *tptr;
  tptr = (struct trade*) malloc (sizeof (struct trade));
  tptr -> price = price;
  tptr -> number = number;
  return tptr;
}
```

In contrast, you want the new version of `construct_trade` to be able to handle the following cases:

- As before, you supply both a price and a number of shares.

- Alternatively, you supply just a price, with the number of shares taken to be 100 by default.

619 Before you define any function that is to take a variable number of arguments, you must provide the C compiler with a certain header-file declaration:

```
#include <stdarg.h>
```

620 To inform the C compiler that `construct_trade` is to take a variable number of arguments, you must supply one or more ordinary parameters, followed by ellipses, `...`:

```
struct trade* construct_trade (int argument_count, ...) {···}
```

Generally, the value supplied for assignment to the first parameter indicates how many arguments follow. In a function such as `printf`, the argument-count indication is through the print specifications buried in a string. In the new version of `construct_trade`, the argument-count indication is much simpler: If only a price is to be supplied, the argument value provided when `construct_trade` is called is 1:

```
construct_trade (1, price )
```

Alternatively, if both a price and a number of shares are to be supplied, the value provided is 2:

```
construct_trade (2, price , number )
```

621 To establish where argument values are located in memory, you first create a pointer using `va_list`, an acronym for *variable* argument *list*:

```
va_list argument_pointer;
```

Even though `va_list` is written with lower-case characters, and there is no asterisk, `va_list` is a macro that declares `argument_pointer` to be a pointer.

With `argument_pointer` declared, you provide an assignment using another macro, `va_start`. The `va_start` macro takes as its arguments both the function's argument pointer and the function's final ordinary argument:

```
va_start (argument_pointer, argument_count);
```

622 You fetch each argument, and move the argument pointer to the next argument, by deploying yet another macro, `va_arg`. The `va_arg` macro takes as its first argument the function's argument pointer. The `va_arg` macro takes as its second argument the type of the argument to be fetched, which `va_arg` needs so that it can properly move the argument pointer. For example, to fetch the first of the optional arguments supplied to `construct_trade`, which is of type `double`, you write the following:

```
va_arg (argument_pointer, double);
```

To fetch the second of the optional arguments, which is of type `int`, you write a similar statement, but with `int` instead of `double`:

```
va_arg (argument_pointer, int);
```

Finally, once all arguments are read, you clean up using `va_end` with the argument pointer as the sole argument:

```
va_end (argument_pointer);
```

623   The required ellipses and calls to all four macros— va_list, va_start, va_arg, and va_end—are shown in the following version of construct_trade:

```
/* Define trade structure */
struct trade {
    double price;
    int number;
};
/* Define constructor for trade structures with variable arguments */
struct trade* construct_trade (int argument_count, ...) {
  va_list argument_pointer ;
  struct trade *tptr;
  va_start (argument_pointer, argument_count) ;
  tptr = (struct trade*) malloc (sizeof (struct trade));
  tptr -> price = va_arg (argument_pointer, double) ;
  if (argument_count = 2)
    tptr -> number = va_arg (argument_pointer, int) ;
  else
    tptr -> number = 100;
  va_end (argument_pointer) ;
  return tptr;
}
```

624   If you need to declare a function prototype for a function with a variable number of arguments, you can provide just the return type and the function name; you do not need type–argument pairs:

```
struct trade* construct_trade ( );
```

625   To understand what the macros are doing, you need to know that function calls push argu-
SIDE TRIP   ment values onto a stack. When construct_trade is called with both a price argument and a number argument, the stack looks like this:

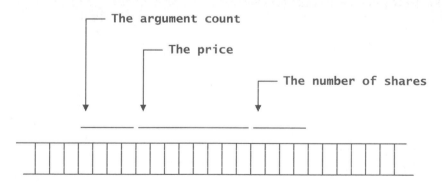

626   The effect of the call to the va_start macro is to place the argument pointer just past the
SIDE TRIP   memory chunk occupied by the final ordinary argument:

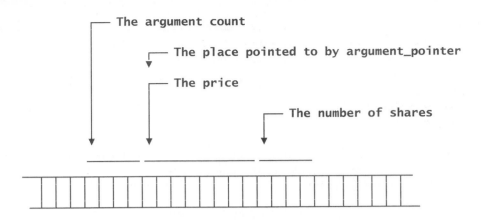

To do its job, va_start needs to have access to both the argument pointer and the location of the final ordinary argument.

627 To produce an argument value and to advance the argument pointer, the va_arg macro
SIDE TRIP needs the current argument pointer, of course. Also, it needs to know the type of the current argument value so that it can advance the argument pointer appropriately:

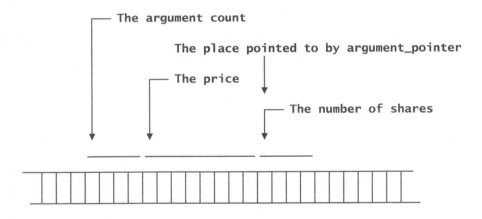

628 The definition of va_list is implementation dependent, but one way to define it uses
SIDE TRIP typedef statement that makes va_list a synonym for a character-pointer specification:

typedef char* va_list;

Thus, the effect of the statement va_list argument_pointer; in construct_trade is to declare argument_pointer to be a character pointer.

629 The definition of va_start is also implementation dependent, but the effect is as though
SIDE TRIP the following were written in the definition of construct_trade:

232

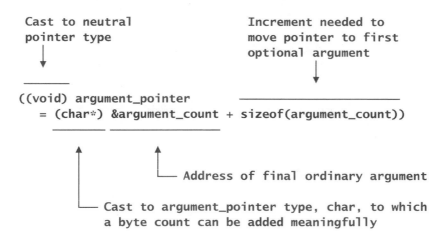

Cast to neutral
pointer type

Increment needed to
move pointer to first
optional argument

```
((void) argument_pointer
   = (char*) &argument_count + sizeof(argument_count))
```

Address of final ordinary argument

Cast to argument_pointer type, char, to which
a byte count can be added meaningfully

The final cast to void is useful only if the va_start expression is embedded in a larger expression.

630
SIDE TRIP Again, the definition of va_arg is implementation dependent, but the effect is as though the following were written in the definition of construct_trade:

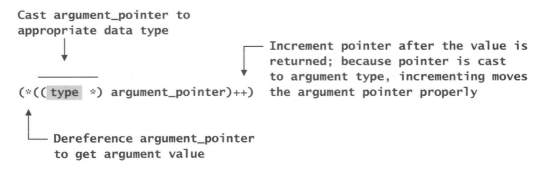

Cast argument_pointer to
appropriate data type

Increment pointer after the value is
returned; because pointer is cast
to argument type, incrementing moves
the argument pointer properly

```
(*(( type *) argument_pointer)++)
```

Dereference argument_pointer
to get argument value

631
SIDE TRIP Finally, the definition of va_end is implementation dependent, but the effect may be just to reset the argument pointer as though the following were written in the definition of construct_trade:

```
((void) argument_pointer = NULL)
```

The final cast to void is useful only if the va_start expression is embedded in a larger expression.

632
HIGHLIGHTS

- If you wish to write functions that take a variable number of arguments, **then** announce your intention by inserting the following declaration in your program:

```
#include <stdarg.h>
```

- If you wish to define a function that takes a variable number of arguments, **then** include ellipses, . . ., at the end of the parameter list:

  ```
  return type  program name  ( ordinary parameters , ...) {
    ...
  }
  ```

- If you wish to define a function that takes a variable number of arguments, **then** use `va_list` to define an argument pointer, **and then** use `va_start` to assign the appropriate value to the argument pointer, **and then** use `va_arg` to fetch the arguments, **and then** clean up using `va_end`.

41 HOW TO ARRANGE FOR CONDITIONAL COMPILATION

633   In this section, you learn how to write compile-time Boolean expressions. Using compile-time Boolean expressions, you can generate a diverse set of run-time program variations.

634   In Section 8, you learned that the C compiler allows you to define macro symbols using `#define`.

The C compiler's preprocessor also allows you to specify that certain lines of code are to be compiled only if a specified macro symbol has been defined. Suppose, for example, that you want certain optional lines of code to be compiled only if you have previously defined VERBOSE to be a macro symbol; otherwise, you want your C compiler to ignore those optional lines entirely.

To arrange for such conditional compilation, you simply sandwich those optional lines of code between a line reading `#ifdef VERBOSE` and a line reading `#endif`:

```
#ifdef VERBOSE
...
...          ◄── Compile if VERBOSE has been defined
...
#endif
```

Symmetrically, the lines between the compiler instructions `#ifndef` and `#endif` are ignored if VERBOSE is defined; otherwise, they are compiled:

```
#ifndef VERBOSE
...
...          ◄── Compile if VERBOSE has NOT been defined
...
#endif
```

635   You use both an `#ifdef–#endif` combination and an `#ifndef–#endif` combination if you want to compile some lines if a definition exists and others if it does not. Alternatively, you can use a single `#ifdef–#else–#endif` combination:

```
#ifdef VERBOSE
...
...          ◄── Compile if VERBOSE has been defined
...
#else
...
...          ◄── Compile if VERBOSE has NOT been defined
...
#endif
```

636   Thus, `#ifdef–#else–#endif` combinations are similar to `if–else` combinations. The key difference is that you use one to control which lines of code are compiled at compile time, and you use the other to control which statements are evaluated at run time.

637   Note carefully that the rules of C syntax require you to place #define, #ifdef, #ifndef, #else, and #endif at the beginning of the line on which they appear—there can be no indentation whatsoever.

638   Although most macros are defined so as to perform text substitutions, you do not need to provide any substitution text for macros defined to control compilation. Thus, you can define VERBOSE as follows:

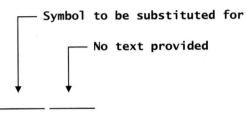

Symbol to be substituted for

No text provided

```
#define VERBOSE
```

The VERBOSE macro does not require substitution text, because the real purpose of the definition is to establish that VERBOSE has a definition, rather than to prepare for substitutions.

639   Suppose, for the sake of illustration, that you have a version of the analyze_trades program that uses two subfunctions, mean_price and mean_size:

```
#include <stdio.h>
/* Define the trade structure */
struct trade {double price; int number;};
/* Define auxiliary functions */
double mean_price (struct trade **array, int length) {
  int counter; double sum = 0.0;
  for (counter = 0; counter < length; ++counter)
    sum = sum + array[counter] -> price;
  return sum / counter;
}
double mean_size (struct trade **array, int length) {
  int counter; double sum = 0.0;
  for (counter = 0; counter < length; ++counter)
    sum = sum + array[counter] -> number;
  return sum / counter;
}
/* Define trade array */
struct trade *trade_pointers[100];
```

```
main ( ) {
  /* Declare various variables */
  int limit, counter, number;
  double price;
  /* Read numbers from the file and stuff them into array */
  for (limit = 0;
       2 == scanf ("%lf%i", &price, &number);
       ++limit) {
    trade_pointers[limit]
      = (struct trade*) malloc (sizeof (struct trade));
    trade_pointers[limit] -> price = price;
    trade_pointers[limit] -> number = number;
  }
  /* Perform analysis */
  printf ("The mean price per share of the trades is %.2f.\n",
          mean_price (trade_pointers, limit));
  printf ("The mean number of shares traded is %.0f.\n",
          mean_size (trade_pointers, limit));
}
```

640 Now suppose that you decide you want two versions of analyze_trades:

- You want one version, the verbose version, to display two complete sentences.

- You want another version, the concise version, to display just two numbers, the mean price per share and the mean number of shares traded.

The verbose version is to display a report such as the following:

The mean price per share of the trades is 10.00.
The mean number of shares traded is 600.

The concise version is to display a shorter report, or perhaps write a shorter report into a file to be read by another program:

10.00 600

641 You certainly should not keep two separate files for the two versions of analyze_trades, because that would make it difficult to keep the two versions moving along together as you fix bugs and make improvements.

642 Accordingly, you should keep just one conditionalized file. To produce the different versions you want, you need only to retain or eliminate the definition of VERBOSE, as in the following example:

```c
/*
Define VERBOSE if you want two complete sentences.
Do not define VERBOSE if you want two numbers only.
*/
#define VERBOSE
#include <stdio.h>
/* Define the trade structure */
struct trade {double price; int number;};
/* Define auxiliary functions */
double mean_price (struct trade **array, int length) {
  int counter; double sum = 0.0;
  for (counter = 0; counter < length; ++counter)
    sum = sum + array[counter] -> price;
  return sum / counter;
}
double mean_size (struct trade **array, int length) {
  int counter; double sum = 0.0;
  for (counter = 0; counter < length; ++counter)
    sum = sum + array[counter] -> number;
  return sum / counter;
}
/* Define trade array */
struct trade *trade_pointers[100];
main ( ) {
  /* Declare various variables */
  int limit, counter, number;
  double price;
  /* Read numbers from the file and stuff them into array */
  for (limit = 0;
       2 == scanf ("%lf%i", &price, &number);
       ++limit) {
    trade_pointers[limit]
      = (struct trade*) malloc (sizeof (struct trade));
    trade_pointers[limit] -> price = price;
    trade_pointers[limit] -> number = number;
  }
  /* Perform analysis */
#ifdef VERBOSE
    printf ("The mean price per share of the trades is %.2f.\n",
            mean_price (trade_pointers, limit));
    printf ("The mean number of shares traded is %.0f.\n",
            mean_size (trade_pointers, limit));
#else
    printf ("%.2f %.2f",
            mean_price (trade_pointers, limit),
            mean_size (trade_pointers, limit));
#endif
}
```

238

643   Alternatively, but perhaps inelegantly, you could use the VERBOSE macro to control displaying in an `if–else` combination. You would compile one version of the program with the VERBOSE macro defined to substitute 1 into a Boolean expression. Then, you would recompile the same program with the VERBOSE macro defined to substitute 0 into that Boolean expression:

```
/*
    Define VERBOSE to insert 1 if you want two complete sentences.
    Define VERBOSE to insert 0 if you want two numbers only.
*/
#define VERBOSE 1
/* ... Bulk of program goes here ... */
  /* Perform analysis */
  if (VERBOSE) {
    printf ("The mean price per share of the trades is %.2f.\n",
            mean_price (trade_pointers, limit));
    printf ("The mean number of shares traded is %.0f.\n",
            mean_size (trade_pointers, limit));
  }
  else {
    printf ("%.2f %.2f",
            mean_price (trade_pointers, limit),
            mean_size (trade_pointers, limit));
  }
}
```

644   Although you can use the VERBOSE macro to control run time conditional statements, you should prefer the conditional-compilation approach for two reasons:

- First, when you use VERBOSE to control `#ifdef–#endif` compile-time combinations, you clearly indicate your intention to produce multiple run-time programs.

- Second, when you use VERBOSE to control run-time branching statements, your compiler squanders time compiling useless code—the unexecuted part of the `if–else` statement—and that useless code squanders run time memory.

645   You frequently see operating-system specific parts of a program bracketed by `#ifdef–`
SIDE TRIP   `#endif` pairs, as in the following example, so as to make those program fragments invisible when the program is compiled for some other operating system:

```
#ifdef SUN
/* ... Program fragment specific to the SUN operating system ... */
#endif
```

646   Modify the program Segment 639 so as to add a macro, PRICE_ONLY. If PRICE_ONLY is
PRACTICE   defined, your program is to compile only those statements needed to keep track of price information. Otherwise, it is to compile as before.

- If you want to have two or more versions of a file, **then** you can arrange for conditional compilation.

- If you want to have certain lines of code compiled conditionally, **then** define a control symbol by instantiating the following pattern:

```
#define control symbol
```

and then surround the lines of code as follows:

```
#ifdef control symbol
lines to be compiled if control symbol is defined
#else
lines to be compiled if control symbol is not defined
#endif
```

42 HOW TO ARRANGE FUNCTIONS IN A MULTIPLE-FILE PROGRAM

648   In general, programs with complex program elements are hard to write, hard to debug, hard to improve, and hard to maintain. Accordingly, when a function definition of any kind becomes too complex to understand, you should think about breaking it up into subfunctions that you can debug and maintain independently.

Also, you should generally divide your large programs into logically separable modules, each of which occupies its own, separately compiled file. In this section, you learn how to construct multiple-file programs.

649   Suppose, for the sake of illustration, that you have a version of `analyze_trades` that uses two subfunctions, `mean_price` and `mean_size`:

```
double mean_price (struct trade **array, int length) {
  int counter; double sum = 0.0;
  for (counter = 0; counter < length; ++counter)
    sum = sum + array[counter] -> price;
  return sum / counter;
}
double mean_size (struct trade **array, int length) {
  int counter; double sum = 0.0;
  for (counter = 0; counter < length; ++counter)
    sum = sum + array[counter] -> number;
  return sum / counter;
}
```

650   Now suppose that you decide to divide this `analyze_trades` program into two files; one containing the `main` function, and the other containing the trade structure declaration and functions that work on arrays of pointers to `trade` objects.

```
main.c                     trades.c

┌─────────────────┐        ┌─────────────────┐
│  main           │        │  mean_price     │
│                 │        │  mean_size      │
│                 │        │  ...            │
│                 │        │                 │
│                 │        │                 │
└─────────────────┘        └─────────────────┘
```

651   But how can the C compiler work on `main.c` without knowing about the trade structure and the functions defined in `trades.c`? Somehow, you need to provide the C compiler with the trade-structure declaration from `trades.c`, and you need to provide function prototypes for `mean_price` and `mean_size`.

652   Fortunately, the C compiler does not need to know about the complete function definitions. You can provide the C compiler with the information it needs to compile the `main.c` file by collecting information about the `trades.c` file in a new **header file** named `trades.h`:

```
/* Trades declaration file (h extension) */
/* Define the trade structure */
struct trade {double price; int number;};
/* Specify function prototypes */
double mean_price (struct trade **, int);
double mean_size (struct trade **, int);
```

Once you have constructed the `trades.h` file, your C compiler can work on `main.c` as long as you provide access to the `trades.h` file via an `#include` declaration in the `main.c` file:

```
...
#include "trades.h"
...
```

As far as the C is concerned, it is as though the complete text of the included file appeared at the place where the inclusion occurs.

653   When a header file specification is surrounded by angle brackets <···>, the C compiler first looks for that header file in a directory known by your C compiler to contain header files for the standard library. Later on, when the C compiler needs the object code corresponding to the function prototypes in a header file, it looks for that object code in a directory known to contain the standard library file.

In contrast, when the file specification is surrounded by double-quotation marks, "···", the C compiler first looks for the header file in the current directory—which is presumably the same one that contains the source-code file.

Whenever the first look produces no header file, most compilers look elsewhere. For file specifications with angle brackets, the second look is likely to be the current directory; for file specifications with double-quotation marks, the second look is likely to be the standard library's directory.

Many compilers also allow you to specify additional places to look by way of a command-line argument.

654   Because definitions allocate memory, whereas declarations do not, you must ensure that your C compiler reads definitions only once. Otherwise, your program will not compile.

Complex programs, involving complex connections between multiple header files, may force your C compiler to read the same header file more than once during a compilation.

Consequently, you should keep definitions out of header files, which may be read more than once; there is no such prohibition against declarations.

Note that structure specifications and function prototypes are declarations, rather than definitions, although many people substitute the word *definition* for the word *declaration* when there is no special need to be precise. The trade-structure specification is a declaration, because it tells the C compiler only what memory to allocate when a `trade` object is created; it does not actually allocate any memory.

655   Also note that, by convention, the file that contains structure declarations and function prototypes has an h extension, for *h*eader, rather than a c extension.

Of course, you are accustomed to including header files, such as `stdio.h`, for functions supplied by C standard libraries.

656   To compile `trades.c`, the C compiler also needs to know about the trade structure declared in `trades.h`. Accordingly, you provide access to the `trades.h` file via another `#include` declaration:

```
/* Trades definition file (c extension) */
#include "trades.h"
double mean_price (struct trade **array, int length) {
  int counter; double sum = 0.0;
  for (counter = 0; counter < length; ++counter)
    sum = sum + array[counter] -> price;
  return sum / counter;
}
double mean_size (struct trade **array, int length) {
  int counter; double sum = 0.0;
  for (counter = 0; counter < length; ++counter)
    sum = sum + array[counter] -> number;
  return sum / counter;
}
```

657   Thus, you must include the `trades.h` header file in both the `main.c` and the `trades.c` files:

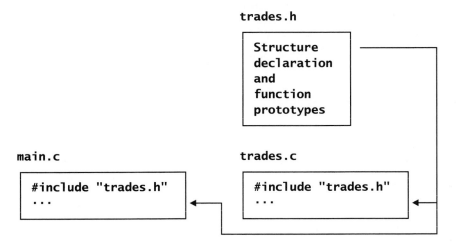

658   In general, you should include each header file in its corresponding source-code file, even if the header includes only function prototypes. That way, should there be any discrepancy between a function prototype provided in the header file and a function definition provided in the source-code file, the C compiler will note the discrepancy and complain.

659   With the header files properly included, you can use the C compiler to compile each source-code file separately, producing object code. The object-code files, by convention, have `o` extensions:

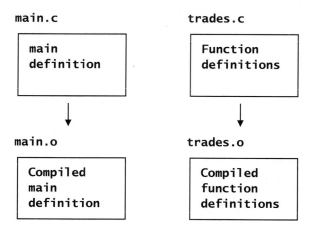

main.c

main
definition

trades.c

Function
definitions

main.o

Compiled
main
definition

trades.o

Compiled
function
definitions

Most of the work required to translate source code into an executable program lies in producing object files. Fortunately, when you make changes in a big, multiple-file program, you need to recompile only the altered files; you leave unaltered files alone.

660   Later, you use the C compiler again to link the object files into an executable program:

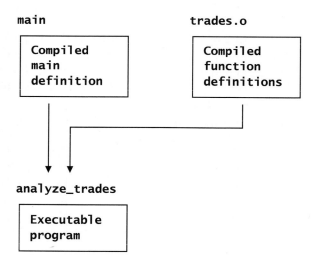

main

Compiled
main
definition

trades.o

Compiled
function
definitions

analyze_trades

Executable
program

The process of linking object files requires relatively little work, compared to the work required to produce object files from source-code files.

661   To produce an object file from a source-code file, you issue a command to the compiler with the -c option. In the following, for example, the compiler and linker, which happens to be named cc, produces a main.o file:

```
cc -c main.c
```

If you want, you can produce several object files at once. In the following, for example, you produce two object files as though you had issued two commands to the C compiler.

```
cc -c main.c trades.c
```

662   Once you have object files ready, you can link them into an executable program file with another command to the C compiler. In the following, the -o option instructs the C compiler to name the executable file `analyze_trades`:

```
cc -o analyze_trades main.o trades.o
```

663   Note that, if you change just one source-code file, you need only to recompile it into an object file and to link it with the object files previously produced from unchanged source-code files. You save time, because you do not have to wait for your C compiler to produce object code from most of your source-code files.

Suppose, for example, that you have a working `analyze_trades` program, but you make a change in the `main.c` source-code file. You therefore need to recompile `main.c`:

```
cc -c main.c
```

Then, you need to relink object files together:

```
cc -o analyze_trades main.o trades.o
```

You do not, however, need to recompile `trades.c`.

664   Of course, you always include other header files, such as `stdio.h`, for functions supplied
SIDE TRIP by C standard libraries. Consequently, when the C compiler links object files to create an executable program, it encounters functions for which it has seen function prototypes but no corresponding function definitions. Whenever that happens, the C compiler looks for the appropriate object code in a **standard library file**. The location of this standard library file generally is provided to the compiler when the compiler is installed.

665   Because there are many header files for the object code in the standard library file, each
SIDE TRIP header file covers only a fraction of the functions in the standard library file. The reason is that many C compilers bring into your program every function mentioned in a header file—even those functions that you do not use. By creating multiple header files, a library's author makes it possible for you to use the library file selectively, reducing the degree to which your programs are bloated with functions that you do not use.

666   Of course, if you change a header file, you must recompile all the source-code files in which that header file is included.

667   For example, you might want to add a prediction function, `predict`, that predicts the price of trade n, given the prices of trades 0 through $n - 1$. You would add the definition of `predict`, along with definitions for any auxiliary functions, to the `trades.c` file. You would also augment the `trades.h` header file with a function prototype for the `predict` function. Assuming that your implementation of `predict` has two parameters—one for a pointer to the trades array and one for the number of trades accumulated in the array—then the addition to the `trades.h` file would be as follows:

```
double predict (struct trade **, int);
```

You do not need to include function prototypes for any auxiliary functions, assuming that those auxiliary functions are not called from functions in other files.

One way to implement `predict` is to use **straight-line extrapolation**. First, you determine values for the slope, s, and intercept, c, of a straight line fit to the prices already in the array. Then, you use the slope and intercept to predict the next price, p_n, the one that would go into the array location n:

$$p_n = s \times n + c$$

To determine values for s and c, you can deploy the following equations for fitting a straight line to a data set consisting of n coordinate pairs:

$$s = \frac{\sum_i y_i \sum_i x_i - n \sum_i x_i y_i}{\sum_i x_i \sum_i x_i - n \sum_i x_i^2}$$

$$c = \frac{\sum_i x_i \sum_i x_i y_i - \sum_i y_i \sum_i x_i^2}{\sum_i x_i \sum_i x_i - n \sum_i x_i^2}$$

Specifically, to predict a price using a trade array, you note that the x coordinate of a trade corresponds to the location, i, of the trade in the array, and the y coordinate corresponds to the price, p, of that trade. Hence, the equations specialize as follows:

$$s = \frac{\sum_{i=0}^{n-1} p_i \sum_{i=0}^{n-1} i - n \sum_{i=0}^{n-1} i p_i}{\sum_{i=0}^{n-1} i \sum_{i=0}^{n-1} i - n \sum_{i=0}^{n-1} i^2}$$

$$c = \frac{\sum_{i=0}^{n-1} i \sum_{i=0}^{n-1} i p_i - \sum_{i=0}^{n-1} p_i \sum_{i=0}^{n-1} i^2}{\sum_{i=0}^{n-1} i \sum_{i=0}^{n-1} i - n \sum_{i=0}^{n-1} i^2}$$

Reducing the specialized straight-line extrapolation equations to functions to be added to `trades.c` file, you have the following:

```
/* Define auxiliary functions */
int sum_of_i (int length) {
  int counter, sum = 0;
  for (counter = 0; counter < length; ++counter)
    sum = sum + counter;
  return sum;
}


double sum_of_p (struct trade **array, int length) {
  int counter;
  double sum = 0.0;
  for (counter = 0; counter < length; ++counter)
    sum = sum + array[counter] -> price;
  return sum;
}


int sum_of_i_squared (int length) {
  int counter sum = 0;
  for (counter = 0; counter < length; ++counter)
    sum = sum + counter * counter;
  return sum;
}
```

```
double sum_of_i_times_p (struct trade **array, int length) {
  int counter;
  double sum = 0.0;
  for (counter = 0; counter < length; ++counter)
    sum = sum + counter * array[counter] -> price;
  return sum;
}

int denominator (struct trade **array, int length) {
  int sum_of_i_result = sum_of_i (length);
  int sum_of_i_squared_result = sum_of_i_squared (length);
  return sum_of_i_result * sum_of_i_result
         - length * sum_of_i_squared_result;
}

double slope_numerator (struct trade **array, int length) {
  int sum_of_i_result = sum_of_i (length);
  double sum_of_p_result = sum_of_p (array, length);
  double sum_of_i_times_p_result = sum_of_i_times_p (array, length);
  return sum_of_i_result * sum_of_p_result
         - length * sum_of_i_times_p_result;
}

double intercept_numerator (struct trade **array, int length) {
  int sum_of_i_result = sum_of_i (length);
  double sum_of_p_result = sum_of_p (array, length);
  int sum_of_i_squared_result = sum_of_i_squared (length);
  double sum_of_i_times_p_result = sum_of_i_times_p (array, length);
  return sum_of_i_result * sum_of_i_times_p_result
         - sum_of_p_result * sum_of_i_squared_result;
}

/* Define prediction function */
double predict (struct trade **array, int length) {
  double d = denominator (array, length);
  double s = slope_numerator (array, length) / d;
  double c = intercept_numerator (array, length) / d;
  printf ("The prediction parameters are: s = %.2f; c = %.2f\n", s, c);
  return (s * length) + c;
}
```

- Header files should contain structure declarations and function prototypes for every structure and function that you expect to appear in more than one file.

- You can declare functions, using function prototypes, as often as you like. You can define them only once.

- If you want to compile a set of files independently, **then** include appropriate header files, **and** instantiate the following pattern:

```
cc -c first source specification ...
```

- If you want to link together a set of independently compiled files to form a working program, **then** instantiate the following pattern on one line:

```
cc -o executable file specification
    first object-file specification
    ...
```

43 HOW TO ARRANGE GLOBAL VARIABLES IN A MULTIPLE-FILE PROGRAM

670 Now that you know how to distribute among files information about structure declarations and function definitions, you need to know how to distribute among files information about global variables.

671 First, however, you should know a little about the proper and improper uses of global variables. Here are a few *improper* uses:

- It is possible to use a global variable to hold a constant such as π. This practice is *usually a bad idea*, because constants are not supposed to change, yet you can certainly reassign a global variable. You should introduce macro symbols using `#define` instead.

- It is possible to use a global variable to return information from a function when there is more than one value to return. This practice is *usually a bad idea*, because passing information out of a function using global variable makes it hard to understand and control the interaction between the calling function and the one that is called. Instead, you should pass out information using pointer parameters, or you should combine multiple values into a single structure object that is returned in the ordinary way.

- It is possible to use a global variable to deliver information from a calling function to a called function. This practice is *usually a bad idea*, because passing information into a function using global variable makes it hard to understand and control the interaction between the calling function and the one that is called. Instead, you should use ordinary arguments.

672 Here, in contrast, is a proper use of global variables:

- You can use global variables to vary the behavior of your functions, thus establishing a sort of context that may vary as a program runs.

673 Suppose, for example, that you want your `analyze_trades` program to have two ways of operating, one fast and approximate and another slower, but more accurate. The `mean_price` function, as defined, is completely accurate:

```
double mean_price (struct trade **array, int length) {
  int counter; double sum = 0.0;
  for (counter = 0; counter < length; ++counter)
    sum = sum + array[counter] -> price;
  return sum / counter;
}
```

Here is another, faster version of `mean_price` that bases its result on only every second element in the array:

```
double mean_price (struct trade **array, int length) {
  int counter, selector; double sum = 0.0;
  for (counter = 0, selector = 0;
       selector < length;
       ++counter, selector = selector + 2)
    sum = sum + array[selector] -> price;
  return sum / counter;
}
```

You can combine the two versions of mean_price, controlling speed versus accuracy via a global variable named mode. If the value of mode is 0, you have high speed; if the value of mode is 1, you have high accuracy:

```
int mode = default value, 0 or 1
...
double mean_price (struct trade **array, int length) {
  int counter, selector, increment; double sum = 0.0;
  if (mode)
    increment = 2;
  else
    increment = 1;
  for (counter = 0, selector = 0;
       selector < length;
       ++counter, selector = selector + increment)
    sum = sum + array[selector] -> price;
  return sum / counter;
}
```

674   Of course, you would never remember whether 0 means fast or accurate. Accordingly, you should test the value of mode against mnemonic enumeration constants. You probably should also replace the if statement with a switch statement, anticipating that you might eventually have more than two possible values for the mode global variable:

```
int mode;
enum {fast, accurate};
...
double mean_price (struct trade **array, int length) {
  int counter, selector, increment; double sum = 0.0;
  switch (mode) {
    case fast:     increment = 2; break;
    case accurate: increment = 1; break;
  }
  for (counter = 0, selector = 0;
       selector < length;
       ++counter, selector = selector + increment)
    sum = sum + array[selector] -> price;
  return sum / counter;
}
```

675 In the `main` function, you can arrange to include the mean-size calculation only if the value of `mode` indicates that you are not in a hurry:

```
main ( ) {
  /* Declare various variables */
  int limit, counter, number;
  double price;
  /* Read numbers from the file and stuff them into array */
  for (limit = 0;
       2 == scanf ("%lf%i", &price, &number);
       ++limit) {
    trade_pointers[limit]
      = (struct trade*) malloc (sizeof (struct trade));
    trade_pointers[limit] -> price = price;
    trade_pointers[limit] -> number = number;
  }
  /* Perform analysis */
  printf ("The mean price per share of the trades is %.2f.\n",
          mean_price (trade_pointers, limit));
  if (mode != fast)
    printf ("The mean number of shares traded is %.0f.\n",
            mean_size (trade_pointers, limit));
}
```

676 You could supply a value for `mode` via a command-line argument. It is more likely, how-ever, that you want to vary the speed-versus-accuracy tradeoff of your program as it is running, especially if your program is in an endlessly repeating loop of the sort you saw in Segment 573. Each time through the loop, you could ask the program user to supply a value for `mode` via the keyboard. Alternatively, you could use functions found in C's time library to keep track of how fast your program is handling files, switching from accurate to fast computing if necessary to keep up with changing information.

677 Figuratively, the information carried by the `mode` variable is **publicly broadcast** to all inter-ested functions. The information carried by an argument or a returned value is *privately sent* to only one destination.

678 Now the question is, Where should you define the `mode` global variable? A reasonable answer is that you should put it in its own file inasmuch as speed-versus-accuracy control is a conceptual unit.

Wherever you define the `mode` variable, you face what seems like a paradox: You use the value of the `mode` variable in both the `main.c` file and the `trades.c` file, but you can define a variable in only one place, just as you can define a function in only one place. But if you define a variable in just one file, how does the C compiler learn what it needs to know about that variable while it is compiling another file that references the variable?

679 Recall that a function prototype is a declaration, because it provides the C compiler with information about a function that is defined elsewhere.

Analogously, you can declare a global variable in one place and define it in another. As explained in Segment 129, when you define a global variable, you tell the compiler to allocate a chunk of memory for the variable. When you *declare* a global variable, you tell the compiler that the global variable is *defined* in an object file available to the C linker when it is time to link together object files into an executable program.

680   The most convenient place to declare global variables is, of course, in a header file that is included in every file where the global variable is evaluated or assigned.

681   To declare a global variable, you must precede its type specification with the symbol extern. For example, if you want to declare the global variable mode, you include the following declaration:

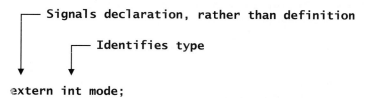

```
extern int mode;
```

Note that you *must not* include an initial value where extern is used. An initial value forces the C compiler to allocate memory for the variable, thus establishing the variable's definition, which can be done only once.

682   In summary, when more than one file uses a global variable, the global variable must be defined in one file and declared in all the others. The declaration may be by way of an included header file:

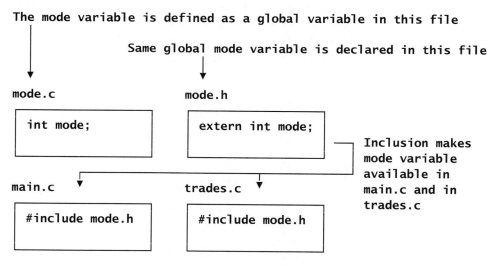

683   Of course, there are occasions when you want to keep the global variables in one file out
SIDE TRIP   of the way of the global variables in another file.

Suppose, for example, that you and a partner have divided into two parts the work of writing a program. Each of you works on a file full of functions. Both of you have employed a global variable named, accidentally, `hack`. Ordinarily, your separate use of that variable name will lead your C compiler to note a multiple-variable–definition error when those files are linked together.

Fortunately, if you add `static` to the definition of a global variable, then the value of that global variable is accessible to only those functions defined in the same file.

Accordingly, one or both of you can define the variable to be static:

The hack variable is defined as a static global variable in this file

A different static global hack variable is defined in this file

```
static int hack;
```

```
static int hack;
```

Because of the use of `static` in the variable definitions, the variables keep out of each other's way.

684   The following general rules will help you to keep global variable declarations and function declarations properly separated from their definitions:

- You must define global variables and functions only once. Accordingly, you should keep definitions out of header files, which are likely to be included into many source-code files.

- You can declare global variables (using **extern**) and functions (using function prototypes) over and over, as long as each declaration is the same. Accordingly, you can place declarations in header files that you use to inform many source-code files about global variables and functions.

685   Note that the declaration–definition restriction on variables does not apply to macro definitions. You can define macros over and over, so there is no harm in having them in a header file.

686   Explain how it is that a header file may be read multiple times as a source file is compiled,
PRACTICE   even though that header file's name never appears in the source file.

687   Using the conditional-compilation idea about which you learned in Section 41, explain
PRACTICE   how to use an `#ifdef`–`#endif` combination to ensure that the material in a header file is provided to the compiler only once, even if the header file is read multiple times as a source file is compiled.

688
HIGHLIGHTS
- Header files should contain global variable declarations for every global variable that you expect to appear in more than one file.

- You can declare global variables as often as you like. You can define them only once.

- **If** you want to declare a global variable, **then** instantiate the following pattern:

  `extern` `data type` `variable name` `;`

- **If** you want a global variable to be accessible from only those functions defined in the same file, **then** instantiate the following pattern:

  `static` `data type` `variable name` `;`

44 HOW TO COMPILE A MULTIPLE-FILE PROGRAM

689   When you build big programs, with many header and source-code files, you eventually lose track of what depends on what. Accordingly, most operating systems that support C provide what is called the `make` utility. The basic idea is that you describe dependencies in a file that a compilation program uses to figure out what needs to be recompiled and relinked.

690   When you compile a multiple-file program using the `make` utility, the file describing dependencies is called a **makefile**.

Over the years, the `make` utility has come to offer more and more features, with a corresponding increase in syntactic complexity. Consequently, expert programmers often write makefiles that are extremely difficult for beginners to read. Nevertheless, simple makefiles are easy to write and read, even for C beginners, and you should learn to use them early on.

691   Recall that the executable file, `analyze_trades`, described in Section 42 and Section 43, depends on three object files. This dependency is reflected in a makefile line in which `analyze_trades` appears, followed by a colon, followed by a list of the depended-on files:

```
analyze_trades: main.o trades.o mode.o
```

A similar line asserts that the `main.o` file depends on the `main.c` file and two included header files:

```
main.o: main.c trades.h mode.h
```

Finally, the following lines assert that the object files containing member functions depend on both source code files and header files:

```
trades.o: trades.c trades.h
mode.o: mode.c mode.h
```

Note that dependency lines *must* begin in the first column—no spaces or tabs are permitted.

692   Makefiles also contain information about what to do when a depended-on file changes. This information is provided in command lines, each of which immediately follows a dependency line. The command line looks like a command that you would issue yourself if you were providing a command line by hand. For example, if you were to relink the object files to produce a new `analyze_trades` program, you would issue the following command:

```
cc -o analyze_trades main.o trades.o mode.o
```

Note, however, that command lines in makefiles *must* begin with a tab character:

```
        cc -o analyze_trades main.o trades.o mode.o
```

693 Accordingly, a makefile for the `analyze_trades` program would contain a dependency line describing `analyze_trades` file dependencies and a corresponding command line:

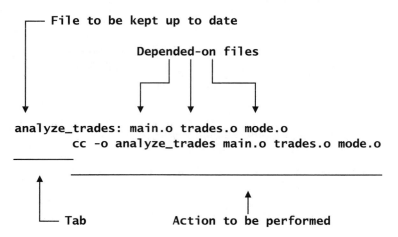

694 The following is a complete makefile for the `analyze_trades` program; note that the `make` utility interprets as comments lines beginning with # characters:

```
# makefile for analyze_trades program

analyze_trades: main.o trades.o mode.o
        cc -o analyze_trades main.o trades.o mode.o

main.o: main.c trades.h mode.h
        cc -c main.c

trades.o: trades.c trades.h
        cc -c trades.c

mode.o: mode.c mode.h
        cc -c mode.c
```

The `make` utility is smart enough to propagate changes properly through the dependencies. For example, noting a change to the `mode.c` file, `make` produces a new `mode.o` object-code file. Then, noting a change to the `mode.o` file, `make` produces a new `analyze_trades` executable file.

695 With the makefile complete, and named `makefile`, you need only to issue the following command to have every file in your program brought up to date:

```
make
```

696 Suppose that want to include a prediction in the program described in Section 42 and in
PRACTICE this section. Further suppose that you move the prediction function, described in Segment 667, into its own file pair, `predict.h` and `predict.c`. Revise the makefile shown in Segment 694 to accommodate the changes.

- **If** you want to keep a multiple-file program up to date, **then** create a makefile named `makefile`.

- **If** you want to express how one program file depends on others, **then** instantiate the following pattern in your makefile, taking care to start in the first column:

  `file name` : `list of depended-on files`

- **If** you want to express what should be done when a change occurs in a depended-on file, **then** instantiate the following pattern, taking care to start with a tab:

    `compiler command`

  └─ **Tab**

- **If** you are ready to recompile a multiple-file program after making changes, **and** you have written a makefile named `makefile`, **then** issue the following command to your computer:

  make

APPENDIX A: PRINT SPECIFICATIONS

698 The following is a representative list of the specifications that are used in C's `printf` statements:

Specification	Argument type	What is displayed
%i	int	integer
%c	int	character
%s	char pointer	string
%f	double	floating-point number
%e, %E	double	floating-point number with exponent
%%		the % character

699 The c, s, and % print specifications are for characters, strings, and the insertion of percent signs.

Display character, percent sign, and string:

```
printf ("The character %c occupies 25%% of the string %s.\n",
                        'a',                            "abcd");
———————————————— Result ————————————————
The character a occupies 25% of the string abcd.
```

700 The i specification is for integers. Note that xs are included in the sample `printf` statements to clarify the placement of padding characters.

If you happen to want an integer printed in octal notation, use the o specification instead of i. If you want hexadecimal, use the x specification instead of i.

Display short or integer or long:

```
printf ("x %i x\n", 816); printf ("x %i x\n", -816);
———————————————— Result ————————————————

x 816 x
x -816 x
```

Display with spaces, if necessary, to fill a six-character field:

```
printf ("x %6i x\n", 816); printf ("x %6i x\n", -816);
———————————————— Result ————————————————

x    816 x
x   -816 x
```

Display with spaces, if necessary, to fill a six-character field; if more than six characters are involved, display them all anyway:

```
printf ("x %6i x\n", 8160000); printf ("x %6i x\n", -8160000);
```
———————————— Result ————————————
```
x 8160000 x
x -8160000 x
```

Display with spaces on the right, if necessary:

```
printf ("x %-6i x\n", 816); printf ("x %-6i x\n", -816);
```
———————————— Result ————————————
```
x 816    x
x -816   x
```

Always include sign:

```
printf ("x %+6i x\n", 816); printf ("x %+6i x\n", -816);
```
———————————— Result ————————————
```
x   +816 x
x   -816 x
```

Always include sign and pad on the right:

```
printf ("x %+-6i x\n", 816); printf ("x %+-6i x\n", -816);
```
———————————— Result ————————————
```
x +816   x
x -816   x
```

701 The f specification is for floating-point numbers. Note that xs are included in the printf statement to clarify the placement of padding characters.

Display float or double:

```
printf ("x %f x\n", 3.14159); printf ("x %f x\n", -3.14159);
```
———————————— Result ————————————
```
x 3.141590 x
x -3.141590 x
```

Display with two digits following the decimal point:

```
printf ("x %.2f x\n", 3.14159); printf ("x %.2f x\n", -3.14159);
```
———————————— Result ————————————
```
x 3.14 x
x -3.14 x
```

Display with spaces, if necessary, to fill a six-character field:

```
printf ("x %6.2f x\n", 3.14159); printf ("x %6.2f x\n", -3.14159);
```
——————————— Result ———————————
```
x   3.14 x
x  -3.14 x
```

Display with spaces, if necessary, to fill a six-character field; if more than six characters are involved, display them all anyway:

```
printf ("x %6f x\n", 3.14159); printf ("x %6f x\n", -3.14159);
```
——————————— Result ———————————
```
x 3.141590 x
x -3.141590 x
```

Display with spaces on the right, if necessary:

```
printf ("x %-6.2f x\n", 3.14159); printf ("x %-6.2f x\n", -3.14159);
```
——————————— Result ———————————
```
x 3.14   x
x -3.14   x
```

Always include sign:

```
printf ("x %+6.2f x\n", 3.14159); printf ("x %+6.2f x\n", -3.14159);
```
——————————— Result ———————————
```
x  +3.14 x
x  -3.14 x
```

Always include sign and pad on the right:

```
printf ("x %+-6.2f x\n", 3.14159); printf ("x %+-6.2f x\n", -3.14159);
```
——————————— Result ———————————
```
x +3.14  x
x -3.14  x
```

702   The e specification is for displaying floating-point numbers in scientific notation. Note that xs are included in the printf statement to clarify the placement of padding characters:

Display float or double:

```
printf ("x %e x\n", 27182.8); printf ("x %e x\n", -0.000271828);
printf ("Using E produces an upper-case E, as in x %E x.\n", 27182.8);
```
——————————— Result ———————————
```
x 2.718280e+04 x
x -2.718280e-04 x
Using E produces an upper-case E, as in x 2.718280E+04 x.
```

Display with two digits following the decimal point:

```
printf ("x %.2e x\n", 27182.8); printf ("x %.2e x\n", -0.000271828);
```
——————————————— Result ———————————————
```
x 2.72e+04 x
x -2.72e-04 x
```

Display with spaces, if necessary, to fill a 10-character field:

```
printf ("x %10.2e x\n", 27182.8);
printf ("x %10.2e x\n", -0.000271828);
```
——————————————— Result ———————————————
```
x    2.72e+04 x
x   -2.72e-04 x
```

Display with spaces, if necessary, to fill a 10-character field; if more than 10 characters are involved, display them all anyway:

```
printf ("x %10e x\n", 27182.8); printf ("x %10e x\n", -0.000271828);
```
——————————————— Result ———————————————
```
x 2.718280e+04 x
x -2.718280e-04 x
```

Display with spaces, on the right, if necessary:

```
printf ("x %-10.2e x\n", 27182.8);
printf ("x %-10.2e x\n", -0.000271828);
```
——————————————— Result ———————————————
```
x 2.72e+04   x
x -2.72e-04  x
```

Always include sign:

```
printf ("x %+10.2e x\n", 27182.8);
printf ("x %+10.2e x\n", -0.000271828);
```
——————————————— Result ———————————————
```
x   +2.72e+04 x
x   -2.72e-04 x
```

Always include sign and pad on the right:

```
printf ("x %+-10.2e x\n", 27182.8);
printf ("x %+-10.2e x\n", -0.000271828);
```
——————————————— Result ———————————————
```
x +2.72e+04  x
x -2.72e-04  x
```

APPENDIX B: READ SPECIFICATIONS

703 The following is a representative list of the specifications that are used in C's scanf statements:

Specification	Argument type	What is read
%hi	short	integer
%i	int	integer
%f	float	floating-point number
%lf	double	floating-point number
%c	int	characters
%s	char pointer	string

704 The scanf function returns a value:

- The value of a call to scanf is the number of read specifications handled successfully. This value is 0 if no read specifications are handled successfully.

- If scanf reaches the end of a file before its work is complete, it returns the value of the macro EOF, which is -1 in most implementations.

705 The i specification is for reading integers of type int. The hi specification is for reading integers of type short.

The following program reads integers of type short and of type int:

```
short sample_short;
int sample_int;
scanf ("%hi%i", &sample_short, &sample_int);
printf ("The short is %i; the int is %i\n",
                    sample_short,  sample_int);
```
———————————————————— Sample Data ————————————————————
```
32000 128000
```
———————————————————————— Result ————————————————————————
```
The short is 32000; the int is 128000
```

706 The f specification is for reading numbers of type float. The lf specification is for reading numbers of type double.

The following program reads integers of type float and of type double:

```
float sample_float;
double sample_double;
scanf ("%f%lf", &sample_float, &sample_double);
printf ("The float is %f; the double is %f\n",
                        sample_float,      sample_double);
```
————————————————— Sample Data —————————————————
```
32.000 128000e+10
```
————————————————————— Result —————————————————————
```
The float is 32.000000; the double is 1280000000000000.000000
```

707   The s specification is for reading characters into an array. In normal use, the s specification tells scanf to skip over any following whitespace characters and to read the characters up to the next whitespace:

```
char input_buffer[100];
scanf ("%s", input_buffer);
printf ("The author's login name is %s.\n", input_buffer);
```
————————————————— Sample Data —————————————————
```
    phw is the author's login name.
```
————————————————————— Result —————————————————————
```
The author's login name is phw.
```

Note that scanf appends the null character, \0, to the characters actually read. Hence, the character array must be big enough to accommodate the characters in the input string plus an additional character.

Note also that you can supply a modifying number with the s read specification, in which case, after skipping any whitespace, scanf reads the input string until that number of characters have been read, or whitespace is encountered, or the end of a file is encountered:

```
char input_buffer[100];
scanf ("%3s", input_buffer);
printf ("The author's friends never call him %s.\n", input_buffer);
```
————————————————— Sample Data —————————————————
```
    Patrick Henry Winston
```
————————————————————— Result —————————————————————
```
The author's friends never call him Pat.
```

708   If you want to skip over material that would otherwise be read by a scanf call, you add an asterisk to the specification:

```
char input_buffer[100];
scanf ("%*s%*s%s", input_buffer);
printf ("The author's surname is %s.\n", input_buffer);
```
―――――――――――――――― Sample Data ――――――――――――――――
```
   Patrick Henry Winston
```
―――――――――――――――――― Result ――――――――――――――――――
```
The author's surname is Winston.
```

709   Often, it is helpful to add spaces in scanf calls to make them easier to read. That white-space matches whitespace in the input, if any. Otherwise, the whitespace is ignored:

```
char input_buffer[100];
scanf ("%*s     %*s     %s", input_buffer);
printf ("The author's surname is %s.\n", input_buffer);
```
―――――――――――――――― Sample Data ――――――――――――――――
```
   Patrick Henry Winston
```
―――――――――――――――――― Result ――――――――――――――――――
```
The author's surname is Winston.
```

710   Finally, other nonwhitespace characters in scanf calls must match corresponding charac-ters in the input; otherwise, reading stops. Two percent signs are a special case; they must match a single percent sign in the input:

```
int i, j;
scanf ("%i%% %i%%", &i, &j);
printf ("The total percentage is %i.\n", i + j);
```
―――――――――――――――― Sample Data ――――――――――――――――
```
   4% 16%
```
―――――――――――――――――― Result ――――――――――――――――――
```
The total percentage is 20.
```

711   The c specification is similar to the s specification, except that no whitespace is skipped and no null character is added. One character is read, unless there is a modifying number, in which case that number of characters is read, unless the end of a file is reached, in which case the value returned by scanf is the value of the EOF macro.

```
char input_buffer[100];
scanf ("%6c", input_buffer);
printf ("The first six characters were:\n%s\n", input_buffer);
scanf ("%*5c%c", input_buffer);
printf ("The twelfth character was:\n%c\n", *input_buffer);
```
———————————————— Sample Data ————————————————
```
   Patrick Henry Winston
```
————————————————— Result —————————————————
```
The first six characters were:
   Pat
The twelfth character was:
H
```

APPENDIX C: OPERATOR PRECEDENCE

712 The following table lists C's precedence and associativity characteristics. Each box contains operators with equal precedence. The table is arranged such that the higher the box in the table, the higher the operator in precedence.

Operator level	Associativity
::	left to right
( ) [ ] -> . sizeof(data type)	left to right
! ˜ ++ -- + (unary) - (unary) * (dereference) & (address of) new delete (data type)	right to left
* / %	left to right
+ -	left to right
<< >>	left to right
< <= > >=	left to right
== !=	left to right
&	left to right
^	left to right
¦	left to right
&&	left to right
¦¦	left to right
?:	right to left
= += -= *= /= %= &= ^= ¦= <<= >>=	right to left
,	left to right

Note that each data type, surrounded by parentheses, is considered an operator—namely, a casting operator. Also, the parentheses following a function name are considered to be the function-call operator.

APPENDIX D: FORMATTED TIME DISPLAY

713   The following is a representative list of the specifications that are used in C's `strftime` statements:

Specification	Argument type
%a	abbreviated weekday name
%A	full weekday name
%b	abbreviated month name
%B	full month name
%d	day of the month
%H	hour (24 hour clock)
%I	hour (12 hour clock)
%m	month (01–12)
%M	minute (00–59)
%p	AM or PM
%S	second (00-59)
%y	year without century
%Y	year with century
%%	%

714   The following illustrates:

```
#include <stdio.h>
#include <time.h>
time_t elapsed_seconds;
struct tm *time_structure_pointer;
char *time_buffer[100];
main ( ) {
  time(&elapsed_seconds);
  time_structure_pointer = localtime (&elapsed_seconds);
  strftime (time_buffer, 100, "%A", time_structure_pointer);
  printf ("Today happens to be %s.\n", time_buffer);
}
```
————————————————— Result —————————————————
```
Today happens to be Friday.
```
———————————————————————————————————————

715   Other examples are shown on the next page.

```c
#include <stdio.h>
#include <time.h>
time_t elapsed_seconds;
struct tm *time_structure_pointer;
char *time_buffer[100];
main ( ) {
  time(&elapsed_seconds);
  time_structure_pointer = localtime (&elapsed_seconds);
  /* Line 1 */
  strftime (time_buffer, 100, "%I:%M %p", time_structure_pointer);
  printf ("The civilian time is %s.\n", time_buffer);
  /* Line 2 */
  strftime (time_buffer, 100, "%H:%M", time_structure_pointer);
  printf ("The military time is %s.\n", time_buffer);
  /* Line 3 */
  strftime (time_buffer, 100, "%d %B %Y", time_structure_pointer);
  printf ("One way to write the date is %s.\n", time_buffer);
  /* Line 4 */
  strftime (time_buffer, 100, "%m/%d/%y", time_structure_pointer);
  printf ("A shorter way to write the date is %s.\n", time_buffer);
}
```
———————————————— Result ————————————————
The civilian time is 01:41 PM.
The military time is 13:41.
One way to write the date is 22 April 1994.
A shorter way to write the date is 04/22/94.

APPENDIX E: HOW TO USE SOCKETS TO CONNECT PROGRAMS

716   Using C, you usually can combine two programs, from diverse sources, to produce a single C program. Sometimes, however, the program-combining option is not available, because two programs are to be part of a distributed system running on two computers. In such circumstances, you need to know how to arrange for those programs to communicate via a network, such as the Internet.

717   Conceptually, the **socket** approach to program communication is straightforward. One program, the **server**, sets up a socket on a particular computer:

Server program

Socket

Statements in here create and name a socket

718   The socket is partially identified by the **network address** of the computer on which the server is running. Because there can be many servers running on a particular computer, the socket is further identified by a **port number**.

719   Once the socket is established by the server, a **client** program can connect itself to that socket, thereby enabling two-way communication:

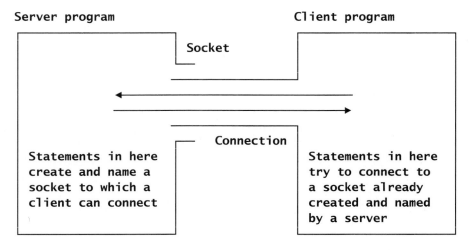

Server program   **Client program**

Socket

Connection

Statements in here create and name a socket to which a client can connect

Statements in here try to connect to a socket already created and named by a server

720   With the socket-based connection fully established, the server can write to the socket, as though that client were writing to a file, and what the server writes can be read by the client, as though it were reading from a file.

Because socket-based communications are bidirectional, the client not only can read, but also can write, and the server not only can write, but also can read.

721   To set up a socket connection, the server must do the following:

- Create the server end of the socket connection, using `socket`.

- Identify the network address of the server and a port number, using `bind`.

- Listen for an attempt by a client to establish a connection, using `listen`.

Then, once the server is listening, the client can do the following:

- Create the client end of the socket connection, using `socket`.

- Attempt to establish a connection to the listening server, using `connect`.

Then, once the client has attempted to establish a connection to the listening server, the server can do the following:

- Accept the offered connection, using `accept`.

Finally, once the connection is accepted, both the server and client can do the following:

- Assign pointer variables to the values returned by calls to `fdopen`, an acronym for *f*ile *d*escriptor *open*.

The pointer variables that are assigned to the values returned from calls to `fdopen` are like the file pointers assigned to the values returned from calls to `fopen`. You soon see, in Segment 733, that a program can read and write to the socket using those pointer variables as arguments to `fscanf` and `fprintf`.

722   Diagrammatically, the sequence of calls has the following shape:

272

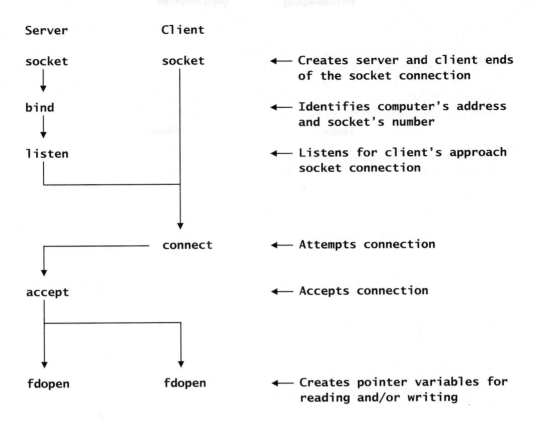

723 Unfortunately, the details that you need to deal with when you set up a socket connection are complex, because the designers and implementers of the socket mechanism have provided for many options, at a low level. Fortunately, you can treat much of the necessary code as ritual that needs to be recited, but not to be understood, at least by beginners.

724 First, you need to include several header files in your server and client programs:

```
#include <stdio.h>
#include <math.h>
#include <sys/types.h>
#include <sys/socket.h>
#include <netinet/in.h>
#include <arpa/inet.h>
```

725 Next, **on the server side of the connection**, inside the main function, you need to declare three integer variables, along with two structure variables and two pointer variables:

```
int socket_number, new_socket_number, client_size;
struct sockaddr_in server_addr, client_addr;
FILE *fm_client, *to_client;
```

The uses of all these variables are explained in the following segments.

726   The `sockaddr_in` structure type is a complex structure containing embedded structures. The purpose of `sockaddr_in` objects—such as `server_addr` and `client_addr`—is to hold information about the socket's type, the computer's Internet address, and the socket's number. All this information is established in assignment statements such as the following, in which `"128.52.36.4"` is the Internet address of the server computer; 6022 is a port number, selected by the author of the server program; and `AF_INET` is a macro symbol that identifies the socket as one that is intended to provide a service over the Internet:

```
server_addr.sin_addr.s_addr = inet_addr ("128.52.36.4");
server_addr.sin_family = AF_INET;
server_addr.sin_port = 6022;
```

Note that the port number must be selected that is different from any port number previously assigned by the operating system or other server program; generally, an integer above 6000 avoids conflict with port numbers assigned by the operating system.

727   The `socket_number` variable is an integer that identifies a raw socket created by a call to the `socket` function, which takes three arguments, two of which are macros defined in `socket.h`:

```
socket_number = socket (AF_INET, SOCK_STREAM, 0);
```

`AF_INET` indicates that the communication is to be between two programs running on the Internet. `SOCK_STREAM` indicates that communication is ordinary in the sense that both the server and the client depend on each other to continue running and communicating. Finally, the 0 indicates that ordinary low-level protocols are to be used in the communication.

728   Once `socket_number` is assigned a value, a call to `bind` associates the corresponding socket with information held in `server_addr`.

```
bind (socket_number,
      (struct sockaddr *) &server_addr,
      sizeof (server_addr));
```

Evidently, the call to `bind` requires a pointer to the `server_addr` structure that has been cast to a pointer of type `sockaddr`. Do not concern yourself with why the casting is needed—consider that detail to be an obscure part of the ritual.

729   Next, you need a call to `listen`; this call causes the server to wait for a client to solicit a connection:

```
listen (socket_number, 5);
```

The first argument, again, is the socket descriptor established by the call to `socket`.

The second argument indicates how may clients are allowed in a queue awaiting a socket connection with the server. In our example, there is to be just one client, so the value of the second argument is not relevant. In more complex situations, several clients may wish to establish a socket connection to the same server. In such situations, the server initiates action with the first client that announces itself after the call to `listen`, and until the server is ready to deal with other prospective clients, those prospective clients are queued. Any clients that try to get into the queue, after it is filled, are told that the server is unavailable.

Most implementation require the second argument of `listen` to be between 1 and 5; many programmers habitually use 5, even if no more than one socket is to be established by their server program.

730 Once a client has sought a connection with the server, it is up to the server to accept the connection. Acceptance is arranged via a call to `accept`:

```
new_socket_number
  = accept (socket_number,
            (struct sockaddr *) &client_addr,
            &client_length);
```

The first argument, yet again, is the socket number established by the call to `socket`. The second and third arguments are supplied via addresses so that the `accept` call can supply the server with information about the client. In the server developed here, this information is not used.

731 The value returned by `accept` is a new socket number assigned, appropriately enough, to `new_socket_number`. In server programs that open sockets with multiple clients, `listen` and `accept` use the original socket, identified by the value of `socket_number`, as a template for the construction of sockets that are actually connected to clients.

732 Once a socket is constructed and is decorated with information, and a client connection has been accepted, then it is time to assign pointer variables that make the socket look like a file from the perspective of functions such as `fscanf` and `fprintf`. The server program developed here both reads from and writes to the socket; accordingly, both a read file pointer and a write file pointer have to be created:

```
fm_client = (FILE *) fdopen (new_socket_number, "r");
to_client = (FILE *) fdopen (new_socket_number, "w");
```

733 At this point, a call to `fscanf` can read in data that have been supplied by the client, and a call to `fprintf` can write out processed data that is to be supplied to the client.

Suppose, for example, that you want to set up a server program that computes the number of years it takes to double money at an interest rate supplied by a client program.

Presuming that the function on the server that actually computes the doubling time is the `doubling_time` function shown in Segment 117, the following `while` loop does the job:

```
while (1) {
  double input;
  fscanf (fm_client, "%lf", &input);
  fprintf (to_client, "%f\n", doubling_time(input));
  fflush (to_client);
}
```

Note that the `input` variable is declared inside the `while` loop; this declaration is legitimate because any block can introduce local variables. Note also the call to `fflush`; this call is needed to ensure that the information supplied in the call to `fprintf` is passed along, and is not left stranded in a buffer.

734 At this point, all the socket apparatus is ready to be put in place on the server side. The following brings together that apparatus by way of summary:

```
/* Server Program */
#include <stdio.h>
#include <math.h>
#include <sys/types.h>
#include <sys/socket.h>
#include <netinet/in.h>
#include <arpa/inet.h>
double doubling_time (double r) {
   return 72.0 / r;
}
main ( ) {
   int socket_number, new_socket_number, client_size;
   struct sockaddr_in server_addr, client_addr;
   FILE *fm_client, *to_client;
   server_addr.sin_addr.s_addr = inet_addr ("128.52.36.4");
   server_addr.sin_family = AF_INET;
   server_addr.sin_port = 6022;
   socket_number = socket (AF_INET, SOCK_STREAM, 0);
   bind (socket_number,
         (struct sockaddr *) &server_addr,
         sizeof (server_addr));
   listen (socket_number, 5);
   new_socket_number
    = accept (socket_number,
              (struct sockaddr *) &client_addr,
              &client_size);
   fm_client = (FILE *) fdopen (new_socket_number, "r");
   to_client = (FILE *) fdopen (new_socket_number, "w");
   while (1) {
      double input;
      fscanf (fm_client, "%lf", &input);
      fprintf (to_client, "%f\n", doubling_time(input));
      fflush (to_client);
   }
}
```

735 Now it is time to look at what is needed **on the client side of the communication**. First, you must declare several variables analogous to those that you declared in the server:

```
int socket_number;
struct sockaddr_in server_addr;
FILE *fm_server, *to_server;
```

736 Next, you need to provide information about the server by assigning appropriate structure variables inside the server_addr object; the required assignment statements are identical to those in the server program:

```
server_addr.sin_family = AF_INET;
server_addr.sin_port = 6022;
server_addr.sin_addr.s_addr = inet_addr ("128.52.36.4");
```

737   Next, your program must create a socket, using a socket statement, again, exactly like the corresponding statement in the server:

```
socket_number = socket (AF_INET, SOCK_STREAM, 0);
```

738   Your program establishes a connection to the server using connect. The connect statement is just like the bind statement, except that connect replaces bind:

```
connect (socket_number,
         (struct sockaddr *) &server_addr,
         sizeof (server_addr));
```

739   Once the server has accepted the connection, then it is time to assign pointer variables that make the socket look like a file from the perspective of functions such as fscanf and fprintf. The client program developed here both reads from and writes to the socket; accordingly, both a read file pointer and a write file pointer have to be created:

```
to_server = fdopen (socket_number, "w");
fm_server = fdopen (socket_number, "r");
```

740   Now, fprintf can write out a request for information that is to be supplied to the server, and a call to fscanf can read in information that subsequently is supplied by the server. Note that the client's request originates with information supplied via the keyboard:

```
while (1) {
  double keyed_number, received_number;
  printf ("Please type an interest rate:\n> ");
  scanf ("%lf", &keyed_number);
  fprintf (to_server, "%f\n", keyed_number);
  fflush (to_server);
  fscanf (fm_server, "%lf", &received_number);
  printf ("Server returned doubling time of %.1f years\n",
          received_number);
}
```

741   At this point, all the socket apparatus is ready to put in place on the client side. The following brings that apparatus together by way of summary:

```
/* Client Program */
#include <stdio.h>
#include <sys/types.h>
#include <netinet/in.h>
#include <arpa/inet.h>
#include <sys/socket.h>
main ( ) {
  int socket_number;
  struct sockaddr_in server_addr;
  FILE *fm_server, *to_server;
  server_addr.sin_family = AF_INET;
  server_addr.sin_port = 6022;
  server_addr.sin_addr.s_addr = inet_addr ("128.52.36.4");
  socket_number = socket (AF_INET, SOCK_STREAM, 0);
  connect (socket_number,
           (struct sockaddr *) &server_addr,
           sizeof (server_addr));
  to_server = fdopen (socket_number, "w");
  fm_server = fdopen (socket_number, "r");
  while (1) {
    double keyed_number, received_number;
    printf ("Please type an interest rate:\n> ");
    scanf ("%lf", &keyed_number);
    fprintf (to_server, "%f\n", keyed_number);
    fflush (to_server);
    fscanf (fm_server, "%lf", &received_number);
    printf ("Server returned doubling time of %.1f years\n",
            received_number);
  }
}
```

742   Note that the server and client programs suffer from a serious defect: Inasmuch as there is much that can go wrong when servers and clients try to get together, defensive-programming code should be added to provide progress information. Accordingly, the following server and client programs are easier to work with in practice, although they are more complex and difficult to read:

```
/* Server Program */
#include <stdio.h>
#include <math.h>
#include <sys/types.h>
#include <sys/socket.h>
#include <netinet/in.h>
#include <arpa/inet.h>
double doubling_time (double r) {return 72.0 / r;}
```

```
main ( ) {
  int socket_number, new_socket_number, client_size;
  struct sockaddr_in server_addr, client_addr;
  FILE *fm_client, *to_client;
  server_addr.sin_addr.s_addr = inet_addr ("128.52.36.4");
  server_addr.sin_family = AF_INET;
  server_addr.sin_port = 6022;
  if ((socket_number = socket (AF_INET, SOCK_STREAM, 0)) < 0) {
    fprintf (stderr, "Server could not obtain a socket !!!\n");
    exit (1);
  }
  if (bind (socket_number,
            (struct sockaddr *)&server_addr,
            sizeof (server_addr))
      < 0) {
    fprintf (stderr, "Server could not bind name !!!\n");
    exit (1);
  }
  listen (socket_number, 5);
  if ((new_socket_number
      = accept (socket_number,
                (struct sockaddr *) &client_addr,
                &client_size))
      < 0) {
    fprintf (stderr, "Server could not accept connection !!!\n");
    exit (1);
  }
  fm_client = (FILE *) fdopen (new_socket_number, "r");
  if (NULL == fm_client) {
    fprintf (stderr, "Server could not open read stream !!!\n");
    exit (1);
  }
  to_client = (FILE *) fdopen (new_socket_number, "w");
  if (NULL == to_client) {
    fprintf (stderr, "Server could not open write stream !!!\n");
    exit (1);
  }
  while (1) {
    double input;
    if (EOF == fscanf (fm_client, "%lf", &input)) {
      fprintf (stderr, "Read from client failed !!!\n"); exit (1);
    }
    if (fprintf (to_client, "%f\n", doubling_time (input)) < 0) {
      fprintf (stderr, "Write to client failed !!!\n"); exit (1);
    }
    fflush (to_client);
  }
}
```

```c
/* Client Program */
#include <stdio.h>
#include <sys/types.h>
#include <netinet/in.h>
#include <arpa/inet.h>
#include <sys/socket.h>
main ( ) {
  int socket_number;
  struct sockaddr_in server_addr;
  FILE *fm_server, *to_server;
  server_addr.sin_family = AF_INET;
  server_addr.sin_port = 6022;
  server_addr.sin_addr.s_addr = inet_addr ("128.52.36.4");
  socket_number = socket (AF_INET, SOCK_STREAM, 0);
  if ((socket_number = socket (AF_INET, SOCK_STREAM, 0)) < 0) {
    fprintf (stderr, "Client could not obtain a socket !!!\n");
    exit (1);
  }
  if (connect (socket_number,
               (struct sockaddr *)&server_addr,
               sizeof (server_addr)) < 0) {
    fprintf (stderr, "Client could not connect !!!\n"); exit (1);
  }
  to_server = fdopen (socket_number, "w");
  if (NULL == to_server) {
    fprintf (stderr, "Client could not open write stream !!!\n");
    exit (1);
  }
  fm_server = fdopen (socket_number, "r");
  if (NULL == fm_server) {
    fprintf (stderr, "Client could not open read stream !!!\n");
    exit (1);
  }
  while (1) {
    double keyed_number, received_number;
    printf ("Please type an interest rate:\n> ");
    scanf ("%lf", &keyed_number);
    if (fprintf (to_server, "%f\n", keyed_number) < 0) {
      fprintf (stderr, "Write to server failed !!!\n"); exit (1);
    }
    fflush (to_server);
    if (EOF == fscanf (fm_server, "%lf", &received_number)) {
      fprintf (stderr, "Read from server failed !!!\n"); exit (1);
    }
    printf ("Server returned doubling time of %.1f years\n",
            received_number);
  }
}
```

743   To experiment with the `server` and `client` programs, suppose you are working with two UNIX computers, and you wish to use one as the server. Once you modify both the `server` program and the `client` program, replacing Internet address `128.52.36.4` with the Internet address of your server computer, you issue the following command on the server computer.

> ┌─ **Tells Unix to run the server program**
> │   **in the background**
> │
> ▼

server &

Then, on the client machine, you issue the following command:

client

At this point, you are prompted to supply an interest rate, and once you provide one, the client talks to the server, the server responds to the client, and the client displays the time it takes to double your money at the supplied interest rate.

744   Of course, what you have learned about sockets in this section is just the beginning. There are many alternatives to the kind of socket communication outlined here:

- You may want to connect a server to a client on the same machine. You can actually run the server and client programs shown in this section on one machine, as is, but there are alternative ways to write such programs that do not require you to provide an Internet address.

- You may want to supply a symbolic Internet address, such as `ai.mit.edu`, rather than a numeric Internet address, such as `128.52.36.4`.

- You may want to have one server supply information to many clients, so that the server continues to do its job even if one of the clients crashes.

To learn how to implement such socket programs, you should explore a book on network programming.

COLOPHON

The author created camera-ready copy for this book using TEX, Donald E. Knuth's computer typesetting language.

He transformed the source text into PostScript files using the products of Y&Y, of Concord, Massachusetts. Pure Imaging, Inc., of Watertown, Massachusetts, produced film from the PostScript files.

The text was set primarily in 10-point Sabon Roman. The section headings were set in 14-point Sabon bold. The computer programs were set in 9-point Lucida Sans bold.

All programs shown with accompanying results were tested using the IBM AIX XL C Compiler/6000 and using the C/C++ compiler produced by the Free Software Foundation, of Cambridge, Massachusetts.

INDEX

SOFTWARE

The programs in this book are available via the INTERNET. To learn how to obtain this software, send a message to books-by-phw@ai.mit.edu with the word "help" on the subject line. Your message will be answered by an automatic reply program that will tell you what to do next.